List of Editors

Patricia East
Karin Inmann
Kurt Luger

This book is printed with support of
Austrian Development Co-operation
Oeko Himal - Society for Ecological Co-operation
Alps-Himalaya, and the University of Salzburg, Austria

ÖKO HIMAL

Österreichische
Entwicklungszusammenarbeit

Patricia East, Kurt Luger, Karin Inmann (Eds.)

Sustainability in Mountain Tourism

Perspectives for the Himalayan Countries

An Oeko Himal Publication

Published by
BOOK FAITH INDIA/Delhi
&
STUDIENVERLAG/Innsbruck-Vienna
1998

Published by
BOOK FAITH INDIA
414-416 Express Tower, Azadpur Commercial Complex
Delhi, India 110 033
&
STUDIENVERLAG
Andreas Hofer Straße 38
P.O. Box: 104
6011 INNSBRUCK, Austria

Distributed by
PILGRIMS BOOK HOUSE
P.O. Box: 3872
Kathmandu, Nepal
Tel. 977-1-424942, 425919
Fax. 977-1-424943
E-mail: info@pilgrims.wlink.com.np

Layout and Graphics: Sherap Sherpa
Cover design: Claudia Koeck & Sherap Sherpa

Front cover picture by Kurt Luger
Backcover picture by Bikash Rauniar

1st English Edition

ISBN : 81-7303-132-0

ISBN 3-7065-1260-2 Studienverlag Innsbruck-Vienna

Printed in India

Table of Contents

Foreword

by the Austrian Ambassador Dr. Karl Peterlik

Austria is the fourth largest tourism destination in the whole world, and we look back on two centuries of experience in receiving guests: every year, about twenty million foreign visitors come to Austria, and the per capita income generated from tourism is larger than in any other country. It has also meant the development of a tremendous tourism infrastructure. This is an experience we would like to share with countries in the Himalaya which have a similar topography to ours. We would like to tell you about the mistakes we have made, to warn you not to follow us in these, and to point out positive paths we think tourism could pursue in future.

The Austrian non-governmental organisation Oeko Himal, which has been active in Nepal for many years in a number of development co-operation projects, is just about to take the first steps for a new project, a small ecologically-oriented programme for developing tourism in the Rolwaling Valley. The philosophy is the same as in all the other Austrian projects in Nepal. It is comprehensive, it is focused on a specific region, and the local population shall benefit from it. It will be a small-scale ecotourism project where sustainability is the first priority. The sociological, cultural and ecological factors will be given due consideration, with the aim of achieving the largest possible economic productivity. The guiding principles must be the protection and preservation of resources. These principles proved to be appropriate when we created the National Park Hohe Tauern in the central Alpine region of Austria; they should also prove effective and appropriate in the Himalaya.

This conference addresses the question how tourism can make use of nature without causing damage to the fragile ecological balance. You will in your discussions and lectures analyse the phenomenon of developing societies chasing after modernisation, and discuss what measures could be taken in order to preserve traditional cultures, the riches of tradition, modalities of cohabitation and the symbiosis of man and nature. We in Europe have learned a lot from many mistakes which led to premature development, and we have now reached a better understanding of the laws of nature and how to adapt to them. The modern trend in the tourism industry is towards tourism compatible with the social, cultural and ecological features of the individual region concerned. Short-term economic profit is no longer the main goal; instead, long-term utilisation of all resources must be at the heart of all development, because ecological concern is synonymous with long-term economic benefit.

Sustainability is the call of the day, and this means balanced development. This is true for the Alps in the same way as it is for the Himalaya. Both are mountainous regions which provide a living space for people even in high regions. In order to initiate a continuous process of development we have to devise tourism strategies which do not simply market protected areas in mountainous regions as exotic destinations. A moderate and measured development of tourism can ensure the preservation of this living space in the mountains for many generations to come. You in Nepal have already taken measures in the right direction by creating natural parks and conservation areas.

Herbert Tichy, Austria's most famous traveller in Asia and Nepal, once called the Himalaya a "Geography of Hope". He and the Sherpa Pasang Dawa Lama were the first men to stand on top of Cho Oyu, in 1954. This joint achievement across all cultural differences should give us confidence for our future co-operation, the co-operation between the Alps and the Himalaya, between the mountain countries Austria and Nepal.

Patricia East, Kurt Luger, Karin Inmann

Himalayan Tourism on the Sustainable Trail?

An Introduction

As Nepal gets going with promotion for "Visit Nepal 1998", and tourists pour into this little mountain kingdom at an annual rate of some 300,000, the gods and the demons and the polluted streets of Kathmandu stand at the gateway to unforgettable holidays in the Himalaya. But while the travel brochures maintain the myth of the hospitable Shangri-La, and 70,000-odd trekkers a year try to believe them, the rose-tinted spectacles have cracked along the socio-economic fault lines. The mountain idyll is succumbing to the seductions and the ravages of the tourists who arrive to delight in it; and ever louder voices are pleading for protection of the goose that lays the golden dollars on which the economies of the Himalayan regions are now so dependent.

So while the sun shone clear and the surrounding mountains glittered enticingly, international delegates gathered for four days in the conference rooms of Kathmandu's Vajra Hotel to consider the development of mountain tourism. The International Conference on Sustainability in Mountain Tourism, hosted by the Austrian non-governmental organisation Oeko Himal, and attended by delegates from the Himalayan and Alpine regions, brought together tourism researchers, practitioners, local and international organisations, development journalists, and politicians to discuss the huge spectrum of issues connected with sustainable tourism development in mountain regions.

How can mountain areas and their communities derive genuine benefit from the tourism industry? How can supply match demand without resources being exhausted? Who bears responsibility, and who should be the engine driving environmental and cultural protection? How can theory be translated into practice? These questions were among those posed and illuminated, and the issues were illustrated by models of sustainable tourism development currently being implemented in the Himalaya and the Alps.

Chasing Sustainability in the Mountains

The growing awareness worldwide in the last few decades of the non-renewable nature of the natural resources which tourism exploits is now coupled with a broadening of the concept of environmental protection to include not only nature itself but also social and cultural resources. This places the emphasis of sustainable tourism development (both in the developed and the developing world) on developing tourism within the context of future-oriented management of all resources, strengthening rather than depleting both the natural and the human environment, in order to realise economic potential and to fulfill the needs both of the present and of the future.

The ingredients of the concept of sustainable tourism development have been extensively if not exhaustively defined since the World Commission on Environment and Development established it in 1987 as "development that meets the needs of the present without compromising the ability of future generations to meet their own needs." In his keynote address, Harka Gurung takes us through the consciousness-shift in the perception of the environment and its conservation, bringing us to the current state of the debate and relating it to the specificity of the Himalayan mountain regions. He demolishes some prevailing misconceptions about the mountain environ-ment as sentimental and exorbitant: to speak of ecological balance in its pristine state is a futile perpetuation of an ancient myth; mountain regions are dynamic, not fragile; soil erosion is only marginally affected by human activity; it is not native ignorance, but economic compulsion which drives local people to hasten environmental degradation in their home areas; and far from being antagonistic to the natural environment, economic development is the key to environmental protection. The signpost to sustainable tourism development thus points towards careful assessment of carrying capacities and the development of appropriate management strategies.

The global challenge of conservation moved onto the international agenda in the second half of the 20th century as increasing concern for environmental issues spurred popular and political pressure. Mac Odell traces the process on the international stage which began with the United Nations Conference on the Human Environment in Stockholm in 1972 and led to the Earth Summit's Agenda 21 and Rio Declaration in 1992. Although attention to the world's mountains was belated, the Earth Summit led to the convention of The Mountain Forum, a collaborative effort by international NGOs to prepare a follow-on initiative focusing specifically on mountain regions, picking up where Chapter 13 of the Agenda 21 left off. The Mountain Forum highlighted the importance of the cultural diversity of mountain regions, the role of ecotourism as an incentive for the promotion of environmental values, and the importance of community management of protected areas. As documented in countless publications in recent years, the global environment arena has thus seen a shift from protection to conservation and a fundamental move toward the involvement of local people, which has brought with it a reassessment of the roles of those involved at all levels in the search for directions for the future.

Nature, society, and economics cannot be considered in isolation. All goals for future development must be based on a holistic approach to tourism, unifying natural, social and economic factors and emphasising co-operation and interaction in a bottom-up process which expands from the local to the national and the global level (Cater/Lowman 1994). Central to this idea is the concept of partnership between public and private actors, considering the interests of all present and future stakeholders.

Friedrich Zimmermann presents a European perspective, illustrating how the holistic approach is followed in a number of projects supported by the European Union's "Partners for the Environment" programme in the touristically overdeveloped Austrian Alps (Williams/Shaw 1996). This programme gives support and subsidies to regional development initiatives linking projects for the development of the economy through partnership, bottom-up participation and building up local capacities by know-how transfer. Examples of projects for sustainable restructuring and eco-labelling include the Bregenz Forest project to stabilise agriculture in an area with a strong demand for tourism, the restructuring of the Lech Valley tourism resort into an ecology-oriented destination, the development of farm holidays in Austria, and eco-labelling programmes for accommodation and catering establishments. Lessons can be learnt from Europe's experience - both positive and negative; the question is whether the Himalayan countries can bypass any of the mistakes made in the Alps, and to what extent the success stories can be replicated in the Himalaya.

Himalayan Tourism: Burden or Benefit?

Whereas the tourism industry in the Austrian Alps looks back on two hundred years of experience of hosting tourists and mountain people have been able to phase in their modern European lifestyle, Himalayan mountain tourism is a relatively new industry that has seen explosive but (in most areas) uncontrolled, demand-led growth in the past three decades: tourists have simply arrived in areas formerly visited only by the occasional trader or pilgrim, and the regions have reacted to meet their needs.

The picture varies, of course, from region to region, and the different segments of the tourism market have led to different types of expansion and brought different types of changes. Nepal, the most popular Himalayan destination, first opened to tourists in the 1950s and saw a trickle of under 1,000 arrivals a year until the early sixties; it now registers some 330,000 arrivals, approximately a quarter of whom (a third if measured in overnight stays) are trekkers and mountaineers. Ladakh opened its doors in 1974 and invited uncontrolled low-cost tourism and trekking: it recorded nearly 30,000 arrivals in 1988, before figures plummeted on account of the Kashmir troubles. Bhutan presents the opposite picture: since it received its first tourist visitors in 1974, it has followed a strict policy of low-volume, high-cost tourism, limiting numbers - in 1995 it reported 4,765 arrivals - and excluding budget tourists through a high levy (US$220 per day in 1996). Sikkim (with 12,000 foreign tourists in 1993) and Arunachal Pradesh in Northeast India are likewise wary of the dangers of unfettered budget tourism growth, and are looking to the top end of the home and foreign market. In the Himalayan regions of India and Pakistan, overseas tourism is insignificant beside domestic tourism. Kashmir had over 700,000 foreign and domestic tourists annually until tourism was hit by the beginning of the militancy in 1989, but pilgrimage tourism is still on the increase. Himachal Pradesh has a huge domestic tourism market (some 3.5 million in 1993) and is fast becoming a popular destination for foreign tourists (70,000 overseas arrivals in 1993); likewise Uttar Pradesh has an enormous amount of domestic tourism, above all to its pilgrim destinations. The figures for Tibet Autonomous Region have risen steadily from some 1,000 arrivals in 1980 to 30,000 in 1995 (with a significant drop to under 4,000 in 1989 and 1990 on account of political upheaval and consequent tourism restrictions): the control of tourism growth here goes hand in hand with the political tensions between the Tibet Autonomous Region and the Chinese central government (Dixit 1995).

With tourism on such a scale, and with the overseas market being wooed as a prime source of foreign exchange, the Himalayan mountain destinations are now waking up - in most cases, being woken up by concerned outsiders - to the fact that uncontrolled tourism growth must be reined in by proactive tourism development towards a future they will be able to participate in. This makes it imperative to tackle the questions of assessment, planning and implementation inherent in the concept of sustainable tourism development.

Himalayan tourists place specific demands on the environment of the mountain dwellers whose home they visit, who live in geographical and climatic conditions which call for particular livelihood patterns: difficult communication networks, limited agricultural space, and lives dominated by seasonality and the need for diversity. The lure of the high Himalaya, with their scenic splendour and their physical and emotional challenge, draws two specific types of visitor: the pilgrim - mainly local or Indian - visiting holy sites, and the sportsman - usually Western - trekking or attempting high mountain peaks. What these two categories of tourists share is that they pass through, of necessity usually on foot, and move on. In addition, there is the increasingly affluent and touristically important "plains tourist" holidaymaker market, frequently overlooked by Western observers.

"Save the spirit of the mountains": to some pragmatists a romantic call, but for many Himalayan dwellers and visitors a heartfelt appeal. The Ghandian environmentalist Sunderlal Bahuguna decries the advent of "a new global religion of economics" and the rape of the Himalaya through commodification of the mountains. "Nature is warning us! The Himalaya should be protected from the onslaught of materialism!" He harks back to the old tradition of pilgrimage tourism in the Himalaya, with pilgrims walking to places of worship in natural settings, journeys whose hardship brings increased spiritual fruits. He propagates an end to commercial exploitation through mining and power stations, and a reduction of luxury (i.e. western-style) tourism - "the last straw on the camel's back" - calling for a return to the spiritual quest and limitation of consumption through austerity and restraint.

Overseas Himalayan tourism represents a culture shock. Unlike Alpine tourism, it is still in the "discovery of exotica" phase, in constant quest of "unspoiled destinations". The much-cited picture is familiar: the Western tourist appears on the scene with needs which clash with those of the host community. His physical requirements - food, lodging, sanitation - draw heavily on the limited resources available. Tourists want to see and experience the mountain environment, while hosts want to derive material benefit from the visitors' presence. Today's Westerner wants to look at the habits and habitat of the "primitive people of Shangri-la", while the local inhabitants want to modernise their lifestyles and emulate the industrialised culture the visitor represents. The tourist wants to gawp at poverty, in order to appreciate his own material superiority (though he often returns home intrigued by the smiling faces); yet the hosts hope for poverty alleviation. The tourist wants to capture this "other world" in photographs which will win him the admiration of his peers; the hosts find themselves serving as photographic subjects for no return.

The view of Western consumerism - embodied in tourism - as a corrupting force which is destroying a hitherto intact mountain culture is at the heart of the ideology of the Ladakh Project as described by Zac Goldsmith. Though tourism was initially welcomed in Ladakh as a source of income, its cultural impact has led to raised and often unrealistic expectations and aspirations. Tourists are unwittingly reinforcing the Ladakhis' image of the West as an affluent paradise, and increasing their dissatisfaction with their own culture. The Ladakh Project has since 1978 been trying to correct this one-sided picture and awaken local understanding of the negative consequences of emulating Western culture (Norberg-Hodge 1992). The project aims to promote traditional culture, medicine, lifestyles and production methods, and to reduce dependence on imported goods and know-how, demystifying the products of the industrial world, and to educate tourists towards more responsible behaviour in an attempt to deromanticise Western life and to teach tourists how to bring real benefit to the local population.

While the Western tourism press focuses primarily on the impact of Western tourists in developing countries, it is the pilgrimage tourism sector which represents the largest volume of Himalayan tourism in terms of numbers. The prime Himalayan Hindu holy sites are in Jammu, Kashmir and Uttarakhand: Jammu's Vishnodevi shrine sees an annual 3.6 million visitors. Uttarakhand's Gangotri Basin is visited every year by over 300,000 pilgrims, compared with some 33,000 trekkers, climbers and porters. Nepal's most frequented holy site is the Gosainkund lakes, which in 1994 recorded over 14,000 visitors over the two-day Janai Purnima period. The economic and social impact of pilgrimage tourism in mountain regions is less significant than that of overseas tourism, as revenue and cultural differences are smaller, and it has received little attention in Western tourism research. The major problems are environmental degradation through deforestation for firewood, and the pollution caused by littering and pilgrims' sanitary needs: programmes such as the Gangotri Conservation Project, described by Captain M.S. Kohli, aim primarily to tackle these two issues.

A voice that demands to be heard: the women of the mountains. Women feature increasingly strongly in the local economies in some of the mountain tourism areas of Nepal, but this is not the case in all regions. The lack of attention paid to the changing role of women as tourism pervades the lives of mountain communities in India is criticised by Nina Rao. Women remain behind the scenes, and while they are called on to participate in playing host to tourists - providing food and accommodation and often also entertaining - their contribution to this new source of income is not reflected in any change in their economic or social status: they usually remain labour at the lowest rung of tourism operations. Experience in Austria, by contrast, shows that women's involvement with tourism - mainly in bed and breakfast and farmhouse tourism, where it tends to be the women rather than the men who develop the entrepreneurial skills - brings them a new role and with it higher status within the family and society (Haas/Hoffmann/Luger 1994).

Tourism's often-cited negative impacts - disruption of traditional cultures, littering, garbage and pollution, firewood demand leading to deforestation - are valid not only for mountain areas but for all third world tourism. At the same time it must be stressed that tourism is by no means the only engine for some of these developments, but must be seen as one factor in the process of modernisation that is rolling inexorably forward throughout the developing world.

A lot of the developments which are now beginning in the Himalaya can be seen in their more advanced stages in the Alpine countries. Kurt Luger and Franz Rest examine the development and social consequences of tourism in the "Alpine Republic" Austria, the world's most tourism-intensive country. Austria looks back on a long tradition of tourism, but the post-war onset of mass tourism has brought fundamental changes to the culture and lifestyles of the small population of 8 million that receives over 20 million guests a year. In rural and mountain tourist destinations, especially in areas which have turned rapidly from an economic system based on subsistence farming into a highly developed, tourist service oriented society, the local population finds itself conforming to the stereotype produced by the media and sought by the visitors, and authentic cultural identity is jeopardised. Yet in many areas Austria's economic dependence on tourism makes it imperative to maintain and expand the industry, and the 1990s have seen a major shift towards consideration of the ecological, social and cultural impact within the debate on the promotion of tourism as a source of revenue.

The natural mountain environment is particularly vulnerable to the forest depletion, erosion and pollution brought about by the changing needs of its local people, with or without the additional strain of tourism. For centuries it appeared to be an infinite resource providing mountain areas with all their daily needs (in addition to supplying markets further afield - the exploitation of the Nepal Himalaya's water resources by India is a well-documented example) - now it must be carefully monitored and budgeted to prevent it from being depleted below renewable levels as it struggles to meet the needs of growing populations. The tourist influx and attendant infrastructure is an added burden, but by no means the main problem.

Mountain regions which for centuries have been isolated by their geographical and political situations are suddenly gaining access to the modern world scene through improved communications and the advent of tv and video, as well as through the direct contact with the Western world imposed on them by overseas tourists (Goldsmith et. al. 1995). Even without the influence of tourism, the socio-cultural systems in mountain regions are readily embracing change: their perceived social and cultural needs are changing accordingly, and they are hungry for progress. Much as Westerners might like to believe in the dream of the simple contentedness and ecological harmony of primitive peoples, no community wishes to preserve itself as a museum of backwardness. Change is inevitable, yet without a full understanding of the nature of this change, a society is unable to control or direct it: "The modern tragedy of the mountain societies is that they enter the global arena not as well-equipped gladiators or well-versed charioteers with a fair chance of success, but as Christians condemned to the lions" (Gyawali 1995). Tourism thus accelerates trends that are already in motion.

Mountain Tourism and Community Development

Yet if successfully managed, mountain tourism should be able to contribute to the ability of mountain societies to control and direct the changes that they are undergoing. Tourism should be able to help promote poverty alleviation, awareness generation, and infrastructure development, thus indirectly staving off the depletion of resources in regions in which underdevelopment and poverty are prime causes of environmental stress. This is the key to turning tourism impact from a burden into a lasting source of benefit. But what are the obstacles preventing this from happening in so much of the Himalaya? Can they be identified, and can they be overcome?

Kamal Banskota and Bikash Sharma outline the specific problems facing mountain tourism in Nepal, of all the Himalayan regions the most tourism-intensive, and analyse the relationship between Himalaya environmental resources, mountain community development and mountain tourism development, discussing the question of carrying capacity within this conceptual framework. As Himalaya environmental resources provide the basis for both mountain community and tourism development, development in mountain areas must be kept within the carrying capacity of the mountain environment, as illustrated in the case study of Nepal's Annapurna region. They conclude that tourism can bring benefits to local communities in remote mountain areas, provided complementary activities are simultaneously undertaken - primarily, the development of tourism supply components and environmental conservation. Axel Schrand suggests a catalogue of socio-economic, sociocultural, sociospatial and socio-ecological indicators to measure the sustainability of tourism in a given area.

The same fundamental problems are addressed by Pitamber Sharma, presenting the findings of research conducted by the International Centre for Integrated Mountain Development (ICIMOD). He outlines the emergent trends and major issues in mountain tourism in the Hindu Kush-Himalaya, and examines the potential of tourism to address the demographic, economic and environmental problems facing Asian regions with the comparative advantage of the mountains. He maintains that - with a few notable exceptions such as the Jomsom-Marpha area of Nepal (Khumbu would be another example) - tourism has so far had very little impact on poverty alleviation, environmental care, and the empowerment of local communities. In addition to environmental degradation, there is a glaring lack of linkage with the local/regional production system; high leakages and low retention of benefits; a high degree of seasonality and dependency; and a real "policy vacuum", a lack of policy and institutional development. Yet the sustainability of mountain tourism in the Hindu Kush Himalaya hinges on the extent to which tourism can contribute to three interrelated objectives: improvement in the livelihoods of the population (and by implication, poverty alleviation), environmental regeneration, and the empowerment of local communities. Though tourism could play a significant role as an element in the strategy of mountain development, it is much neglected as a potential positive force. Overcoming this deficit places a tall order: it would require a long-term policy perspective, developed on the basis of a comprehensive appreciation of the value of mountain environmental resources, to co-ordinate complementary sectoral policies; more baseline information on carrying capacity; integrated development for the major economic sectors in the mountains (agriculture, forestry, energy, etc.); the institutionalisation of a framework for monitoring impact; sustainable local institutions playing a key participatory role; and human resource development and training among the local population in each area.

A tall order indeed, yet the urgency is acknowledged by all with eyes to see. The identification and acknowledgement of these core problems is the cornerstone of the visions of possible ways towards a sustainable future.

Trickling down the Benefit

Where does the money go? Mountain tourists exploit the resources of the areas they visit, yet the mountain regions themselves are unable to retain much of the revenue that the visitors generate. Instead of trickling down, tourism earnings widen the gap between rich and poor. Domestic tourism does not bring in significant revenue; and most of the money that overseas Himalayan travellers leave behind locally is in the main cities, where hotels, tour operators and other tourism facilities benefit from the sought-after foreign exchange. The lion's share stays in the tourism industry of the sending countries.

Without material benefit, local mountain communities are degraded by the resource depletion that tourism helps to cause, and increased poverty and outmigration are the inevitable result. The problem is illustrated with reference to the Nepalese trekking industry within the case study presented by Kamal Banskota and Bikash Sharma. A full service group camping tour which enters a region carrying the food and fuel it requires will use trails, water, and sanitary facilities if available, but will hardly bring any material benefit to the local community. Foreign individual tourists (FITs) at least buy food and accommodation, and sometimes hire the services of local people as porters etc. along the way, even though they are generally low-budget travellers who turn every rupee over twice. Yet very few dollars are left in the local area: The average trekker only pays a total of under US$18 a day for a trekking holiday, and of this only a fraction - an estimated 6% - trickles down to his hosts in the areas he visits (Nepal 1996).

Mac Odell and Wendy Brewer Lama discuss the impact of this so-called "tea-house trekking" in Nepal (i.e. back-packing, with travellers eating and sleeping in simple village homes along their routes rather than camping and living off their own supplies), showing that it can significantly benefit the rural economy. As a form of modern tourism, tea house trekking follows a centuries-old indigenous, grass-roots tradition in a country where walking has always been the principle - if not the only - means of travel. The authors examine Nepal's four main tea house trekking areas (Khumbu, Annapurna, Langtang/Helambu and Makalu-Barun), and conclude that this form of tourism represents a model for development which promotes environmental and cultural conservation and which above all generates direct revenue for the villagers living in the mountains and hills. Unlike other forms of tourism, the real beneficiaries of tea house trekking are people who operate largely outside the formal economy.

However, the very nature of mountain tourism, in which the environment itself is the prime element of the tourism product, and the local population only has access to limited resources, makes it very difficult for these mountain areas to diversify their product and to exploit tourism more effectively as a potential source of income. Services hardly go beyond guiding, portering, and simple accommodation; and products are limited to basic foodstuffs.

Benefit retention is thus one of the central problems of sustainable tourism development in mountain regions. Although a number of the development projects currently being implemented include education programmes to make local communities more aware of their potential for generating material benefit from the tourists who visit them, in practice the issue remains unresolved.

Marketing and Management

Tourism marketing and environmentalism, at one time perceived as forces working in opposite directions, have now recognised the mutual advantages of joining ranks. Using the eco-label as a marketing instrument is not necessarily a contradiction or an underhand deception - provided the "eco" represents a genuine move and is not simply an empty buzzword to catch consumers with a vague idea of "anything that calls itself green is good".

Renton de Alwis takes this idea one step further: all tourism should be ecotourism, he argues, and thus "good" should become synonymous with "environmentally beneficial". The global travel market involves over 530 million travellers and $3 trillion a year, and it is growing fast. Major shifts in travel patterns can be observed, with increasing individual, custom-designed, experience-oriented, quality travel. But Nepal's mountain tourism has been wrongly placed on the market for many years: a Nepal trek today costs an average of US$18 a day, only a fraction of what it cost in the eighties. Although product development is an integral part of marketing, there is too little understanding of the market and its dynamics. Renton de Alwis sees possible solutions in improvement of quality instead of an increase in volume, more effective promotion, and competition with other destinations rather than within the country. "All tourism, including ecotourism, is business," he reminds us.

Although Nepal's market image abroad may have suffered from negative press, for example, on account of the pollution in the Kathmandu valley bewailed by Ludmilla Tüting, the New Zealand tourism consultant Les Clark suggests that this is part of the cycle of needing to stress the negative in order to impress donors and justify projects. In the hope of breaking out of this cycle by highlighting some of the successes, he presents the marketing and management question in terms of seven practical planning principles for tourism as a successful development tool in integrated conservation and development planning in mountain environments: the planning process must be driven by clearly defined goals; it must be set in a wide perspective; and tourism resources need to be assessed with tourism markets in mind. Simple diagrams showing future tourism development concepts can be very effective in local area planning. Professional resource managers are needed on-site, watching for problems and dealing with them before they get out of hand. Partnerships are the key to tourism management, involving local communities, NGOs and special interest groups; and this principle of shared responsibility must be extended to regional co-operation.

On the national park level, Guenter Mussnig provides some examples of projects incorporated in Austria's Hohe Tauern National Park which are potentially replicable - in some cases already being implemented - in Himalayan tourism areas: the concept of zoning the protected areas, the integration of the local population in running the park, visitor management through visitor centres and a network of environment-friendly accom-modation facilities, and the establishment of a training centre for park rangers and others working in the tourism industry.

Management has become a central challenge in all fields of tourism development, with tourist trends changing constantly, and the different sectors of the tourism industry becoming more and more closely knit. The problems are becoming more comprehensive, calling for holistic answers. The hotel sector, as an industry totally dependent on tourism, is a major point of impact and interaction between the host and the guest communities. A hotel can bring in revenue if it fills its beds; but if it remains empty, it can cause financial ruin. Overcapacity in the hotels of Kathmandu is a glaring example of misdirected planning in tourism development. Narendra Bajracharya and Yogendra Shakya look at the problems of the hotel industry in Kathmandu and examine the implications of global tourism trends for this sector.

The tourism industries of the Himalayan countries are urgently seeking know-how and management expertise as they struggle to cope with their business problems. The role of outside assistance in sustainable tourism development is crucial and at the same time controversial. It would be an arrogant misconception to believe that it is easy or even possible to come in and teach people how to change and improve their business styles without due regard to their cultural background and their own problem-solving capacities. Local experience and expertise are what are needed, just as at the community level it is not for outsiders to tell local people how to change and better their lives. However; a wider perception of the environmental and social issues is essential, and above all funding for certain measures can only come from outside sources. NGOs working together with local organisations and with government organisations can play an important role as external catalysts in this process.

Harsh criticism has been levelled in the context of mountain tourism at high levels of corruption, lack of democracy, the state's inability to regulate the tourism industry effectively, and the centre's ignorance about the mountain regions. Mismanagement is alas a widespread feature of Himalayan tourism. This criticism forms the core of the view of Kanak Mani Dixit, the chief editor of "Himal" magazine, in his pessimistic assessment of the media oversight of the tourism sector in Nepal, where issues languish for want of media attention.

Projects of Hope

The specificity of the different regions, and of tourism policy in each - outlined by Pitamber Sharma in his overview of the whole Hindu Kush-Himalaya, and presented in greater detail for Northern Pakistan by Basit Khan – confront the different projects for sustainable development with different challenges. The final section of the book gives examples of approaches to putting the principles of sustainable tourism development into practice: in Nepal, the Annapurna Conservation Area Project (Siddhartha B. Bajracharya), the Centre for Community Development and Research CCODER (Karin Inmann) and Oeko Himal (Karin Inmann/Kurt Luger); in India the Himalayan Environment Trust and Gangotri Conservation Project (Captain M.S. Kohli) and the LEDeG/Ladakh Project (Zac Goldsmith).

Varied as their approaches may be, these projects of hope in the Himalaya all aim to translate the theoretical basis of sustainable tourism development into practice. These contributions take us out into the field and illustrate some of the hurdles to be overcome and the difficulties encountered in building up democratic frameworks for village development and community-driven sustainable tourism. Projects such as these are breaths of fresh air and offer a spark of hope for the village people in the remote mountain regions of the Himalaya. Tourism alone will never be able to lift people out of the poverty trap, but it can become an instrument towards opening up new sources of cash income. Tourists must be made aware of the impact of their holidays on the lives of the local population, and they must learn how to make their contribution tip the positive rather than the negative side of the scales. Local experience is the core resource, communication and knowledge transfer are indispensable at all levels, and bottom-up strategies with full participation are clearly the only viable paths to a brighter future. It is the mountain people themselves who must ultimately take on the task of minimising the negative impact of tourism and determining the pace and direction of the development process. Helping them to meet this challenge, and encouraging them forward on the path to self-confidence and empowerment will in the long run prove to be more profitable than aiming for short-term gain. This is the essence of sustainable tourism development, and this is the chance that mountain communities must take into their hands.

The publication of "Sustainability in Mountain Tourism" has involved Alpine-Himalayan co-operation at every level and stage of the venture: all the contributors are closely connected with one or both of these two mountain regions, and the two publishing houses (Pilgrims Book House and Studienverlag) are based in Kathmandu, Nepal, and Innsbruck, Austria. The editors would like to thank the Austrian Development Co-operation (Ministry of Foreign Affairs) as well as the contributors and everyone whose expertise and assistance have helped them through the mountainous terrain of the production process.

Salzburg/Kathmandu, December 1997

References

Cater, Erlet/Gwen Lowman (Eds.): Ecotourism. A Sustainable Option? John Wiley & Sons, Chichester 1994

Williams, Allan/Gareth Shaw (Eds.): Tourism, Leisure, Nature Protection and Agri-Tourism: Principles, Partnerships and Practice. The EPE Workbook Series, Tourism Research Group, University of Exeter 1996

Dixit, Kanak Mani: Tourism Trends and Issues accross the Himalaya. In: Luger/Inmann 1995, pp 203-222

Gyawali, Dipak: Challenge of Mountain Economy. Managing Marginality or Risk Resilience. In: Luger/Inmann 1995, pp 223-238

Luger, Kurt/Karin Inmann (Eds.): Verreiste Berge - Kultur und Tourismus im Hochgebirge. Studienverlag, Innsbruck 1995

Norberg-Hodge, Helena: Ancient Future. Learning from Ladakh. London 1992

Haas, Hanns/Robert Hoffmann/Kurt Luger (Eds.): Weltbuehne und Naturkulisse. Zwei Jahrhunderte Salzburg-Tourismus. Pustet, Salzburg 1994

Goldsmith, Edward/Martin Khor/Helena Norberg-Hodge/Vandana Shiva & Others: The Future of Progress. Green Books Ltd., Dartington 1995

Nepal, Sanjay K: Tourism, Environment and Sustainable Development - Reflections on the Nepal Himalayas. In: Weiermair, Klaus (Ed.): Alpine Tourism: Sustainablility Reconsidered and Redesigned. Proceedings of the International Conference at the University of Innsbruck. May 1996, pp 156-174

Sunderlal Bahuguna

Save Himalaya!

अस्तुतरस्याम् दिशि देवातात्मा, हिमालयो नाम नागाधिराज ।
पूर्वा परौ तोतनिधि वगाहय, स्थित: पृथिव्या ईव मानदण्ड ।

"The Abode of Gods, King of mountains, Himalaya!
You bound the ocean from east to west.
A northern yardstick to measure the Earth."

Thus is the Himalaya described by the great Sanskrit poet Kalidas. The glories of the Himalaya are still sung by many. For sages and saints the Himalaya was a place for penance, peace, meditation and self-realisation. History and mythology are full of the accounts of great sages who left an everlasting influence on humankind with their work in the Himalaya. Bhagirath, the king-turned-ascetic who performed penance to bring the Ganga down to the Earth, was the first among these. The great scholar Vyas Dev, the author of Mahabharata, was another. Hundreds and thousands of pilgrims, caring nothing for the hardships of the journey, have for centuries visited the places of pilgrimage situated in remote areas like Muktinath, Amarnath, Kedarnath and Gomukh. The Himalaya remained so till the middle of this century. All the great teachers of India visited this great mountain range at least once to get strength and energy for their mission. Rabindranath Tagore—the great poet and Nobel laureate—had his summer resort in Ramgarh, Nainital, from where he gazed upon the snowy peaks and composed songs. Mahatma Gandhi completed his commentary on the Gita which he named Anashakti Yog (yoga of detachment), sitting in Kausani from where there is a magnificent view of the panoramic Himalayan ranges.

That the Himalaya has long been a source of spiritual inspiration for humankind and that it continues to play this role even now is widely recognised; the Ganga-Himalaya Mohonk Mountain Society in 1986 stressed this aspect in its first resolution and called for the preservation of this unique cultural heritage of humankind.

But with the advancement of material civilisation, especially during the second half of this century, the Himalaya has gained a new importance. Extending to and influencing the ecology and economy of eight countries of Asia, the peaceful Himalaya has become one of the most disturbing regions of the world. Sages no longer meditate in the caves here, but soldiers with guns sit in bunkers guarding national frontiers against their neighbours. Himalayan peaks attract adventure-seeking mountaineers, trekkers, and even more than these the pleasure-hunting luxury tourists who throng the many tourist spots in the Himalaya.

Apart from these, a new class of lovers of the Himalaya has appeared. They are the wealth-hunters, who see great potential for earning in the Himalaya—by cutting its forests, extracting minerals, damming the rivers and setting up five-star hotels. These four activities are being encouraged in the Himalaya in the name of development. Especially since the concept of development underwent a tremendous change after the second World War, when President Harry Truman in an address to the U.S. congress on June 20th, 1949 defined development as economic growth for the poor countries.

In the Himalayan region, the commercial exploitation of forests started in the middle of the nineteenth century, when Fredric Wilson, a British bird-hunter, floated down timber from Tehri-Garhwal to Haridwar. Thus the razing of forests on hill slopes started, because rivers were an easy and cheap mode of transport.

The commercialisation of the forests converted the originally mixed natural forests into timber mines—monoculture pine stands. This affected both the economy and the ecology of the Himalaya. With deforestation, precious top-soil—the flesh and blood of the hills—flowed down to the plains. The Garhwali folk singer Jeevanand Shriyal sings:

पहाड़ु क् ल्वै मासु, माटो बगीगे ।
खाण सेण को अब घाटो पड़ीगे ।

The flesh and blood of the hills have flowed down.
There is no place to live, no food to eat.

This reflects the basic principle of ecology - "Men follow their soils". Mass scale migration from the hills to the plains started, and continues unabated even today. The forests had been the main source of the prosperity of the people. Thus destruction of forests led to the destruction not only of nature but also of culture in the Himalaya. This trend continues. Now in the name of afforestation, soil-depleting and water-sucking commercial species are being encouraged with international monetary and technical aid. This activity is in a hidden way uprooting the people from the soil and making them dependent on outside sources of income.

With the expansion of roads, the hunt for minerals like magnesite, dolomite, limestone, soapstone etc. in remote hill areas has started. The mining activity has converted hill slopes and fertile valleys into deserts. The villagers' slogan is:

Wherever there is mining on the hills,
Down below the cropland has become desert!

This can best be seen in the Doon valley in India, where limestone quarries have converted the fertile basmati rice producing valley into a desert. And deserts know no national boundaries. I have seen a desert spreading in North Bengal from a dolomite mine of Bhutan in Samchi district. The Himalayan state of Himachal Pradesh in India has a programme to start 27 cement factories in the hills, even though factories near Paonta in Sirmoor district and Darala in Bilaspur have done irreparable damage to the farms, forests and the health of the people.

Economic benefits often overweigh ecological considerations. The Supreme Court of India, in a judgement ordering the closure of limestone mines in Doon valley, observed that trees are more valuable than stones. But the Government of India did not take a cue from this to stop mining in other hill areas.

The latest 'developmental' activity is the construction of large dams in the mid-Himalayas. There were already two large dams in the Himalayan foothills—Bhakra and Pong—in India, and Mangla and Tarabela in Pakistan, but to quench the thirst of big cities, industries and commercial crops, and to generate energy for these royal consumers, a series of high dams have been planned in the Himalayan region. The first of these is the killer Tehri dam which, in spite of peoples' protest for the last 31 years, is being pushed ahead simply to satisfy the national vanity that India has built the first mega (260.5 metre high) dam in Asia. The others to come are Mahakali (288 m), Chisapani (270 m) in Nepal and more than two dozen in the Indian Himalaya. These dams will flood the beautiful valleys and change the geography of the Himalaya, eliminate much flora and fauna besides adding more than a million development refugees to the already existing twenty million. The Himalaya lies in a seismic zone. There have been big landslides and avalanches in the past like Belakoochi (1970) and Kanodiagad (1978). The possibility of more such disasters in the future cannot be ruled out.

The main attraction of the Himalaya is its enchanting scenic beauty. This beauty can be maintained only if there is no interference with nature and the landscape is kept intact. Already, on account of the abovementioned activities, and a network of roads which are eulogised by development pundits as life-lines of the Himalaya but in a real sense are only death traps, the landscape has been completely changed. In spite of slopes with dense tree-cover, ugly scars are visible everywhere. Landslides have become frequent and there are several such zones where roads are often blocked for days together. In the midst of these, ugly concrete structures are appearing, which have turned once beautiful Himalayan towns into concrete jungles. These are all sliding down. Nainital and Shimla in India are two prominent examples. Mussoorie is also going the same way.

All this has happened with the advent of a new global religion of economics. When economics becomes the religion, everything becomes a marketable commodity. The commodification in the Himalayas has not been limited to forests, mines and rivers, but in this 'era of environment', the scenic beauty of the Himalaya has become the most precious commodity. In the era of the religion of economics, where the marketplace is the temple, experts and technocrats are the high priests and the dollar is the supreme God, the importance of luxury tourism has increased because it can bring in dollars. But luxury tourism, if it comes to flourish in the Himalaya, will prove to be the last straw on the camel's back. It will drain scanty natural resources, especially water, because the luxury tourist belongs to an affluent society, which maintains a high level of consumption. While the travel companies and the hotels earn, the local people have to bear the burden of a rise in prices.

In some areas, like Leh in Ladakh, land use has been totally changed. The scarce agricultural land, which was used to grow barley and provided a rich diet to human beings and cattle alike, is now used to grow vegetables to cater to tourist demand. There is no fodder for the cows, thus no butter for tea and no cow-dung for fuel. The people now eat rice and wheat; the change in diet will in the long run reduce the vitality and strength required for the hardy life of the hills. All their earnings go to the market to buy food, butter and cooking gas. The transfer from an economy of sustenance to a market economy, and the adoption of a different lifestyle, because the tourists tend to leave an impression of superiority over the local populace, ultimately deprives them of the self-confidence which in the past created adventurers, mountaineers, explorers, and people with many admirable qualities in the mountains. This loss can never be made up.

Sudden changes in food, clothing and housing patterns which had evolved after centuries of practical experience to suit the local climatic and geographical conditions, are creating a new class in the mountain region. The members of this class think themselves closer to the foreign and affluent Indian tourists than to the local populace. I have noticed this particularly in India and Nepal. The ugly cement buildings of hotels and tourist lodges in the midst of wooden houses may be seen at many places. Imagine the manner in which bread and butter and chickens have to be lugged by porters to remote Himalayan tourist resorts.

The spread of AIDS and drug abuse is not a hidden fact. The luxury tourist usually comes from a social background where bodily pleasure is the ultimate objective of life; he hunts far and wide for the satisfaction of this. The poor, whose life is already too full of hardships, fall an easy prey. And no legislation can check this.

In this respect the Alps are safe, because there is not such a vast difference between the living standards and the life-style of the tourists from outside and the local people, their traditions and religious outlook. Even in the Alps, though, much damage has been done to nature and ecology, especially due to skiing. When skiing areas started being overrun by tourists and the hotel industry began to flourish around these, artificial ski-resorts were created. But the chemicals used to create artificial ice later spoiled the water downstream; this then had to be remedied. Fortunately, the European Parliament is there to save the Alps and the countries around the Alps have adopted the Alpine Convention, whereas the countries in and around the Himalaya are in a blind race to earn more. Politically it is difficult in India, as the owners of big hotels in Jammu & Kashmir, Himachal Pradesh, and now in the Uttar Pradesh hills are themselves political leaders. They violate the laws with impunity. In one case the course of the river Beas was diverted to serve the interests of a big hotel in Manali, owned by the relative of a minister. Practically every top politician or his relatives own a hotel in this region. The race for opening new hotels is such that an ex-minister occupied a site for his relative's hotel in advance, by putting up a temporary structure at Gauchar (Chamoli Uttar Pradesh), where an air-strip is being constructed—evicting more than 200 farmers.

The tradition of tourism in the mountains is very old in the Himalayan region. The Aranya culture believes in the worship of nature. The Earth itself is regarded as a deity, a divine Mother. Thus the sage sings:

समुद्र वसने । देवि । पर्वत स्तनमण्डले ।
विष्णु पत्नी । नमस्तुभ्यम् पाद स्पर्श क्षमस्व मे ।

O Mother! Wife of Lord Vishnu!
Pardon me as I tread upon you with my feet.

Places of worship were traditionally located either on the banks of rivers, especially near their points of origin or on the hill tops. Millions visited these places. Prominent among these are Amarnath, Sharda Kshetra (Kashmir), Manikarnika, Kinnar Kailash, Trilokinath (Himachal Pradesh), Yamunotri, Gangotri, Kedarnath, Badrinath, Tungnath (Uttarakhand), Tholing Math, Kailash-Mansarovar (Tibet), Pashupatinath, Muktinath (Nepal).[1] Mountain peaks were named not after the names of individuals, but according to their location and structure or their connection with some deity e.g. Bander Poonch (tail of monkey), Satopath, Nanda Devi, Panchachuli, Annapoorna, Sagarmatha. Pilgrimage to these places was motivated by religious feelings. The objective of this was to obtain inner, spiritual happiness which is permanent but can be achieved only after much physical hardship. The fruits of a pilgrimage are in fact considered proportionate to the hardships. Though IUOTO (International Union of Official Tourist Publicity Organisation), London (1947) and the World Tourist Organisation (1975) were initially formed to facilitate cultural, social and educational exchange, this gradually changed into the mere earning of money. The objective of modern tourism is to provide physical pleasure and luxuries and for this the tourists themselves are fleeced indiscriminately.[2]

Thousands of pilgrims visit the Uttarakhand region every year. Most of these are either from the poor or lower middle classes. The following chart gives an idea of the economic status of the pilgrims:

13.5% High income group (above Rs. 4000 per month)
44.5% Low income group (below Rs. 1000 per month)
18.5% Upper middle class (Rs. 2000 to Rs. 4000 per month)
21% Lower middle class (Rs. 1000 to Rs. 2000 per month)

Out of these, the percentage of those who had come for sight-seeing was only 11.6 %.[3]

Badrinath is connected by a motor road, but for Kedarnath one has to walk about 19 km from Gaurikund. The earnings of the local people, as pony drivers, dandi and basket carriers and porters in one season totalled Rs. 44.9 million. Besides this, the income of the Pandas (priests), who also act as guides to the pilgrims, and the temple was Rs. 6.5 million. Employment was given to 3500 persons.[4]

A Policy for the Future

The Himalaya has already started groaning under the burden of luxury tourism. Even the Alps and other regions of the world are threatened with the disastrous impacts of tourism. The gifts of tourism in poor countries have been: Aids, flesh trade, drug abuse, economic disparities, robbery & depletion of common resources of land, water and forests for the benefit of a few by displacing the poor, theft of idols and other cultural artefacts, and loss of confidence and faith in the traditional lifestyles and cultures. Thus promotion of tourism only to earn money leads to total disaster. This should be stopped forthwith.

The vision of a new policy, not only for the Himalaya but for the Alps and other mountainous regions as well, may be found in the experience of spiritual seekers and literary men who spent their youth wandering in the Himalayas. They have written excellent descriptions of Nature and its impact upon them. Prominent among these were Swami Ram Tirtha[5], Swami Tapovanam[6], Swami Sivananda[7], (spiritual seekers), Rahul Sanskrityayan[8] (the famous Himalayan wanderer), Kaka Kalelkar[9] (Gandhi's associate and famous writer). Unfortunately the all-important aspects of the Himalaya that they highlighted were deliberately ignored by English writers and foreign travellers. Thus the Himalaya came to be seen as a place fit for mere sensual pleasures and upon this idea stands the prevailing concept of tourism.

Swami Ram Tirtha walked from Yamunotri to Gangotri along a route which nobody from the plains had ever before trod upon. He stayed in the lonely caves along the route for three nights. He was all alone except for the shepherds, who often met him at the confluence of Bander-poonch and Hanuman-poonch. He could see a veritable flood of flowers covering the whole path. The fragrance of these flowers makes one's inner self happy. It seemed as if beautiful and intricately woven carpets had been spread all over the landscape.[10]

Swami Tapovanam has related his experiences thus:

"The silent grandeur, the enormous extent, and the unshakeable firmness of the mountain, and the divine beauty and fragrance of the flowers that fascinate even birds and beasts... these are in themselves hymns to God. The music, of course, is not vocal. But vocal music is harsh and grating, compared with the silent music of those sights around me here. Melodies heard are sweet, those unheard are sweeter! The perennial stream, Alaknanda, and this waterfall, Vasundhara... what are they doing here? They too are loudly and ceaselessly singing the glory of God...

These streams are gratefully singing the praise of the Creator who makes them flow. These fine birds sweeping along the skies are proclaiming the matchless glory of the Lord. Look at those charming flowers, bright with many colours, blooming here on the meadow. They too proclaim nothing else. In this holyland everything seems to join in that universal harmony...

I attained a state of meditation in which I became unconscious of the material world around me... Without eating aught I was filled; without friends and things to gladden, my heart was filled with bliss. Intoxicated with the Divine Joy, I forgot all distinction between me and the world around me. All sense of duality disappeared. I was now one with the Vasudhara, the Himalayas, the World itself. In that union I felt the fullness of Divine Joy. That Oneness is the Truth, the Blissful Truth. O! Himalaya! I find no end to your spiritual greatness."[11]

Today we wonder how we can protect places of scenic beauty from being spoiled by litter and filth. Swami Tapovanam, on his way to Dodi Tal (in 1928), relates how the local villagers warned them:

"It was from there (Gajoli) I learnt all about the lake. It was only natural that some of the headmen of the village should accompany us for guidance and help. But some of the women and the old people in the village objected to our attempt. They said that the lake was the abode of gods, that it was hidden from impious eyes and men could not reach it. If somebody arrived there in a spirit of adventure, the place was sure to be desecrated by excretions and by cooking, sleeping and such unholy acts. And to remove the stains the gods would send down heavy hailstorms, destroying all the crops in the villages."[12]

In a world full of dust, noise, smoke and tension, humankind will need more and more places with peace and tranquillity. The Himalaya and other mountains, if visited with the right attitude and manner, can provide that much-needed peace and tranquillity. Thus the Himalaya should be protected from the onslaught of materialism. Instead of bringing to this holyland the marketplace with all its luxuries, austerity and restraint should be observed during Himalayan travels. That is why austerity has always been cherished as an essential element in the eastern culture.

Use less and less of everything. More than that, use only what is available from your surroundings. So far as food is concerned, the tradi-tional meals of the mid-Himalayas are not lacking in nutrition; dal-bhat, jhangora (a rainfed millet), corn, koda (ragi), kadhi (prepared from buttermilk and gram powder), local soyabean (not the soyabean encouraged by governments for export as cakes to be used for cattlefeed in Europe), stinging nettle vegetable, and amranthus (both very rich in protein). Such food will keep the tourists in good health. I would recom-mend walnuts to replace meat, as 100 grams of walnut contains calories equivalent to 500 grams of meat. Sattu (ground roasted barley) and salty Bhotia (Tibetan) tea with butter are the best diet for higher altitudes. Sattu is a good and very nutritious 'fast food' traditionally used in Tibet, Ladakh and other high-altitude areas.

The local handspun-handwoven clothing, chubba in Tibet, bakkhu in

Kashmir & Ladakh, mirjai and pyjama in Uttarakhand and Nepal are best as one can sleep with these on. The invasion of western dress forms is a tragedy. It has not only thrown the local weavers and tailors out of their jobs, but has also created an inferiority complex in those who still wear traditional apparel.

The ecological degradation of existing tourist centres can only be halted if trekking is encouraged and the tourists are diverted to lesser-known places. Big hotels should be equipped with all facilities to house visitors. Visits to certain places, especially the glaciers, which are receding at an alarming rate and which are the sources of rivers, should be completely banned. Similarly, felling of trees, mining, and damming of rivers should be stopped. It is shameful that international agencies like the World Bank and Asian Development Bank and the rich countries of the west as well as those of Asia like Singapore, Korea and Japan are coming forward to finance these disastrous projects. The worldwide campaign to save the Himalaya should be intensified. The Save Himalaya Movement's declaration has offered a blueprint for the survival of the Himalaya.

Following widespread destruction of forests and the consequent soil erosion, water from glacier-fed rivers is now the one remaining resource which holds immense potential if tapped for hydro-electricity generation. However, what is needed is to tap this resource in a permanent and sustainable manner, by constructing on a priority basis smaller hydel projects which would not inundate fertile valleys or displace people. The first use of electricity should be for lifting water, for driving ropeways, and for domestic and small-scale industrial use. It should be ensured that these schemes are eco-friendly and have employment potential. Of the power generated for export, Uttarakhand should get a 20 per cent share, of which 10% should be given to local bodies for development. However, the primary use of available water resources should be to supply irrigation and drinking water to scarcity-hit hill villages. The present policy of exporting water while denying it to the local hill populace would not be acceptable.

The main objectives of a Himalayan policy should be:

1. To ensure that the Himalaya remains a living space for its permanent residents, spiritual seekers, pilgrims and tourists visiting for peace and to enjoy scenic beauty.
2. To ensure that resources are used for regional economic self-sufficiency. There should be a ban on indiscriminate exploitation and export of resources (mining, deforestation, and construction of big dams etc.).
3. To maintain the local landscape for a number of economic activi-

ties, especially for tourism connected with scenic beauty.

4. To preserve the genetic biodiversity of the flora and fauna of the Himalayan region.
5. To ensure more autonomy for the development of local institutions, which is essential for their appropriate utilisation, sustainability and cultural development.[13]

Efforts should be made to evolve such a Himalayan policy sponsored by the countries in and around the Himalaya and supported by the UNO.

I conclude with an appeal made by VIPRO [a youth organisation of Garhwal University, Srinagar. The acronym stands for "Stop Destructive Tourism"]:

"Wander, with great joy, but not disturbing the joy of others, for all have an equal right over the gifts of nature - the gifts of trees, birds and animals, fresh air and water. Do not interfere with the rights of others by polluting or destroying these. Remember that our ancestors left this society, culture and environment secure for us, so we have to maintain it for the coming generations. To find happiness while comforting others is to be humane, but to find happiness by harming others is to be downright devilish. To wander is a natural right, but the abuse of the right is a violation of the laws of Nature."

Footnotes

1. Tapovanam, Swami: Wanderings in the Himalaya. Central Chinmaya Mission Trust, Bombay 1990, 400 072.
2. Kala, Dr Shankar: Visitors' Impact on Environmentally Sensitive Areas of dist. Uttarkashi & Chamoli 1989-1995.
3. Ibid.
4. Ibid.
5. For Swami Ram Tirtha's writings see Complete Works of Swami Ram Tirtha, Swami Ram Tirtha Pratishthan, Lucknow.
6. Tapovanam, Swami: Wanderings in the Himalayas.
7. Mother Ganga by Swami Sivananda. For Swami Sivananda's writings contact: Divine Life Society, Sivananda Nagr, PIN - 249 192. U.P.
8. Complete Works of Rahul Sanskrityayan published by Radhakrishna Prakashan, Daryaganj, New Delhi - 110 002. See especially the travelogues on H.P., Garhwal, Kumaon, Nepal and Tibet.
9. Kaka Kalelkar, Himalaya Ki Yatra, Ganhi Hindustani Sahitya Sabha, Sannidhi, Rajghat, New Delhi - 110 002.
10. S. Puran, Singh: The Story of Rama, Ram Tirtha Pratishthan, Lucknow.
11. Tapovanam, Swami: Wanderings in the Himalayas, pp. 65-66.
12. Ibid., pp. 27-28.
13. From "The Himalayan Threat", lecture delivered by Sunderlal Bahuguna at the Indian Institute of Technology. New Delhi in August 1996.

I

Sustainable Tourism:
Theories for the Mountains

Harka Gurung

Sustainability and Development in Mountain Tourism

I wish to thank Oeko Himal (Society for Ecological Co-operation Alps-Himalaya) for providing this opportunity to share my views with you. The theme is about sustainability and development in mountain tourism. I will approach the task from theory to situation analysis and conclude with practicalities. These are capsulized into five sections: (1) defining development, (2) mountain environment, (3) tourism impact, (4) carrying capacity, and (5) management strategy.

1. Defining Development

One might begin with clarification of the concept regarding development. There has been a considerable shift in the paradigm, i.e. mode of perception around which reality is perceived, of what is deemed development. This will involve tracing the evolutionary sequence in order to contextualize the current thinking.

1.1. Growth to Development

In broadest terms, development means a process of directed change and various definitions deal with objectives of this process and means of achieving them. Conventionally, development used to be equated with, or even held to be synonymous with economic growth, that is growth in consumption and output. Since the 1960s, growth and development have been considered as disparate processes. Growth basically pertains to quantitative increment which may be achieved even without qualitative change in the process. The prognosis addressed by The Club of Rome was to dramatize such a linear progression as incompatible with available physical resources. Development, on the other hand, refers to processes of economic and social transformation accompanied by structural change. It encompasses increasing productive potential (growth) as well as equality of opportunity (equity). Development rather than growth connotes an explicit orientation and upgrading of the level of integration of social, ecological and economic concerns in planning.[1]

The distinction between growth and development evolved from differing philosophies of the nature-man relationship debated as economics/development versus ecology/conservation. Development takes place in the context of the relationship between nature and society that necessarily involves change in this relationship. This was highlighted by the Club of Rome whose findings on the physical limit imposed by the finiteness of the world system was first reported in summer 1971 at Moscow and Rio de Janeiro.[2] It was soon followed by the UN Conference on Human Environment (Stockholm, 1972) that drew global attention to managing the relationship between nature and human activities for the future. Further emphasis on careful management of biophysical resources for 'sustainable development' was provided by the World Commission on Environment and Development[3] and the Earth Summit (Rio de Janeiro, 1992).

1.2. Development and Environment[4]

Theoretical considerations that emphasize either economics or ecology can best be illustrated by the five paradigms summarized in Table 1 as:

1. Frontier economics (FE);
2. Environmental protection (EP);
3. Resource management (RM);
4. Eco-development (E-D);
5. Deep ecology (DE).

Table 1: Paradigms on Environment and Development*

Paradigm **Aspects**	**Frontier Economic**	**Environment Protection (EP)**	**Resource Management (RM)**	**Eco-development**	**Deep Ecology (DE)**
1. Nature-Man Relation-ship	Very strong anthropo-centric	Strong anthropocen-tric	Modified anthropocen-tric	Eco-centric	Bio-centric
2. Dominent Imperative	'Progress' as infinite economic growth	'Trade-off' in ecology vs economic growth	'Sustainability' as constraint to growth	'Co-development' of man and nature	'Eco-topia', anti-growth
3. Problem	Poverty	Endangered species	Resource degradation	Ecological change	Ecosystm collapse
4. Main Theme	Exploitation of natural resources as infinite	Remedial/ defensive	Economize ecology	Ecologize social systems	Back to nature for symbosis
5. Limitation	Mechanis-tic, ignores limited resource	Lacks vision of abundance	Downplays social factors	May generate false security	Organic but not creative

*Adapted from Colby 1990, Table 2.

1. *Frontier economics*, which prevailed in industrial countries until the late 1960s, treated nature as an infinite supply of physical resources to be used for human benefit as well as a sink for by-products of development and consumption of these benefits. Capitalism and communism both held visions of infinite economic growth and human progress.
2. *The environmental protection* paradigm was born of the necessity to make compromises between economic growth and ecological perception. Incorporation of the environmental impact statement was inherently a remedial measure rather than ameliorative. It is a modest variation of 'frontier economics' with unbridled faith in technological progress.
3. The third paradigm, *resource management*, was more in response to resource depletion in developing countries and survival priorities of the poor. The basic idea is to incorporate all types of resources to be managed for potential use. Resource managers view the stabilisation of population levels in developing countries and reduction in per capita consumption in industrial nations as absolutely essential to achieving sustainability.
4. *Eco-development* believes in restructuring the relationship between nature and society by making human activities synergise with natural processes. Eco-development attempts to provide a positive vision for both human development and nature by making social, ecological and economic criteria explicit.
5. Finally, *deep ecology*, on the other hand, emphasizes ethical, social and spiritual aspects and recognizes mutual dependence, and the need for co-operation between nature and man. Its world view is more 'biocentric' with philosophical strains of 'small is beautiful' and 'green politics'.

The five paradigms enumerated above have both negative and positive linkages. Deep ecology may be taken as the polar opposite, or rather as a reaction to consequences, of frontier economics. Environmental protection and resource management are progressive responses to the predatory propensity of frontier economics. Eco-development that aims to restructure the nature-man relationship into a 'positive sum game' attempts at convergence between efficiency economists and deep ecologists. It is directed towards "*ecological transition*: from the notion of an always-renewable nature (and naive confidence in its permanence) to a revolt against over-exploitation of its resources, its purity, and its beauty".[5]

1.3. Towards Sustainability

In recent years, the phrase 'sustainable development' (SD) has become so pervasive as to acquire the status of cliché or jargon. But what is SD, as it has become "an article of faith, a shibboleth; often used, but little explained."[6] The interpretations of SD vary so widely that some call it a "contradiction in terms" or "another development truism." Most equate SD with environmentally-sound development. Sometimes it is assumed to be 'sustained growth', 'successful development' or even to have a social connotation. In fact, the phrase "sustainable society" was used as early as 1974 in the report of an ecumenical Conference on Science & Technology for Human Development (convened by the World Council of Churches).[7]

The central idea of SD had an environmental basis as defined by the World Conservation Strategy: "the overall aim of achieving sustainable development through conservation of living resources."[8] It addressed only the issue of ecological sustainability rather than sustainable development. Since then, SD has acquired a broader connotation as defined by the World Commission on Environment and Development:

Sustainable development is development that meets the needs of the present without compromising the ability of future generations to meet their own needs.[9]

The WCED report stressed the inter-generational nature of sustainability along with exploitation of resources as a key aspect and institutional change involving the people. However, the mainstream formulation of SD still suffers from incomplete understanding of the links between poverty and environmental degradation, conceptual vagueness relating to the role of economic growth, and lack of clarity between conservation of natural resources and sustainability of development.[10] SD can be seen as the logical conclusion of the paradigmatic progression from frontier economics to deep ecology through resource management and eco-development.[11]

The concept of sustainability has multiple dimensions – economic, environmental and social. Thus, a holistic view is a sine qua non for sustainability. And it is futile to talk of sustainability without addressing the problem of poverty.[12] Poverty is at the root of environmental degradation as poor people are forced to overuse their habitats in order to survive. Therefore, poverty alleviation seems essential for environmental sustainability. As argued above on the distinction between growth and development, economic growth that cannot be sustained is not development. The original meaning of the word 'development', derived from the Old French, is to envelop or unfold more fully. Sustainability is, therefore, about the survival of people through the unfolding of their potentials for development.

2. The Mountain Environment

Section one touched on aspects of development and sustainability. The next step is to explore what constitutes the characteristics of the mountain environment. However, a clearer picture can emerge only after surmounting the fog of some bland notions.

2.1. Notion versus Reality[13]

The first task is to demolish some prevailing misconceptions about the mountain environment that are the making of sentimentality and exorbitance. These relate to platitudes on ecological balance, the fragility of mountains, erosion equated with deforestation, native ignorance of the environment, and development-environment as confrontational (Table 2). It is necessary to traverse these conceptual crevasses.

Table 2: Notion and Reality

Notion	Reality
1. Nature-man balance	Technological development to adapt/control nature Temporal Sequence: a. Dominance of nature over man; b. Adaptation of man to nature; c. Balance between man and nature; d. Adaptation of nature to man; e. Dominance of man over nature.
2. Mountains are fragile	Mountains are dynamic
3. Deforestation = Erosion	Erosion mainly due to steep slope
4. Native ignorance of the environment	Intimate knowledge of environment, but economic compulsion
5. Development is anti-environment	Environmental protection possible only through development.

I. *Ecological Balance*: To speak of ecological balance in its pristine state is a futile perpetuation of an ancient myth. The spoliation of the natural eco-system is inevitable with human intervention. The progression of human civilization has been a continuous effort to be free from the shackles of nature. It is the level of technology that enables man to exploit and control nature. The degree of imposition on the natural environment varies in rapacity both in time and space depending on whether it is for survival (poverty) or conspicuous consumption (affluence). The quantum leap in science and technology has, however, obliterated the Middle Path between traditional immobility and materialist heedlessness.

II. *Fragility of Mountains*: Gravitational law ordains that objects must come downhill from higher to lower elevations. Mountain peaks and pinnacles are outliers of extreme resistance in terms of the geomorphic process. In the geological time-scale, highlands represent an intermediary or even dramatic stage between the alluvial plain which is the organic womb, and the plateau when mountains are tired of dominating the landscape. Excessive exposure to natural elements makes mountains a high energy area for mass wasting. Therefore, it would be more realistic to consider mountain areas as dynamic.

III. *Erosion due to Deforestation*: Most statements attribute soil erosion entirely or directly to loss of vegetation. The presumed intimate relationship between deforestation and soil erosion is not necessarily true in the mountains. The instability of the mountain is related more to steep slopes. At excessive heights above the tree-line, mass wasting takes place independently of vegetation cover. Soil creep, soil erosion, solifluction, land slips and slides are common in the highlands whether there be vegetation or not. Human activities do contribute to deforestation but the extent of human impact on consequent land degradation is marginal compared to the natural processes.

IV. *Native Ignorance*: Generally, the natives are said to be ignorant of the adverse consequences of environmental degradation. First, it is said that the highlanders should not multiply so fast. Here the philosophical question is–if the land could not support them, how was this population growth possible? Shifting cultivation is said to be a bad land use practice. But this is the only practical mechanism of utilizing forest fecundity. Tree felling for fuel wood certainly leads to forest depletion. Then how can the highlander contend with the cold and cook his food when there are no alternative sources of energy to wood, and when even if available they are beyond his means? Mountain people have an intimate knowledge of their natural world through accumulated experience. But one needs to appreciate their compulsions to toil on harsh land, not in order to achieve a certain standard but for survival itself.

V. *Development vs Environment*: The relationship between the natural environment and economic development is generally considered to be antagonistic. This notion is based on the observation that the more advanced the economy, the greater the pressure on resources. In fact, the relationship between the environment and development in the mountains should be considered inverted since some of the environmental stresses there are the result of extreme underdevelopment. Here, poverty is the basic cause of poor land management, and the consequence of poor management is deepening poverty.[14]

2.2. Mountain Specificity

The above clarifications imply certain conclusions. These can be summarized as (1) the environment needs careful management, (2) mountains are more exposed to dynamic processes, (3) in which erosion is elemental, (4) natives impose on the environment to survive, and (5) development is a pre-condition for conservation. Beyond these, it is also necessary to appreciate some essentials or specificities[15] of the mountain environment. They are conspicuity, diversity and marginality.

I. *Conspicuity.* A mountain, strictly speaking, is a conspicuous elevation of small area. A mountain range provides a pedestal to an array of high summits. Therefore, an essential element in the definition of a mountain is its conspicuity. This conspicuity is the product of the initial uplift and the subsequent erosion process. Conspicuity in altitude imparts to mountains an air of mystery (pilgrimage) and beauty (tourism). Ascending the elevation against the pull of gravity as a physical challenge is what alpinism is all about. Hence the high potential of mountain areas as tourist destinations.

II. *Diversity.* Since mountains are the culmination of ascending land surface, they encompass various ecological zones with associated diversity. Climatic variations from sub-tropical to temperate and nival (snow) zones reflect abundant biotic diversity. These not only represent a biodiversity bank but also generate a variety of livelihood patterns that include nomadic herding, shifting cultivation, settled agriculture and trade. Poor soil productivity is compensated by use of diverse spaces with seasonality. The Sherpas of Khumbu shuttle between winter ghunsa and summer yarsa while Bakarwals of Western Himalaya range 250 km from Kathuwa (500m) in Jammu to Dras (4,000 m) in northern Kashmir. Diversity of lateral dimension, between the arid west and the humid east of the Himalaya, is to be seen in the shifting cultivation of Assam where jhum is the simplest technique of exploiting natural soil fertility. The diversity of mountain products sustains trade and even smuggling. Again, it is the scenic variety that draws hordes of tourists to the mountain.

III. *Marginality.* Mountains everywhere are marginal areas for human occupancy. This has two contradictory consequences. One may be considered positive as a space for refuge. This breeds independence of attitude and a refuge for ancient cultures. Another may be considered negative as the frontier of innovation as well as for political access. These have adverse effects on the development of mountain areas. A classic example of the slow pace of change in mountain areas is the long interval of time in potato introduction. The first potato planted in the Himalaya was in Bhutan by George Bogle in June 1774. It reached Kumaon in the mid-1850s through Henry Ramsay and then Jumla only in 1889 through Tej Bikram Rana (Bada Hakim).[16] Inaccessibility limits external linkage both for product marketing and technology transfer.

As people on the frontier, mountain people have continued to survive by contending with natural risks as well as exploitation from the centres of economic and political power. Mountain dwellers must remain mobile with the season and forage for more land resources to survive. It is poverty that compels them to become migrant labourers, and even soldiers of fortune epitomized by the guards at the Vatican or Buckingham Palace!

3. The Impact of Tourism

Since tourists are outsiders, they will have impact on the areas they visit, both positive and negative. These may be classified as environmental, social, and economic.

3.1. Environmental

Tourism affects the mountain environment, more so when a large number intrude on uninhabited areas and exert pressure in areas of sparse population. The most obvious direct effects are in forest depletion and pollution. But these negative effects are not due to tourism alone. Tourism activities exacerbate the situation. The clearing of forest for cultivation in mountain and hill areas has been an ongoing process that began long before the advent of tourism. Tourist demand for fuel may be minuscule compared to the aggregate demand of the local population. Despite the insignificant level in absolute terms, a concentration of tourists in limited areas makes significant impact. Moreover, the fuel wood requirement for tourists is much higher than the local level. The critical factors that affect levels of fuel wood consumption are the type of activity, length of trip, number of staff and the extent of substitutes used. According to one estimate for Nepal, this averages 138 kg per tourist, varying from 55 kg for an individual trekker, to 186 kg for an agency trekker and

1,116 kg for a mountaineer. The increase in demand for fuel wood also varies from area to area depending on the tourist volume. Of the total local need estimated for 1987, 85.2 percent in Khumbu and 18 percent in Langtang were from tourist demand. Deforestation due to wood harvesting not only affects the natural landscape visually, the loss in biomass can have a damaging effect on the natural habitats of flora and fauna.

Another obvious negative impact of tourism on the mountain environment is pollution. The problem is accentuated by the inflow of large numbers of visitors during certain peak periods and at particular locations. Littering is not dangerous to health as such but is visually intrusive. Littering with plastic, tin, and non-degradable materials has turned some popular trek routes into virtual 'garbage trails'. Solid waste is another pollution problem with a health hazard. Using water courses for garbage disposal, including faecal waste, is common in most trek areas. These give rise to hygiene problems. Even within national parks, there is inadequate provision for waste disposal or portering out of recyclable waste. With growing numbers of tourists, garbage disposal can be a serious problem as waste decomposition is a slow process in mountain areas.

3.2. Socio-cultural

Tourism has economic benefits with social costs. Unlike other exporting activities where producers and consumers rarely meet, the distinguishing feature of tourism is that tourists have to come to consume the product. Hence the inevitable socio-cultural impact.[17] Impacts differ according to the quality of encounter between the tourist and the host. Generally, three stages of such encounters are recognized: discovery, initiation and institutionalization. Socio-cultural maladies become apparent at the institutionalization stage.

Basically, the problem is one of schism between leisured tourists and the impoverished natives. This superimposition of a highly competitive profit-based industry serving a high income, foreign clientele has significant impact upon every aspect of culture. On the other hand, it is also true that cultures do change; thus it is necessary to enquire:

- How much of the change is a direct consequence of tourism?
- And, which aspects of this change are beneficial and which are harmful to the indigenous population?

For example, tourism is blamed for commercialization of art, culture and religion. But there are also many instances where tourism has helped to revive traditional art and culture and provided new markets for crafts and musical traditions once threatened by extinction. "It is an interesting sidelight to the impact of tourism that even among governments notably uninterested in protecting ethnic diversity, tourism operates to enlarge the government's interest and involvement in culture."[18] This, in turn, gives the ethnic groups a leverage they otherwise would not enjoy.

Societies even in mountain enclaves will change with outside exposure whether there be tourism or not. There is a world of difference between living in tradition and viewing it from outside, just as one might decry the disappearance of the horse-drawn cart and yet enjoy the efficiency of the milk van. Similarly, whatever their sentimental value, the bamboo blower (dhungro) and iron tongue (chimta) will disappear with the introduction of improved stoves into mountain hearths. The so-called demonstration effect–the economist's concept –attributed to tourism is, in fact, mostly due to mainstream development, e.g., westernization/modernization.

3.3. Economic

The economic benefits of tourism have much value particularly for mountain areas. These are mainly in the form of employment and income. In fact, without tourism, some mountain communities would have either withered or outmigrated. Tourism provides opportunities for seasonal and permanent employment and generates handicraft industry. For example, total employment generated by mountain tourism in Nepal is estimated to range from 536,935 to 1,115,345 man days.[19] The number of those employed in hill and mountain tourist establishments totals 24,524. Estimates of income generated for one year (1988) average Rs.10.6 million from individual tourists and Rs.46 million from group tourists. These have a positive impact on the local as well as the macro economy.

During two decades (1975-95), Nepal experienced a 3.9-fold increase in tourist arrivals. (Table 3). There were 6.7 times as many arrivals for trekking and mountaineering, their share among total visitors rising from 13.6 percent in 1975 to 23.3 percent in 1995.

Foreign exchange earnings from tourism increased 53-fold from Rs.170.6 million in the fiscal year 1974/75 to Rs.8,973.2 million in 1994/95. Such earnings as a percentage of total value of merchandise export grew 2.6-fold and as a percentage of GDP 4.3-fold. Data on income from mountaineering in Nepal for the last decade also show a positive trend. Nepal experienced no increase in the number of climbing expeditions and had less climbers in 1995 than in 1985 (Table 3). Yet the amount collected as climbing royalty increased eleven-fold and the amount from expedition expenditure over six times. There are also other sources of tourism revenue. In 1988, total income from four sources was Rs.15.6 million (Table 4).

Table 3: Nepal Tourism Data

	1975	1995	Change 1975-95 Absolute Increase	Times
a. Arrivals				
Tourist arrivals (Number)	92,440	363,395	270,955	3.9
Trekking & Mountaineering (Number)	12,587	84,524	71,937	6.7
Percent for Trekking & Mountaineering (%)	13.6	23.3		
b. Foreign Exchange Earning	1974/75	1994/95		
Total earning (Rs. Million)	170.6	8,973.2	8,802.6	52.6
As % of total value of merchandise export	19.2	50.0		2.6
As % of total foreign exchange earning	30.2	17.2		-1.8
As % of GDP	1.0	4.3		4.3
c. Mountaineering	1985	1995		
Number of Expeditions	91	91	0	0
Number of Climbers	824	6242	-200	-1.3
Royalty, Rs. 1000	3,298	37,307	34,009	11.3
Expedition expenditure, Rs. 1000	17,870	116,600	98,730	6.5

Source: Finance Ministry, Economic Survey 1995/96, Kathmandu 1996, Tables 3.11, 3.12, 3.13 & 3.16

Table 4: Tourism Revenue by Source, 1988

Source	Revenue (Rs)	Percent
1. Trek permit fee	4,852,680	31.1
2. Mountaineering royalty	4,615,106	29.5
3. Park entrance fee	4,606,623	29.5
4. Trek peak fee	1,548,220	9.9
Total	**15,622,629**	**100.0**

Source: Gurung 1991, Table 7.

Khumbu accounted for 58.8 percent of the mountaineering royalty and 46 percent of the trek peak fee collected. Nearly two-thirds of trek permit fee came from the Annapurna area, while Chitwan led in park entrance revenue. These revenues are much higher now due to the increase in climbing royalties and entry fees along with more visitors. The basic issue is how to utilize such revenue in areas where they are generated. This will be discussed as one of the management strategies in the concluding section.

4. Carrying Capacity

The term 'carrying capacity' was first used in the context of determining the maximal population of a given species that its environment can support indefinitely. Since this depends not only on population per se but permutations of the population-technology-consumption combination, the Independent Commission on Population and Quality of Life (ICPQL) qualifies the definition as the "maximal sustainable load that humankind can impose on the environment before it loses its capacity to support human activity".[20]

4.1.Contrasting Samples

The case of Austria and Nepal, two mountain countries, exemplifies divergent carrying capacities in the tourism sector. Nepal is 1.8 times bigger in area and 2.5 times larger in population than Austria (Table 5). On the other hand, Austria caters to 65.2 times more international tourists. Again, Nepal has 40 more natives per km² while Austria has 226 more tourists per km². In 1991, the ratio between the native and the tourist population was 1:0.01 for Nepal and 1:2.4 for Austria.

Table 5: Country Comparison, 1991

Select Indicator	Unit	AUSTRIA	NEPAL	Variance
1. Land area	Km²	83,856	147,181	Nepal 1.8 times bigger
2. Population, mid-1991	Million	7.82	19.6	Nepal 2.5 times larger
3. GNP per capita	US$	20,380	180	Austria 113 times richer
4. International visitors	In 000	19,092	293	Austria receives 65.2 times more
5. Tourism receipts	Million US$	13,956	126	Austria exceeds 110-fold
6. Tourism expenditure	Million US$	7,449	38	Austria exceeds 196-fold
Population density	Persons/Km²	93.3	133.2	Nepal has 40 more per km²
Tourist density	Persons/Km²	227.7	2.0	Austria has 226 more per km²
Population/Tourist ratio	1:2.4	1:0.01		Austria exceeds Nepal's ratio 240-fold
Receipt per tourist	US$	731.0	430.0	Austria earns 1.7 times more
Expenditure per tourist	US$	390.2	129.7	Austria gains 3.0 times more

Source: WTO, Compendium of Tourism Statistics 1987-91 Madrid 1993, pp.10, 106, 201 & 203.

There is an obvious contrast in the tourism revenue of these two countries. Austria exceeded Nepal 110-fold in tourism receipts and 196-fold in tourism expenditure (Table 5). The receipt per tourist for Austria was nearly double and expenditure per tourist was three times that of Nepal.

The per capita income from tourism is said to be higher in Austria than in any other country. And the environmental situation of tourist locations in Austria remains superior despite the immense tourist volume. The success of Austrian tourism seems to lie in a long tradition of hospitality service, dual seasonality marketing, multi-faceted packaging and increasing environmental awareness.[21] Initially known for its summer resorts, 40 percent of tourism income now comes from winter activities. Austrian promotional slogans range from 'Austria–a wander and wonderland' to 'Festival Country Austria' and 'Servus in Oesterreich (Hallo in Austria)'. Finally, there are strict capacity restrictions for environmental protection on visitor volume by location.

4.2. Dynamic Aspect.

The notion of carrying capacity is generally concerned with the capability of available resources to meet the created demand. Since tourism itself is an expression of externality in the local economy, application of this notion in mountain tourism needs qualification. Mountain tourism is basically an act of getting closer to wilderness in remote areas. Therefore, most mountain economies are sustained through outside linkages of seasonal migration and product import. Since transport infrastructure influences where tourists go, improvement in access can induce a larger volume of visitors. Their optimum number is dependent both on physical space and created facilities. The unique value of the tourism industry is the local processing through services that enhance the income of such marginal economies.

The concept of carrying capacity does not have a single fixed value. There can be different levels of carrying capacity based on local values for tolerance of outsiders. The limits of carrying capacity are determined by the combination of three factors: environmental threshold, investment options, and management policies.[22] Assessment of the environmental threshold will determine the extent and type of investment, while management policies have to be strategized according to the local context and situation. The primary concern is efficient utilization of limited space for sustainable tourism activities.

5. Management Strategy[23]

Tourism is an important economic activity, and even a prime engine of development, for mountain areas with limited resources. But it also has environmental and social costs if not controlled. Hence the emergence of new awareness under the rubric of such terms as alternative, responsible, eco-friendly or gentle tourism. Basically, they refer to the protection of the environment as well as the interests of the locals and visitors. Some of the management strategies for a sustainable mountain tourism are enumerated briefly below.

5.1. Regulation of Volume

Mountain ranges provide a panorama and each mountain peak has its own personality. These may be extensive and widespread but tourists tend to concentrate and crowd in particular seasons and regions. Hence the need for regulating their volume by seasonality and geographic spread. The mechanism should include both the absolute number permitted and differential rate for user charges.

(i) *Seasonal*

Most Himalayan destinations experience extreme high pressure of tourists during the autumn and spring seasons. The beauty and human activity of the monsoon season remain unsung. Therefore, each tourist area should be assigned an optimum number by seasonality according to the available infrastructure. The guiding principle should be to minimize the wide disparity between the valley of low season and high peak season. An element of price mechanism can be introduced to influence tourist choice with different rates for permit fees by season. In other words, tourists opting for the peak season would have to pay more and vice versa. There is also scope for encouraging more tourists to visit the rain-shadow areas of the Himalaya during the summer.

(ii) *Regional*

A rational approach for the regulation of volume would be to adopt a policy of regional dispersal. In fact, much of the negative image of tourism in the Himalaya is based on problems of a few overcrowded areas. An effective measure to divert tourists from crowded areas would be to limit their number during the peak season and promote new areas. Promotion of new destinations would involve both differential costs for permits (cheaper for new areas) and government initiatives. The latter would include exploring/facilitating new destinations, decentralizing the permit issue and the provision of incentives to private agencies that promote new destinations.

5.2. Revenue Sharing

The case study of Nepal shows an annual revenue of over Rs..15 million a year from tourism fees (Table 4). Normally, such revenues accrue to the central exchequer, be it in Nepal, India or Pakistan. The exception is the Annapurna Conservation Area Project (ACAP) where all revenue from entrance fees is directed to environmental manage-ment in collaboration with local communities. Since the poor govern-ments themselves need resources, and also in order to sustain their policy interest in such endeavours, a more viable mechanism would be to share tourism revenue between the central exchequer and the areas where it is generated. This formula has the carrying capacity rationale. The more visitors to an area, the more the pressure and need for higher management costs, but also the higher the related revenue. The share retained in the area should be utilized for environmental protection and local development activities.

5.3. Priority Concerns

Tourism in mountain areas is also dependent on the scale of the economy. Attracting more tourists will entail a higher level of development intervention and ameliorative activities. The first relates particularly to energy alternatives to wood and the second to pollution control. Vegetative resources are facing increasing pressure for firewood in most mountain areas whether trekked or untrekked. Since tourists accentuate the demand for firewood, the additional energy requirement should either be met from outside or developed locally. This means a supply of kerosene or gas and the development of hydro, solar or wind power in tourist areas.

Pollution can be controlled only through a regular system of collection and disposal. Garbage should be burnt or buried, recyclable waste disposed of and non-degradable waste transported out. Involvement of local people in these activities will enhance their income. Mountain tourism generates economic benefit for locals as well as satisfaction to the visitors. The only path to its regenerative capacity is controlled management through judicious policy and local involvement.

Footnotes

1. Colby 1990, 24
2. Meadows et al, 1972, 186
3. WCED 1987
4. Colby 1990
5. ICPQL 1996, 38
6. Tolba 1984
7. Dowdeswell 1994, 144
8. IUCN 1980
9. WCED 1987, 43
10. Lele 1991, 610-611
11. Franks 1996
12. Samad, Watanabe & Kim 1985
13. Gurung 1987
14. Piers Blaikie & Harold Brookfield 1987
15. Jodha (1995) at ICIMOD devised six mountain specificities: inaccessibility, fragility, marginality, diversity, niches, and adaptation mechanisms. One might note conjunction between inaccessibility and marginality on one hand and niches as expression of diversity on the other.
16. Gurung 1980, 69
17. Gurung 1993, 139-140
18. Richter 1984, 193
19. CREST 1995a
20. ICPQL 1996, 97
21. Luger & Rest, forthcoming
22. CREST 1995b, 16
23. Gurung 1991, 22-24

References

Blaikie, Piers/Brookfield, Harold: Land Degradation and Society, London 1987

Centre for Resource & Environmental Studies (CREST): Mountain Tourism in Nepal: An Overview, ICIMOD, Kathmandu 1995a

Carrying Capacity of Himalayan Resources for Mountain Tourism Development. ICIMOD, Kathmandu 1995b

Colby, Michael E.: Environmental Management in Development: The Evolution of Paradigms. World Bank Discussion Paper No.80, Washington, DC 1990

Dowdeswell, Elizabeth: "A global view". In Partnerships in Practice. Department of Environment, U.K., London 1994, 143-146
Finance Ministry (Nepal): Economic Survey, Fiscal Year 1995/96. Kathmandu 1996
Franks, T.R.: "Managing sustainable development," Sustainable Development, Vol. IV, No.2, August 1996, 53-60
Gurung, Harka: Vignettes of Nepal, Kathmandu 1980
Gurung, Harka: "Protection of Himalayan environment: traverse and bivouac" Nepal Himalaya Annual Journal, Kathmandu 1987, 9-11
Gurung Harka: "Environmental Management of Mountain Tourism in Nepal. Bangkok ESCAP 1991
Gurung Harka: "Tourism with social consideration," PATA '93, 42nd Annual Conference Record, Honolulu 1993, 131-143
IUCN (International Union for the Conservation of Nature and Natural Resources): World Conservation Strategy: Living Resource Conservation for Sustainable Development, Gland 1980
Independent Commission on Population and Quality of Life (ICPQL): Caring for the Future: A Radical Agenda for Change, New York 1996
Jodha, N.S.: "The Nepal middle mountains" Regions At Risk: Comparisons of Threatened Environments edited by Jeanne X. Kasperson, Roger E. Kasperson & B.L. Turner, UNU Press, Tokyo 1995, 140-185
Lele, S.M.: Sustainable development: a critical review. World Development, Vol.XIX, 607-621
Luger, Kurt/Franz Rest: Culture and tourism in the Second Republic. In: Larkey, Edward/Kurt Luger (Eds.): Beyond Habsburg. Forthcoming
Meadows, Donella/Dennis Meadows et.al.: The Limits of Growth. A Report for The Club of Rome's Project on the Predicament of Mankind. New York 1972
Richter, Linda K.: The Politics of Tourism in Asia. Honolulu 1984
Samad, S.A./T. Watanabe/S.J. Kim (Eds.): People's Initiatives for Sustainable Development: Lessons of Experience. Asian & Pacific Development Centre, Kuala Lumpur 1995
World Commission on Environment and Development (WCED): Our Common Future, New York 1987

Pitamber Sharma

Sustainable Tourism in the Hindu Kush-Himalayas

Issues and Approaches

Introduction

The mountain areas of the Hindu Kush-Himalayas (HKH) at the present time are facing a formidable array of problems: rapid population growth, food deficit and energy shortages, declining productivity of agriculture, increasing unemployment and underemployment, and a host of environmental problems resulting from the accelerated degradation of renewable resources. These demographic, economic and environmental problems facing the Hindu Kush-Himalaya region call for the promotion of activities that are based on the region's comparative advantage, that help in the diversification of the mountain economy, provide alternative livelihood opportunities for mountain people and at the same time actively promote environmental care so that the twin issues of poverty and environmental degradation can be simultaneously addressed. Tourism in the mountains has the potential of addressing all these concerns and providing alternative and environment-friendly income and employment opportunities all across the HKH. It is this potential that makes mountain tourism (which includes all tourism activities for which mountains manifest a comparative advantage) and its sustainability a singularly important aspect in integrated mountain development.

Sustainable tourism has been perceived and interpreted in different ways (Nepal 1996), much of it emanating from the literature on tourism and the environment. For the World Tourism Organization sustainable tourism has to fulfill three objectives: improvement in the quality of life of the host population, a high quality experience for the visitor, and maintenance of the quality of environment on which both the visitors and the host community depend (WTO 1993). Others consider the promotion of local economic development which conserves local natural, cultural and built resources as the key mechanism for the realization of sustainable tourism (Hunter and Green 1995). Concepts such as ecotourism, alternative tourism, green tourism, soft tourism etc. have often been interpreted as synonymous to sustainable tourism. Sustainable tourism, like sustainable development, is a multidimensional concept. Further, sustainability is a process and not an end state. In ecological terms sustainable tourism means that the level of tourism and tourist activities has to be compatible with the maintenance and enhancement of biological resources and their diversity so that the capacity of the environment to regenerate itself is not impaired. In social and cultural terms, sustainable tourism development needs to ensure that it is compatible with the culture and values of the people, that its benefits are broadly shared, and that it strengthens community identity, promotes wider participation in decision-making related to development and management of natural resources and enhances people's control over their own lives. In economic terms, sustainable tourism development needs to facilitate a process of development that is economically efficient, has positive backward and forward linkages that relieve pressure on fragile resources, and allows and promotes management of resources in ways that not only support present needs but which can also support the needs and aspirations of future generations (WCED 1987).

The objective conditions obtained in the mountains also have implications for the sustainability of tourism. These objective conditions include their general inaccessibility, the fragile and diverse nature of their resources, the comparative advantage afforded by specific niches, their "marginality" in terms of political and economic decision-making, and the variety of human adaptations of activities and institutions evolved by mountain societies (Jodha 1991). Sustainability of mountain tourism requires a positively reinforcing response to these objective conditions. Mountains, by virtue of their geological, altitudinal and therefore climatic characteristics impose considerable constraints on the "type" and "volume" of tourism that can be promoted. Also, mountains have historically remained marginal to the centres of decision-making and have consistently suffered the consequences of adverse terms of trade and undervaluation of their resources. Therefore, while fragility and marginality often remain as constraints to be overcome, relative inaccessibility, diversity, niche and resiliency of human adaptations afford opportunities to be tapped.

In such a context, how can tourism be made a vehicle of sustainable economic and environmental development of areas and communities in the HKH? What have been the approaches to tourism development in the region and what are the issues that require prioritized attention? The present paper attempts to highlight some of these concerns on the basis of the studies and reviews made by ICIMOD. The following section presents the trends in tourism development in some countries of the HKH. The major issues in terms of sustainability are then elucidated in the next section. This is followed by a brief review of the approaches to mountain tourism pursued by some countries of the region, and finally initiatives required for sustainable mountain tourism are briefly presented.

Tourism in the HKH: Emergent Trends

Tourism is the fastest growing industry worldwide and accounted for 3.4 trillion dollars in 1994, employing about 10 percent of the global workforce (PANOS 1995). Although the database on tourism in the Himalayas in general remains extremely poor, indications are that tourism as an activity and as a contributor to the economies of the mountain areas is quite significant. For larger countries and economies of the Hindu Kush-Himalaya region such as China, India and Pakistan, the share of domestic tourism is overwhelming in the total tourism scene. In Himachal Pradesh and the Uttar Pradesh hills, in India, for example, 95 to 96 percent of the total tourist flow (of 3.5 million and 25 million respectively in 1992/93) is domestic. In the NWFP and Northern Areas in Pakistan, 85 to 90 percent of the total tourist flow is domestic. A similar situation prevails in China, where, for the country as a whole, the volume of domestic tourism exceeds 300 million compared to around 38 million foreign tourists. In smaller economies of the region such as Nepal and Bhutan the concept of domestic tourism is not properly accounted and remains ignored in official statistics. Tourism in these countries essentially means foreign tourists. In 1993 Nepal, for example, received a little over 334,000 foreign tourists. Bhutan received about 3,000 tourists in the same year.

The magnitude of tourist flows also testifies to the increasing economic importance of tourism. In Himachal Pradesh the sector is estimated to contribute IRs 2 to 2.5 billion annually to the state economy. Similar figures for the U.P. hills are IRs 2.5 to 2.75 billion (AME 1995a). Above 20 percent of the domestic product in each case is contributed by tourism. For economies like Nepal tourism is also a major source of foreign exchange earnings. Tourism accounted for as much as 20 percent of all foreign exchange earnings and in 1992 comprised 3.8 percent of the GDP. In Pakistan foreign exchange earnings from tourism amounted to 120 million USD in 1992 and was the ninth largest foreign exchange earner. China in the same year earned 3,947 million USD from tourism (Jian 1995). The contribution of mountain tourism in both cases remains only conjectural.

The magnitude of tourism and the economic implications of tourism notwithstanding, relatively little is known about the impacts and implications of mountain tourism in the Hindu Kush-Himalayas. A number of key environmental and economic issues related to the sustainability of mountain tourism, however, emerge from the literature as well as the case studies that have been conducted by ICIMOD. These show that tourism has not been a complete blessing for the economically poor and environmentally fragile economies of the HKH. Indeed, the need to protect the product as it is being marketed is nowhere more conspicuous than in the case of mountain tourism. This is more so if the promotion of mountain tourism is to be seen as an economic compulsion derived from the hard economic and environmental realities of the region. The unfolding development scenario in the Hindu Kush Himalaya region makes it evident that mountain tourism cannot be sustainable without fostering a positively reinforcing linkage with the economic and environmental development of local communities.

Major Issues in Mountain Tourism in the HKH

There appear to be six substantive issues that contribute to the unsustainability of tourism in the mountain environment: 1. exploitation of environmental resources and environmental pollution, 2. lack of linkage with the local/regional production system, 3. very low retention of benefits in tourist areas and regions, 4. high degree of seasonality, 5. socio-cultural impacts resulting from tourism, and 6. problem of policy and institutional development.

1. Exploitation of Environmental Resources and Environmental Pollution

Mountain areas are inherently unstable due to slope and elevation and therefore the potential of soil erosion, landslides and mass wasting is intrinsically high. Even without the intrusion of tourists, many mountain areas are under tremendous pressure due to the demand made on environmental resources by a growing population (Sharma 1994). The most obvious examples of the environmental stress are forest degradation and deforestation resulting from the increased demand for fuel wood and timber to cater for tourist needs; loss of bio-diversity in areas with endemic species of flora and fauna, many of which might not even be known; environmental pollution due to garbage and littering along trekking routes and campsites; pollution of creeks and rivers, and water bodies; overburdening of the basic infrastructure and sanitation systems of destination settlements etc.

Deforestation and forest degradation due to tourism is a widely reported issue (ERL 1989, Sharma 1990; Gurung 1990). In the Everest area in Nepal, for example, it has been reported that the tourist demand increases the local demand for fuel wood by an estimated 85 percent. Many tourist destinations receive tourists in numbers that are at least two to three times the number of native inhabitants. The demand for timber for construction, and the very short growing season add to the problem of forest degradation and deforestation.

The lack of alternative energy sources, lack of monitoring of energy use by trekking parties in areas where the use of fuel wood is banned, and the problem of design and dissemination of efficient energy technologies have been some of the issues associated with the problem of forest degradation and depletion. The trekking areas of Nepal elucidate these problems (CREST 1995a).

Environmental pollution along trekking routes, campsites, and settlements is a universal problem associated with mountain tourism. Increased amounts of bio-nondegradable garbage and littering, inappro-priate disposal of human waste and contamination of water supply and pollution of creeks and rivers are some of the most negative effects of tourism in the mountains. Ecological stress in terms of pollution and destruction of natural vegetation have been noted from all across the HKH (Sharma 1995a). A study in Nepal shows that an average trekking group of 15 people generates about 15 kg of bio-nondegradable and non-burnable garbage in about 10 trekking days (Lama and Sherpa 1993). The littering and solid waste disposal problem has reached crisis proportions in the Everest region in Nepal. Between 1979 and 1988 about 770 mt of garbage is reported to have been disposed by about 840 mountaineering teams. This included 422 mt of disposable garbage, 141 mt of non-degradable garbage and about 207 tons of oxygen cylinders. In higher altitudes where decomposition is a slow process and the assimilative capacity of the environment remains quite limited, the problem is further exacerbated.

ICIMOD studies show that the problems of land degradation, of the constraints of water supply, basic infrastructure and sanitation due to tourism in resort areas and pilgrim centres, and of the maintenance of biodiversity in high altitude meadows or bhugyals are quite pronounced in the Uttar Pradesh hills and parts of Himachal Pradesh (AME 1995b). In many hill resorts and pilgrim centres the build-up of infrastructure such as road, electricity, water supply, large civil constructions and rapid urban expansion have occurred at the expense of the natural beauty and the environment, the very assets which supposedly attract tourists to these destinations. In the North West Frontier Province and Northern Areas of Pakistan, the environmental impacts of mountain tourism are manifest in terms of water and river pollution, pollution of soils and glaciers, deforestation and problems due to congestion in selected resort locations in the Swat valley, Kagan valley and Kalam valley, and trekking/ mountaineering areas (DRG 1995a). The problem of garbage and littering has been reported from over a dozen staging camps between Skardu and the base camp of K2 in Pakistan (Mirza 1991, Groetzbach 1989).

2. Lack of Linkage with the Production System

The state of forward and backward linkages of tourism with the production sectors has been a major issue of concern in mountain tourism. Often the promotion of tourism in these environments is rationalized on the basis of the multiplicity of impacts on the production regime. But with the exception of petty trade, lodge keeping and catering for tourists, productive activities linked with the agro-ecological resource base have rarely been induced through tourism.

Tourism almost everywhere has impacted on land use along trekking routes or more often in and around destination settlements, whether they be tourist resorts, or scenic villages. The most obvious effect on land use and therefore on the production regime has been through conversion of forest land to agriculture; encroachment on public open space to build lodges, tea stalls etc.; the tendency to leave land fallow to rent as camping sites etc. (Banskota and Sharma 1994). Tourism is often blamed for the neglect of traditional resource management systems such as the management of upland pastures and livestock upkeep in the Rolwaling area in Nepal. Also, in spite of the employment created by tourism in certain pocket areas such as the Khumbu region in Nepal, the income generated rarely finds its way to induce local resource-based productive activities in these areas.

The positive effect of tourism on land use and production systems is also noted in a few cases. The preference for fruit and vegetable farming as opposed to traditional crops is a noted phenomenon in the trans-Himalayan areas of Nepal. The most noted case of the development of a production base in which trekking tourism played a major role is the case of the Annapurna area, which receives upwards of 40,000 trekkers each year. Tourism, particularly in the Jomsom area, has induced a number of economic activities such as lodge and hotel keeping, farming of apples and other temperate fruits, fruit processing, commercial vegetable farming, cottage craft and mule transportation, the latter because most of the goods have to be transported from Pokhara or Baglung, both hill towns quite some distance away (K.C. et al 1992, ICIMOD 1992). The area has an airstrip but is not connected by road. However, these activities together have opened up novel off-farm employment and income opportunities in this basically food-deficit region, and have contributed to significantly raising the living standards of the local people. The Jomsom area, which was basically an area of outmigration, is one of the richest transhimalayan areas of Nepal today. A number of factors have contributed to the "success" of the Jomsom-Marpha area, including its peculiar ethnic blend, the extension support in temperate horticulture provided by the government, selective barrier to entry into the area created by formal and informal institutional set-ups, thus effectively shielding the area from the influence of big business from outside, and so on. The region elucidates the advantages that can be derived spontaneously from relative inaccessibility.

There remains a very wide scope for such developments in most areas of the HKH. Development of horticulture, vegetable farming, livestock, poultry, commercial wood lots, cottage craft etc. are areas where the activities could thrive because of the demand created by tourists. Also, if the prospects for local food purchases by tourists were to be enhanced, this would further add to the strength of the local economies in favourable areas. Domestic tourism, which is quite significant in the HKH areas of India and Pakistan, offers greater scope for such development.

3. Lack of Retention of Benefits from Tourism in Tourist Areas

The lack or very low level of the retention of benefits from tourism, particularly income, has been a matter of serious concern in mountain tourism in the HKH. The employment effect in many areas is limited to portering, but often porters hail from areas far from tourist destinations. In Nepal, for example, most porters in mountaineering come from the Khumbu region irrespective of the location of the peak to be climbed. Further, portering is only a seasonal occupation although the total number of man-days involved is estimated to be quite considerable. It is estimated that the total employment from mountain tourism, basically trekking and mountaineering, ranged from a high of 2.3 to a low of 1.1 million man-days in Nepal in 1994. Porterage accounted for about 21 percent of this total employment (Sharma 1995b).

The experience from trekking and mountaineering areas in Nepal suggests that the bulk of the income that accrues in mountain areas is not retained locally, as lodge owners are often from outside the region, foods and other essential goods have to be imported, and income is remitted to family members living in urban areas (Banskota and Sharma 1994). There are also considerable income leakages in the form of benefits to large city-based trekking and travel agencies, and in the form of royalties, taxes and fees of various kinds to the central government (Sharma 1992).

There seems to be in general a lack of integration of tourism sector activities with local resource-based economic activities, with the result that not much economic benefit is retained at the local level. Studies in Pakistan show that the benefits of tourism tended to be higher at the national level than at the level of local mountain communities who bore the brunt of the economic and ecological problems resulting from tourism (DRG 1995b). Thus a situation arises where outsiders have been successful in "capturing the benefits" of mountain environmental resources while the resultant environmental costs have been "externalised" to the local communities (Bhadra and Sharma 1995). In the Annapurna area in Nepal, studies show that as much as 60 to 65 percent of the local tourist expenditure leaks out; in the Kalam valley in Pakistan this figure is in excess of 80 percent. Over 40 percent of the trade in the Badrinath pilgrimage circuit is directly controlled by outsiders (AME 1995b, Sharma 1995c).

While this issue in general has tended to be ignored, innovative schemes such as the Annapurna Conservation Area Project (ACAP) in Nepal have shown that there are ways through which the dual aims of resource conservation and maximization of economic benefits of tourism to local communities can be simultaneously achieved (ACAP 1989, CREST 1995b). While meeting the needs of the local people, the ACAP seeks to conserve the natural and cultural resources of the area, promote sustainable social and economic development, and develop tourism with minimum negative environmental impact. The ACAP philosophy is to involve local people in all aspects of conservation and development, including tourism, so that the villagers are enabled to improve their quality of life and to strengthen their cultural integrity. The community empowerment approach pursued by the ACAP relies on the formation of grass roots level conservation and development committees. Although not all areas in the ACAP evidence the same degree of success as in the Ghandruk area, the ACAP approach has elicited considerable attention. ACAP's activities are sustained among other sources by the entry fee levied on tourists who enter the ACAP area. The ACAP is managed by King Mahendra Trust for Nature Conservation which functions as an NGO with links nationally and internationally.

Learning from the ACAP experience, recently the Nepal government has decided to provide revenues generated from entry fees in the National

Parks and Conservation Areas for environmental and community development activities in other tourist areas. A decision also has been made to replicate the ACAP experience in the Manaslu region of Northern Gorkha.

Other HKH countries have also experimented with other means to retain income from tourism locally. Among these are the Village Guest House schemes variously tried in the Indian Himalayas and also in Pakistan. The issue of the retention of benefits locally is one of the most important issues in mountain tourism and needs to be adequately addressed if tourism in the mountains is to be sustainable.

4. High Degree of Seasonality

Tourism in the HKH is a highly seasonal activity. In Nepal, for example, October through November and February through March are the two peak seasons for tourist arrivals. Almost 40 percent of trekkers and mountaineers come in the months of October-November. In the Darjeeling area of West Bengal, April-June and September-October are the two peak seasons. This is a pattern typical of many hill resorts in the Indian Himalayas. Pilgrimage tourism is affected by the temple opening seasons. In the NWFP and Northern areas of Pakistan, where monsoons gradually become weaker, the tourist season extends from June to September. A distinct seasonality is evident in all tourist areas of the HKH.

There are two, often conflicting, implications of seasonality. The most obvious implication is that tourist capacity in these areas remains unutilized during the slack season. Since the income and employment is dependent on tourist flow, the incomes earned during the tourist season have to compensate for the non-tourist seasons. Seasonal unemployment and slackness in commercial activities is a noted phenomenon in all tourist centres. Also, the concentration of tourist activities in a limited time and space means congestion, overcrowding, pollution, and bottlenecks and frequent breakdowns in the provision of infrastructural services, a situation not uncommon in resort towns, pilgrim centres and favoured trekking routes. Ideally, therefore, an even flow of tourists throughout the year remains desirable. In many areas marketing strategies and promotion of appropriate tourist activities to attract tourists during the off-season are lacking. The seasonality factor makes it all the more important to link tourism to local production systems.

Although seasonality is generally perceived as a major problem, recent studies, however, indicate that seasonality may also be a blessing in disguise in an environmental sense (CREST 1995a, AME 1995a). The fact that the tourist flow dries up during the monsoons in much of the HKH means that the environment gets a period of rest and regeneration precisely during the period when the ecological metabolism is at its peak. Also, since the monsoons signal the period of hectic agricultural activity, a lowered tourist flow is also a period for the population to contribute to agriculture, on which much of the economic well-being of the communities depends.

5. Socio-cultural Impacts resulting from Tourism

Tourism, after all, entails contact with, and by implication encroachment by people from other countries, regions, social systems and cultural practices. This contact has the potentiality of bringing about changes in people's ideas, behaviour patterns, lifestyles, social systems, institutions, values and norms, expectations and other manifestations of material and non-material culture. Decline in the support and participation in local cultural practices and institutions, commercialization of traditional cultural practices, pollution of sacred places, introduction of alien architecture styles and building materials are some of the noted negative impacts of tourism on society and culture. Awareness regarding the maintenance and upkeep of cultural and historic monuments, increased pride in one's cultural identity, and resurgence in the observation of some cultural festivals, like the Mani Rimdu in Khumbu, are some of the positive impacts. It remains difficult, however, to differentiate between the impact made by tourists and the impact resulting from increased incomes, increased exposure to the worldwide television network, for example, and of course the educational system.

Profound changes, both negative and positive, have taken place in the Khumbu area in Nepal. The Sherpas, a traditional Buddhist highlander society of pastoralists-cum-subsistence agriculturists and traders who traded in Tibetan salt and wool and grain across the high passes between Tibet and Nepal to supplement their meager income from agriculture, have transformed themselves in a matter of decades into modern-looking, intelligent, widely traveled individuals endowed not only with the skills of mountaineering but also with the art and science of running a tour and trekking business (Sharma, P.R. 1995). This change has been accompanied by, the critics argue, a decline in the number of Lamas entering the monasteries, decline in traditional craft and agricultural practices, and the absence of what used to be a vibrant family and cultural life of the Sherpas (Haimendorf 1984).

The commercialization of culture due to tourism has been noted almost everywhere. The symbolism of many festivals has been lost. In Ladakh, Indian religious festivals traditionally celebrated during the winter season are reported to be observed during the summers to cater to the tourists (Sharma 1995c). Inflation due to tourism hits the local economy hard. The poor and the disadvantaged who derive little benefit from tourism are often the ones affected the most. Objects and artefacts venerated for their cultural and religious values are often stolen and sold on the black market. Such cases are reported from all across the HKH (Singh et al 1986). In the Chitral area in Pakistan, the culture and life styles of the Kalash people is being negatively impacted due to the influx of tourists, and it is the domestic tourists who seem to be having a stronger impact (DRG 1995a).

A major socio-cultural aspect of tourism that is often ignored is the impact of tourism on women. Among the Sherpas, for example, in spite of the relative prosperity that it has brought, the burden on women has increased as menfolk are away for most of the year on mountaineering expeditions or in urban areas. In the Annapurna region in Nepal the overall impact, as reported by women in the case study areas, appears to have been positive as it has increased women's participation in direct income-earning activities that are less strenuous than subsistence agriculture (Gurung 1995). Slowly the social and psychological barriers against women's participation in tourism activities are giving way to quiet acceptance in parts of the Nepal and Indian Himalayas. In Pakistan, however, for cultural reasons women's participation in tourism activities remains negligible although mountain societies have a better integration of women in their economies. In all cases greater efforts are called for in developing the requisite skills and capabilities of women. What is required is main-streaming gender issues in local development efforts in general, and tourism in particular (Bhadra and Sharma 1995).

6. Problem of Policy and Institutional Development

The fact that many of the above issues remain far from adequately addressed in the HKH countries clearly demonstrates what might be termed a policy vacuum. There is no defined policy perception on the role of tourism in mountain development in respective contexts, and the kind of tourism that is desirable. Also, the impact and implications of mountain tourism do not seem to have been thought through and woven into the policy fabric. Most often policies appear to be guided by revenue and foreign exchange earning considerations rather than the need to reinforce positive linkages of tourism to the mountain economy and the environment. Existing policies and regulations in most cases remain ad hoc and the understanding and analysis required to enforce policies and regulations remain absent. Most policies, further, are control oriented rather than based on a system of incentives and disincentives for correcting problems arising from market failure (McNeely 1988). It has been argued that regulations are given too much time to fail while economic incentives are given too little time to succeed (Banskota and Sharma 1994).

The problem of policy basically appears to be one of limited comprehension of the ramifications of the environmental, economic and related issues emerging from mountain tourism, lack of a sectorally integrated perspective, and the lack of a perception of the desired objectives of tourism development. The relevance of tourism to the objective conditions, constraints and opportunities afforded by mountain environments needs to be brought in much sharper a policy relief than has been the case hitherto. Tourism can be a catalyst of development only when it is integrated with the overall development concerns of mountain areas. ICIMOD case studies in the region clearly indicate that a positive linkage between mountain tourism and the central development concerns in the mountains, namely, poverty alleviation, environmental regeneration, and empowerment of local communities is not a spontaneous process, but needs to be deliberately planned and managed through an effective partnership with all the actors concerned. This is where the policy orientation at all levels becomes so crucial.

The second policy-related problem is with respect to institutions for the development and promotion of tourism. Tourism development requires institutions at different levels that are capable of promoting, marketing, facilitating, monitoring, regulating and orienting the impacts and effects of tourism in desirable directions. This requires that the role of the government, of non-governmental organizations, of community groups and of the private sector in translating the policies into actions through incentives and initiatives at each level be clearly defined so that an environment of trust and partnership can be built for the promotion of tourism in the mountains. This does not seem to be the case in most mountain areas of the HKH. The comparative advantage of each actor in the tourism policy-programme-implementation continuum with respect to defined tasks and objectives has still to be adequately appreciated.

Co-ordination and complementarity among different sectoral agencies is a must for the success of a tourism policy because tourism, in practice, is not the responsibility of a single agency but of a number of agencies. For example, the diversification of tourist destinations may be the official policy but it will have no meaning unless there is a co-ordinated planning between the tourism agency, agencies responsible for infrastructural development, and the private sector.

Approaches to Tourism in the HKH

It has been indicated above that the policy and institutional response and approaches to mountain tourism in the HKH countries have been far from consistent. An overview of the policy response in the countries of the region reflects both the diversity as well as the ad hoc nature of the approaches to mountain tourism development. Also, in many cases the policy pronouncements have little bearing on the realities on the ground. The cases of Bhutan, India, Nepal and Pakistan elucidate this.

BHUTAN

From the beginnings of tourism in Bhutan in 1974 the Royal Government has taken a very cautious approach to its growth and development. The tourism policy has been based on the principle of high value, low volume. This has been guided by the objective of minimizing the adverse impacts of tourism by keeping the volume of tourists to manageable levels while ensuring a steady flow of foreign exchange. The Bhutanese tourism industry is based on the principle of sustainability, which means it must be environmentally and ecologically friendly, socially and culturally acceptable and economically viable. The tourism policy is therefore designed to cater to a select clientele of high income, mostly group tourists.

Only 287 tourists visited Bhutan in 1974; the number increased to 3,971 in 1994. Most tourists until recently were cultural tourists with special interest in Buddhism. In 1988 the Royal Government declared some important monasteries and dzongs closed, as tourist activities were believed to be marginalising the importance of these institutions in the day to day life of the people. Also, mountaineering, an activity initiated in 1983, has been stopped since 1994 at the behest of the people of the northern regions who consider the peaks to be sacred. Trekking has emerged as an important activity in recent years, particularly after the closure of the more important monasteries and dzongs, and accounts for about 25 percent of the total tourists. Efforts are now being made to develop other activities based on the judicious use of natural resources. Principal among these are the development of nature treks, botanical tours and ornithology trails (TAB 1995).

Clearly, Bhutan has opted for a rather exclusive path to the development of tourism. This cautious approach is motivated by the desire to conserve the country's pristine natural heritage as well as its culture. The linkage and the impact of tourism on the socio-economic development of mountain communities is therefore not an area of major concern because the activity itself is so restricted. The tourism industry has been privatized since 1991 and licenses are issued to private tour operators. The

Tourism Authority of Bhutan has been strengthened as the public sector organization overseeing tourism activities.

INDIA

Tourism in India has received increasing attention after the enunciation of the Tourism policy in 1982 and the 1986 report of the National Committee on Tourism. In 1992 a National Action Plan for Tourism was inaugurated. Tourism in India, given its federal character, remains a State subject and therefore the policies of the states concerned have a greater bearing on the aspects of policy implementation.

The Eighth Plan (1992-97) document lays emphasis on the participation of the private sector in the expansion of tourism. The thrust areas in terms of their implications for mountain tourism include diversification from culturally related tourism to holiday and leisure tourism, development of trekking, winter sports and wildlife tourism, exploring new source markets to lure high-spending tourists, providing inexpensive accommodation in different tourist centres and improving the service efficiency of the public sector, among others. The National Action Plan for Tourism places emphasis on enhancing the socio-economic linkages of tourism including the socio-economic development of tourist areas, increase in employment opportunities, developing budget category domestic tourism, diversification of the tourism product and the preservation of the national heritage and environment. A number of concessions and special assistance from the centre are provided to improve infrastructure and other facilities.

The central government has also recommended a Special Areas Programme for the hill areas. These initiatives, however, have not been followed by a policy-programme-plan-action continuum. Critics argue that ad hocism has been rampant. State governments have not undertaken detailed assessment of the tourist resources nor has tourism been put in perspective in relation to the larger development concerns in the mountains. Incentives provided by the government are reportedly fuelling the menace of 'subsidy skimming'.

The policy pronouncements of the central government are also reflected in the policy statements of the state governments including Himachal. The Himachal tourism policy is guided by the considerations of the availability of greater employment opportunities through tourism, reduction in intra-state economic disparities, equitable distribution of tourism benefits and the build up of infrastructure, thus increasing the pace of overall development. In Himachal Pradesh the emphasis in tourism policy has been on the creation of basic infrastructure and transport, facilitating the private sector in the development of accommodation and other tourist facilities, and the diversification of tourist destinations through the development of adventure as well as cultural heritage tourism. Comparatively speaking there appears to be a policy void in the Uttar Pradesh hills although a number of steps in lieu of a tourism policy have been identified. These include the promotion of tourist activities in the off-season, diversification of tourist destinations into unexplored areas from overcrowded centres, improvements in the facilities at pilgrimage centres, and promoting the involvement of local entrepreneurs in tourism development (AME 1995a).

In India the role of the government in tourism is not limited to policy formulation alone. Through the Tourism Development Corporations the government plays a direct role in the provision of tourism facilities and infrastructure and also competes with the private sector.

NEPAL

In Nepal the importance of the tourism sector was first reflected in the Tourism Master Plan formulated as early as 1972. The plan put forward a comprehensive set of policies to promote tourism. Subsequent policy initiatives in various periodic plans have largely been guided by this Master Plan. It enunciated policies, priorities and guidelines for the development of various types of tourism including sightseeing, trekking, resort development and recreation, pilgrimage and conservation and management of natural and environmental resources. It envisaged investment flows from the public and private sectors, the former creating the necessary infrastructure and the latter creating accommodation and related facilities. The government was supposed to play a leading role in diversifying tourism by opening the bottlenecks perceived by the private sector. But as noted by a 1984 review of the Master Plan, the government largely failed to share its responsibilities in directing and promoting tourism in a planned manner. The result was a demand-driven development mainly concentrated in the Kathmandu Valley in the case of pleasure and sightseeing tourism, and over-exposure and overcrowding in the three major trekking routes in mountain tourism: Annapurna, Khumbu and Langtang. The government's role in regulating and monitoring mountain tourism products, in marketing Nepal and in encouraging and orienting the private sector was and is largely conspicuous by its absence (CREST 1995a).

The Nepal Tourism Development Programme prepared by Touche Ross consultants on behalf of the Asian Development Bank has resulted in the identification of about fifty tourism-related projects and action plans designed to release the bottlenecks in Nepal's tourism industry, increase tourist expenditure and establish Nepal as a premium tourist destination.

Much of mountain tourism in Nepal takes place in National Parks and Conservation Areas which are not under the Ministry of Tourism. Most tourism operations in mountain areas are regulated through trekking permits issued by the Department of Immigration. The problem of park-people interface is an important issue in many areas. Recent policy initiatives in tourism seek basically to diversify tourism to new areas, address environmental issues resulting from tourism, promote community participation, encourage the private sector to invest in and benefit from tourism infrastructure, and focus on research and development related to issues of carrying capacity, and enhancing the linkages between tourism and other sectors of the economy.

Liberal economic policies in recent years have resulted in the opening of domestic airline routes and helicopter operations in the private sector. Mountaineering royalties and fees have been revised. For example, the royalty for Mt. Everest has been fixed at $ 50,000. The new policy also classifies trekking areas, singularly the most important mountain tourism activity, by the level of ecological sensitivity. Also, following the Annapurna Conservation Area Project experience, the policy to plough back some proportion of the tourist revenue to destination areas is being extended to include other trekking areas.

A Tourism Council has been set up under the chairmanship of the Prime Minister to co-ordinate activities related to tourism at the highest level.

PAKISTAN

Prior to 1993, when a National Tourism Policy was formulated, tourism in Pakistan was not guided by any comprehensive policy initiatives. Interventions for the development of tourism were few and far between and the overall impression was that tourism was not taken seriously by the government (Richter 1989). The National Tourism Policy enunciated in 1993 for the first time accorded to it the status of an industry with similar benefits, concessions and treatment. Concessionary loan financing for tourism projects in mountain areas and pilgrimage centres; five-year tax holidays for the tourism industry throughout the country; "deemed export" status to tour operations and travel agents; import concessions for adventure tourism-related coaches and other equipment; introduction of chartered flights and liberalization of the visa policy are some of the salient features of the 1993 tourism policy (DRG 1995a).

Following these policy initiatives the government outlay for the tourism sector has also been raised considerably. These structural changes are expected to result in a rapid increase in tourist flows into Pakistan: a growth rate of as much as 15 percent annually is expected for the next few years.

Tourism in Pakistan is essentially a central subject and remains the responsibility of the Ministry of Tourism, which looks after the planning and policy, research and development, controlling standards, monitoring, supervision and training related to the tourism industry. A number of public sector institutions exist for facilitating the marketing, promotion and infrastructure development for tourism. These include the Pakistan Tourism Development Co-operation (PTDC) which has developed a chain of accommodation and related facilities at tourist destinations. For broadening the base of tourist facilities in the NWFP in particular, and for promoting domestic tourism, the Sarhad Tourism Co-operation (STC) was set up in the early 1980s. The mandate of the STC is basically to address the needs of mountain tourism. The organization is not as yet fully operational.

The approaches to tourism in the HKH countries has been diverse. With the exception of Bhutan, which has clearly remained partisan to selective tourism, the other countries appear not to disfavour mass tourism. Tourism in these instances is seen as an economic imperative as well as a corollary to mountain development. While sustainable tourism is invoked as the major objective of policies, there have been precious few attempts at weaving together the environmental, social, economic, cultural, and participatory aspects of sustainability. As a result, the idea of pursuing mountain tourism from the perspective of economic, environmental and social development of local communities does not find a coherent and consistent expression in most official policies and approaches. A reorientation of policies from the mountain tourism for local community development perspective and the working out of mechanisms for their translation into a policy-programme-action continuum is definitely warranted. A policy environment for mountain areas to benefit from mountain tourism needs to be created, or else tourism would have little meaning for the development of mountain areas.

Towards Sustainable Mountain Tourism

The sustainability of mountain tourism in the HKH hinges pretty much on the extent to which tourism can contribute to three interrelated objectives: improvement in the livelihoods of the population (and by implication poverty alleviation), environmental regeneration, and the empowerment of local communities. Sustainability is not an end-state but a process that has to be set in motion through a series of initiatives in a number of areas of policy and programmatic action. Some of the major initiatives required for sustainable mountain tourism in the HKH are highlighted below:

- Long-term policy perspective: Tourism development occurs within the policy framework provided by the state. A long-term policy perspective regarding the role tourism is expected to play in the overall development process in the mountain and the type of tourism that may be desirable in particular mountain environments needs to be articulated. Such a policy can be developed on the basis of a comprehensive appreciation of the value of mountain environmental resources. A long-term perspective is needed because the benefits from tourism can be maximized only through a co-ordinated set of complementary sectoral policies. This perspective is essential also because tourism development requires the investments in infrastructure as well as the production apparatus of tourist areas.

- It has to be appreciated that different types of tourism have different kinds of requirements. Policies should allow for rational planning in accordance with a region's natural and human resources. Policies should provide clear guidelines with respect to monitoring and management of environmental as well as economic and cultural impacts. Experience suggests that the benefits of tourism do not automatically flow in desirable directions and that mechanisms need to be created to enable the poor and the disadvantaged to benefit from tourism.

- Tourism resource inventory and carrying capacity consideration: Baseline information on most tourist destinations and routes and the inventory of tourism resources of the areas remain lacking in most cases. Most tourist areas in the HKH are fragile and diverse with a wealth of often endemic flora and fauna species. There is no accounting or appreciation of the value of what is lost and what remains. In order to derive maximum benefits from tourism resources and to allow tourism product diversification, baseline information on ecology, economy, social and cultural systems etc. is required. This means that more emphasis needs to be placed on tourism-related research. It is on this basis that tolerable limits of acceptable change, or environmental, economic and social carrying capacity considerations can be brought to bear in the planning and management of tourism. Such baseline information can also provide the basis for mobilizing NGOs, local community groups etc. in monitoring and dealing with the impacts and implications of mountain tourism. Mass tourism is not the only possible policy. Carrying capacity considerations can warrant a search for other forms of tourism that are soft on the tourist resources of an area.

- Integrated programme development: Tourism planning and development has to be conceived in the context of the overall development of areas. The linkage of major economic sectors in the mountains - agriculture, horticulture, forestry, energy etc. – with tourism has often been ignored, resulting in the problem of the lack of integration of tourism with the local economy, low linkages and high leakages, problems of land use conflicts and so on. The demands of the tourism sector on other sectors and vice versa need to be better appreciated if tourism is to be developed in an integrated fashion.

- Institutionalization of impact monitoring framework: The development and institutionalization of an environmental, economic and cultural impact monitoring framework related to tourism needs to be urgently developed. Such a framework provides the basis for assessing the impacts, and allows better feedback and planning of activities and action projects to mitigate the adverse consequences. ICIMOD studies reveal very clearly that in spite of a plethora of anecdotal evidence, the understanding/ analysis of environmental effects and impacts resulting from tourism remain very limited. It is obvious that without a proper understanding and analysis, sustainable systems of environmental pollution control, alternative energy, sanitation and building technology and a whole host of related issues cannot be developed or addressed.

- Sustainable local institutions: If mountain tourism is to aid and complement the process of local development, participatory institutions need to be nurtured at the local level that can monitor impacts, orient the benefits accruing from tourism to environmental regeneration and provision of basic services, and initiate requisite efforts to bring the poor and the disadvantaged groups to benefit from tourism. The experience in mountain development in various countries of the region shows that local receiving mechanisms need to be strengthened to benefit from the various kinds of support that the government may provide. In the case of tourism in remote mountain areas, a system also needs to be developed whereby the revenues from tourism can be shared with local bodies, community groups etc. for local level environmental, economic and community development work. Participatory local institutions could play a key role in the planning of tourism activities, in raising popular awareness among the host population and the tourists, in discouraging pollution, monitoring proper sanitation, encouraging and disseminating new energy and building technologies, in maintaining cultural integrity, and in advocating the cause of sustainable tourism.

- Human resource development and training: The creation of skills locally to cater to tourist needs is an extremely important aspect of promoting tourism for local development. Impetus for local enterprise development and provision of quality services is essential for realizing the large revenue potential of mountain tourism. A well-conceived HRD strategy can also be a way of minimising the economic and social inequities that often accompany tourism development, and of ensuring the participation of the disadvantaged groups in tourism-related activities.

References

ACAP: Programme for Conservation and Sustainable Development. King Mahendra Trust for Nature Conservation. Kathmandu (1989)

AME (Academy for Mountain Environics): Mountain Tourism in Himachal Pradesh and the Hill Districts of Uttar Pradesh: An Overview. MEI Discussion Paper Series 95/6. ICIMOD, Kathmandu 1995a

AME Mountain Tourism for Local Community Development. Report on Case Studies in Kinnaur District, H. P. and Badrinath Tourist Zone, U. P. MEI Discussion Paper Series 95/13. ICIMOD, Kathmandu 1995b

Banskota, K./B. Sharma: Carrying Capacity of Himalaya Resource for Mountain Tourism Development. Paper presented at the Regional Conference on Sustainable Development of Fragile Mountain Areas of Asia, 13-15 December. ICIMOD, Kathmandu 1994

Bhadra, B./S. Sharma: Tourism for Local Community Development in Mountain Areas. A Synthesis Report. ICIMOD Internal Document, 1995

CREST (Centre for Resources and Environmental Studies): Mountain Tourism in Nepal: An Overview. MEI Discussion Paper Series 95/7. ICIMOD, Kathmandu 1995a

CREST: Tourism for Mountain Community Development. Case Study Report on the Annapurna and Gorkha Regions of Nepal. MEI Discussion Paper Series 95/11. ICIMOD, Kathmandu 1995b

DRG (Development Research Group): Mountain Tourism in the North West Frontier Province and the Northern Areas of Pakistan: An Overview. MEI Discussion Paper Series 95/8. ICIMOD, Kathmandu 1995a.

DRG: Tourism for Local Community Development in the Mountain Areas of Pakistan: Case Studies of Kalam and Hunza. MEI Discussion Paper Series 95/12. ICIMOD, Kathmandu 1995b

ERL (Earth Resources Ltd): Natural resource Management for Sustainable Development. A Study of Feasible Policies, Institutions and Investment Activities in Nepal with Special Reference to the Hills. A Report Prepared for the Asian Development Bank and National Planning Commission, Nepal 1989

Groetzbach, E.: Mountain Tourism in North Pakistan Region and Problem of Further Development. Tourism, Recreation, Research. Vol. XIV, No. 2/1989, pp 67-74

Gurung, H.: Environmental Aspects of Mountain Tourism in Nepal. Paper prepared for the International Trade and Tourism Division of ESCAP. Bangkok 1990

Gurung, D.: Tourism and Gender: Impact and Implications of Tourism on Nepalese Women. MEI Discussion Paper Series 95/3. ICIMOD, Kathmandu 1995

Haimendorf, C. Von Fuerer: The Sherpas Transformed: Social Change in the Buddhist Society of Nepal. Sterling, New Delhi 1984

Hunter, C./Green, H.: Tourism and the Environment: A Sustainable Relationship. Routeledge, London 1995

ICIMOD: Off-farm Employment and Mountain Development. Report of the International Workshop on Mountain Off-farm Employment. ICIMOD, Kathmandu 1992

Jian, Liu: Introduction to China's Mountain Tourism and Regional Development. Paper presented at the HKH Regional Workshop on Mountain Tourism for Local Community Development. ICIMOD, Kathmandu June 1195.

Jodha, N. S.: Mountain Perspective and Sustainability: A Framework for Development Strategies. In: Jodha et al. (Eds.): Sustainable Mountain Agriculture Perspectives and Issues, New Delhi – Oxford IBH, Vol. 1, 1991, pp 41-82

K. C., J. et al.: Off-farm Employment in Nepal: A Case Study of Marpha-Jomsom VDCs, Mustang District. MPE Discussion Paper No. 18. ICIMOD, Kathmandu 1992

Lama and Sherpa (1993). Quoted in Banskota and Sharma (1994)

McNeely, J.: Economic and Biological Diversity: Developing and Using Economic Incentives to Conserve Biological Resource. Gland, IUCN 1988

Mirza, Q. A.: Pollution in the Himalayas. Inaugural Issue 1991

Nepal, Sanjay K.: Tourism, Environment and Sustainable Development: Reflections on the Nepal Himalayas". Paper presented at the International Conference on Alpine Tourism: Sustainability Reconsidered and Redesigned. Innsbruck, Austria, May 2-5 1996

PANOS: Panos Briefing: Ecotourism. 1995

Richter, L. K.: The Politics of Tourism in Asia. University of Hawaii, Honolulu 1989

Sharma, P.: Tourism and Sustainable Development. In: Banskota, Sharma et al.: Economic Policies for Sustainable Development in Nepal. ICIMOD, Kathmandu 1990

Sharma, P.: Who Climbs Whom, Himal, November-December 1992

Sharma, P.: Population and Employment Challenges in the Mountains. In: International Symposium on Mountain Environment and Development: Constraints and Opportunities. ICIMOD, Kathmandu 1994

Sharma, P.: Sustainability of Mountain Tourism in the Hindu Kush-Himalayas. Towards an Agenda for Action. Paper presented at the

International Himalayan Environment Programme and Action Projects Conference. Indian Mountaineering Foundation. New Delhi, 10-12 February, 1995a.

Sharma, P.: Equity and the Nepali Porter. Paper presented at Hard Livelihood: Conference on the Himalayan Porter. 3, 4 August. Kathmandu, 1995b

Sharma, P. (Ed.): Tourism for Local Community Development in Mountain Areas: Perspectives, Issues and Guidelines. Proceedings of the HKH Regional Workshop on Mountain Tourism for Local Community Development. ICIMOD, Kathmandu 1995c

Sharma, P. R.: Culture and Tourism: Defining Roles and Relationships. MEI Discussion Paper Series 95/2. ICIMOD, Kathmandu 1995

Singh, T. V./J. Kaur: The Paradox of Mountain Tourism: Case References from the Himalaya. UNEP Industry and Environment. January-March 1986, pp. 21-26

TAB (Tourism Authority of Bhutan): Paper Presented at the HKH Regional Workshop on Mountain Tourism for Local Community Development. ICIMOD, Kathmandu June 19-21 1995

WCED (World Commission on Environment and Development): Our Common Future. New Delhi – Oxford 1987

Friedrich M. Zimmermann

Nature, Society and the Economy in Partnership

European Perspectives in Mountain Tourism

1. The Diversity of Challenges in Tourism

Tourism at the end of the 2nd millennium presents environmental, social and economic challenges in both new and existing (traditional) tourism and leisure destinations:

- In existing tourism areas, environmental and social deterioration can be the cause and the effect of a declining competitiveness of tourism. The challenge is how to revitalise such areas by initiating projects which are able to upgrade the environment and improve the quality of life for the local people.
- In new destinations the challenge is to integrate lessons from abroad into the planning process and learn from practical experiences in the past.

In both above-mentioned cases the necessary goal for future development will be to initiate a holistic approach based on principles and best practice of sustainable tourism within an organisational framework founded in partnerships.

The parts of the paper dealing with the holistic approach are based on the author's membership in a European Union expert team in 1995-96, aiming at the implementation of sustainability in European tourism management (Williams, Shaw, Zimmermann et. al. 1996).

2. The Holistic Approach to Sustainable Development

Holism is the reunification of nature and society, which have been divided within the concept of modernisation. Holism is considered as a basis for practical action, with following important dimensions:

- The idea of partnership between the stakeholders in the environment and the economy, as an attempt to build consensus based on mutual respect and work towards common goals.
- the incorporation of all the principal stakeholders: hosts and guests, public and private bodies and NGOs, environmental, social and economic interests

- The consideration of the interests of all stakeholders, both in the present and in the future
- The internalisation of external costs and benefits by the partners to bridge the gap between individual and social costs and benefits
- The integrated approach is based around a community or region because realism dictates that the quest for holism should begin at the local level to be able to extend to the global level.

Fig 1: The Holistic Approach to Sustainable Development

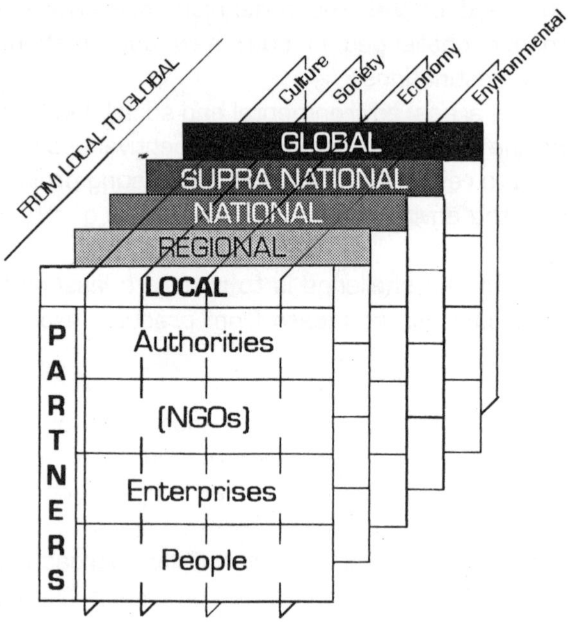

3. Contents of a Holistic Sustainable Tourism Program

As an attempt to provide a practical guide to assist the move towards holism, the recommendations of the EU Commission paper Taking Account of the Environment in Tourism Development, modified by the author, can be summarized in basic terms as follows:

- Treat the region/area as a system by defining development strategies as common goals and encouraging co-operation and co-ordination
- Improve control at the supra-national level, using the experiences of the local level (hierarchy principle)

- Limit capacities and establish acceptable development objectives
- Co-ordinate entities with impact on environmental and human resources. Use partnerships for defining regulations and measures as well as eco-labelling to integrate development, marketing and environmental policy
- Reduce peaks and enforce seasonal spreading by using price strategies, facility limitations, special interest offers and visitor management
- Implement responsible marketing of the environment, e.g. educational programs, promotion of environmental quality aspects, information
- Create product improvement towards a tourism lifestyle, with emphasis on local identity and integrating socio-cultural and environmental issues into a co-operative-oriented production system
- Give priority to flexible and 'open' planning, favouring modular solutions with space for future modifications
- Establish strategic marketing plans and operative actions to select target groups, compatible with local development and resources (nature as a unique selling proposition)
- Encourage local people and individual operators to adopt environmental measures, by using media campaigns, educational programs and information systems for the diffusion of tourism–environ-ment know-how. Special awards, tax benefits and other financial instru-ments help to improve environmental measures
- Encourage the tourists to act environmentally responsibly and become part of the local socio-economic system
- Stimulate environmental competition (public presentation of merit awards)

This agenda is an ambitious set of actions which needs a professional organisational framework to co-ordinate the programs and the required partnerships – a problem to be solved is the territorial level.

4. Levels for a Holistic Approach

Individual establishments or companies may develop a holistic program in a region, but in isolation, e.g. lack of consensus with possible partners. However, a single enterprise cannot be genuinely holistic, whenever the guests are off the hotel premises, there may be no more opportunity to be environmentally responsible.

Similiar problems apply to the policies of an economic sector as a whole, because the influence on other sectors involved in tourism is limited.

There are different positive lessons in developing a holistic program for regions. The best known example is the planning for the Lillehammer/ Norway Winter Olympics. The objective was the creation of a showcase for environmental policy with respect to the relations between the environment and major sporting events. "Co-operation between developers, national, regional and local authorities and NGOs was the most important factor to success in our environmental work." "Co-operation... has generated new environmental expertise, new environmental service and new environmental products of national and international interest. Trade and industry, businesses and organisations have been able to create stronger environmental profiles for themselves, which has given them competitive advantages in the market" (UNEP, Olympics '94).

In contrast to the economic globalisation and to centralisation tendencies, there is a strong movement in the European Union to strengthen small regional units. Enforced by the EU Regional Policy and by the debate on subsidiarity, the level for certain aspects of regulation and responsibility is moving towards the local community.

Applying a holistic approach means founding action programs at different levels with the result that it is not always possible to match these levels. For example, the Alps require partnerships and action at a range of levels from supranational to community level. Therefore it is useful to create a hierarchy of programs, integrating different layers using holistic principles.

5. The European Alps: Experiences from the Past – Solutions for the Future

5.1. Changing challenges and current day situation

The Alpine Arc, a mountain system with an area of 240,000 sq. km, a length of 1,000 km and a width of 130 to 250 kms, is centrally located in Europe and encompasses parts of France, Italy, Switzerland, Austria, Germany, Liechtenstein and Slovenia (fig. 2). This is one of the most important tourist regions worldwide – about 25 % of global tourism turnover is generated in the Alps.

Although there are a number of shared features of Alpine areas, developments in individual countries have been typified by contrasting tourism and regional development ideologies and strategies, based upon different political, legal and organisational frameworks. Some special features are:

- When traditional tourism structures in Switzerland encountered difficulties in the 1980s, an intensive discussion of economic and ecological issues was initiated, based upon certain research projects (e.g. UNESCO Man and Biosphere).

- In the 1960s and 1970s Austria made substantial profits out of mass tourism development. The development of tourism facilities was extremely dynamic until the end of the 1980s, when ecological concerns led to a politically initiated end of quantitative growth.
- In Germany, a restrictive tourism development strategy for the Bavarian Alps was introduced at the beginning of the 1970s, when the "Alpenplan" was created so as to protect certain Alpine areas.
- In France the pattern of Alpine tourism development is based on an ex-nihilo creation in high altitude zones with very weak links to local economies and societies.

Since the late eighties, these features have been subject to external effects and changing internal constraints, which has led to immense restructuring processes.

Fig. 2: The Alps: Changing Challenges and Present Day Situation

Changing Challenges	Facts
The former preserve of mountain agriculture, has become the **"Roof Garden of Europe"**, a major recreation and sports area for the urban population.	▪ 50 million tourists with ▪ 500 million overnight stays ▪ more than 150 million short-term visitors per year
The importance of traditional **sustainable agriculture** has been and **is decreasing**, recently in Austria enforced under EU-conditions.	▪ agricultural income is too low to secure sustainable farming in the alps ▪ fallow areas are increasing
The exponential growth of tourism caused a spatial diffusion of facilities and **land-use competition** between agricultural needs and tourism infra and supra-structures.	▪ 5 million tourist beds ▪ approx. 12,000 ski lifts can transfer 1.2 million persons ▪ 40,000 ski slopes with an area of 1,000 sq. km and a length of 120,000 km
The intensive use of Alpine regions for tourism causes **ecological problems**, like scarring of the ground, noise, air pollution, waste.	▪ Settlement areas in Alpine tourism regions quintupled within the last 50 years ▪ Population density in tourism centers lies between 1,000 and 2,000 persons per sq. km during peak season
The fragile environment of the Alps is **criss-crossed by** more than 400,000 km of **transportation** lines, connecting some of the major economic areas of Europe.	▪ Cross – Alpine traffic (1993) ▪ 105 million tons of goods (60% on roads) ▪ 200 million people (80% on roads) ▪ = more than 100 billion km driven on Alpine roads ▪ 13 million cars and trucks use one major freeway across the Alps annually.
The local population face the threat of a **decreasing attraction of the landscape, a loss of their cultural identify** and **traditional economic basis** (disintegration of the local social-economic system)	▪ increasing hostility in tourism ▪ more and more young people are not willing to take over tourism enterprises ▪ younsters increasingly refuse to work in tourism

Source: Friedrich M. Zimmermann, 1996; statistical data: CIPRA.

5.2. Examples of best practice in terms of sustainability, partnership and a holistic approach

The changing challenges need reactions and solutions on different regional scales. Therefore initiatives which can be seen as "examples of best practice" are based on a hierarchical view:

- The supra-national level: "Alp Action" and the "Alpine Convention".
- A program at the provincial level and an example for eco-labelling: The Tyrolean Environmental Seal of Quality.
- The regional level 1: Nature and Life – Bregenzerwald – A European Union Regional Policy Initiative.
- The regional level 2: The Lech-Valley: Ecology oriented life and economy – sustainable restructuring of a major winter sports resort.
- The community level: Green Villages in Austria: Eco-labelling on the community scale.
- The level of co-operating enterprises: Farm holidays in Austria.

5.2.1. The supra-national scale

Two initiatives seeking to include the entire ecosystem of the Alps into future sustainable development strategies should be mentioned:

Alp Action aims to encourage tourism based on quality by promoting sustainable development by co-operation between tourism authorities, mountain communities, scientists, environmental organisations, businesses and governments. Projects include the preserving of nature, promotion of rail transport, use of renewable energy, and revitalisation of ancient building crafts.

The Alpine Convention was signed by Austria, France, Germany, Italy, Liechtenstein, Slovenia and Switzerland and the European Union. It aims to provide a global policy for the conservation of the Alps based on transnational co-operation and specially states that a key objective is to "...agree upon a common development strategy based on ecological and sustainable objectives."

The Alpine Convention, the model for sustainable regional development, contains specific protocols for agriculture, forest ecosystems, regional planning and sustainable development, traffic, nature protection and conservation, soil protection, water and energy, and tourism:

"... ensure that tourism and leisure activities are in harmony with ecological and social requirements whilst, at the same time, restricting those activities which are harmful to the environment through restriction of certain zones."

The signatory nations and the European Union share the responsibility for the uniqueness of the Alps by enacting European and national laws, and enforcing standards and regulations which are detailed in the Alpine Convention.

5.2.2. The Tyrolean Environmental Seal of Quality: A program for the provincial level and an example for eco-labelling:

The Tyrol is Austria's leading tourist province, it has some 370,000 tourist beds and 45 million overnight stays per annum. In order to better integrate tourism and environmental management, the Tyrolean Environmental Seal of Quality was initiated as an eco-incentive program for all accommodation and catering establishments.

This is based on persuading businesses that 'green' behaviour means 'being in the black'. The broad aims are to make a lasting contribution to environmentally and socially minded Tyrolean tourism, through an eco-labelling award scheme. 'In the knowledge that ecology and the economy are not antagonists, but partners, the Tyrol wishes to send out signals to emphasise the necessity of environmental action under the motto 'deeds are born of knowledge'.

The more specific objectives are:

- Providing an orientation aid for environmentally-conscious hosts and guests
- Improving ease of tourist choice of environmentally sensitive accommodations and other facilities
- Creating and maintaining competitive advantages by emphasising environmental qualities
- Providing incentives and encouragement for the tourism suppliers
- Achieving concrete cost savings for tourism-related enterprises
- Reduction of disposal problems and costs
- High positive image and marketing benefits for firms and the whole region
- Occupying a pioneering position in the general shift to sustainable tourism
- Image improvement with local people, staff, and guests
- Providing an instrument for ecological – oriented quality tourism
- Voluntary adherence to the demands of environmental conservation helps to anticipate and perhaps negate the need for statutory regulations.

Operations procedures and conditions of entry are:

- All entrants must undertake to observe the currently valid environmental seal criteria
- When advertising the award to their establishment, entrants must undertake to clearly indicate the time period for which the award is valid
- Entrants must also undertake to return the environmental plaque loaned to them if the seal award is revoked or rescinded

The participants include hotels, the catering trade, farm holidays, holiday apartments, camp sites and Alpine refuges. The assessment of the business usually takes place during the peak season when the establishment is operating to capacity. The Assessment Commission tests the establishment on the basis of a checklist of obligatory criteria for each sector:

- The fundamental criterion is the observation of all state laws and regulations on the environment. The general principle of environmentally responsible management has to be observed
- The use of local products is to be enforced
- Environmental policies on waste, air, energy, soil, transport, noise, information for visitors and staff have to be applied

Enterprises need to meet all the criteria in order to be eligible for an award. The validity of the seal is limited to one year duration only and it must then be re-applied for establishments are continually assessed and inspected. This helps to ensure that companies do not become complacent. Failure to observe the criteria means that the environmental seal is revoked. Beside these, the general specifications and the overall ideas for the environmental seal, underpinning this innovative and ambitious program, are:

- The concept is drawn up on a broad basis, and on a voluntary principle
- Attention is paid to the specific nature of Tyrolean tourism
- The 'seal of quality' criteria are not static, they are dynamically conceived on the basis of increasing environmental sensitivity shown by local people and visitors, international criteria, and technical developments.
- Highest attention is paid to the required qualifications of the seal assessors and to the quality of advice they provide (Source: Tyrolean Environmental Seal of Quality)

5.2.3. Nature and Life – Bregenzerwald: A European Union regional policy initiative

The European Union regional policy aims at the reduction of disparities among regions and the development of disadvantaged rural areas by strengthening comparative advantages. There are different objectives for areas to be eligible for structural funding:

Objective 1: Regions of lagging development
Objective 2: Declining industrial areas
Objective 5b: Development of fragile rural areas
Objective 6: Regions in Scandinavia with very low population density

One of the most important initiatives is called LEADER (LEADER I: 1990 – 1993; LEADER II: 1994 – 1999), a regional initiative linking actions for the development of the rural economy by

- partnership
- bottom-up participation and development
- "capacity building" (improved information and education, know-how transfer)

Objectives

- to ensure that support for local initiatives involving local development continues from LEADER I
- to support operations that are innovative, suitable as a model and transferable, and that illustrate the new directions that rural development may take
- to step up exchanges of experiences and the transfer of know-how through a European rural development network
- to back transnational co-operation projects developed by the local bodies in rural areas which reflect their solidarity

LEADER II has 4 eligible measures:

Measure A:

Acquiring skills – step prior to the development of rural innovation programs in areas where the practice of local development is new. This measure concerns actions such as analysis of the local area, motivating and training local people to participate actively in the development process, drawing up a strategy, and finding finance.

Measure B:

Rural innovation program - these models and transferable programs are promoted by local action groups or, in some cases, by other collective bodies. They are extremely innovative in terms of method and content and in relation to the policies conducted in the same area, particularly in the context of operational programs. Rural innovation programs are multiannual, they can be comprised of a set of very diversified measures in terms of:

Technical support for rural development,
Vocational training,
Support for rural tourism,
Support for small businesses,
Local exploitation and marketing of agricultural, forestry and fisheries products,
Preservation and improvement of the environment and living conditions.

Measure C:

Transnational co-operation: the objective is to facilitate the devising and development of joint projects by groups and other local bodies from at least two Member States.

Measure D:

European network for rural development: The different components of LEADER II make up a European network for rural development (co-ordinated by the LEADER European Observatory), constituting a permanent tool for the exchange of achievements, experience and know-how (databases, publications, electronic network, seminars, symposiums,...). The Observatory's primary task is to analyse and make known the innovations arising out of LEADER II.

The Community's financial participation for LEADER II has been set at 2 billion US $ for the duration of the new period of reform of the Structural Funds from 1994 to 1999. The beneficiaries are "local action groups", rural collective bodies, public or private partners (local authorities, consular chambers, co-operations, associations, etc.), jointly devising a strategy and innovative measures for the development of a rural area on the local/regional scale (less than 100,000 inhabitants)

(Source:http://www.rural-europe.aeidl.be).

LEADER in practice: Nature and Life – Bregenzerwald

The regional initiative "Nature and Life – Bregenzerwald" is designed to support partnership between tourism, agriculture, manufacturing and trade businesses, based on sustainability and using a holistic approach. This is a project pilot for the Vorarlberg province and could be applied in other regions of the Alps.

Bregenzerwald has a population of 28,000 living in 24 communities. Agriculture, tourism, and other services account for one third of the economy each. Mountain agriculture is under pressure, and low prices and low incomes lead to a further decrease of active farmers. In contrast, there is strong demand for tourism, and there are about 300 tourism enterprises and more than 330,000 tourists spend 1,7 million overnight stays in the area.

The Project aims are:

- Stabilisation of agriculture by improving the co-operation between farmers, tourism entrepreneurs, local and regional businesses so as to increase farm incomes
- Promotion of sustainable agricultural production which protects the cultural and natural landscape that is the most important prerequisite for gentle summer tourism activities
- Support of emerging partnerships which will help to increase communications and enforce a holistic approach which is important for innovations
- Set up professional marketing fulfilling the needs of steadily changing markets.

This initiative is characterized by numerous partners such as the Provincial Association of Innkeepers, the Provincial Chamber of Agriculture, the Provincial Association for the Promotion of Natural Products, the Regional Planning Corporation, the Regional Tourism Bureau, 22 municipalities, farmers, retailers, restaurants, etc.

The main achievements to date have been:

- Provision of a quality seal for regional products
- Offering local specialities in local restaurants
- Opening of farmers' shops in restaurants and hotels
- An annual fair to improve information for the local population and the guests, and to increase co-operation between partners

Similar projects can be found in several mountain areas in Germany (Regain, Bavaria), Italy (Arca Umbria; Alta Val di Non), Ireland (Ballyhoura), Austria (Waldviertel, Eisenwurzen, Hohe Tauern), Switzerland (LaNaTour, Wallis), Slovenia (Logarska dolina) etc.

Fig: 3 Pressures of Tourism: Input-Output Analysis

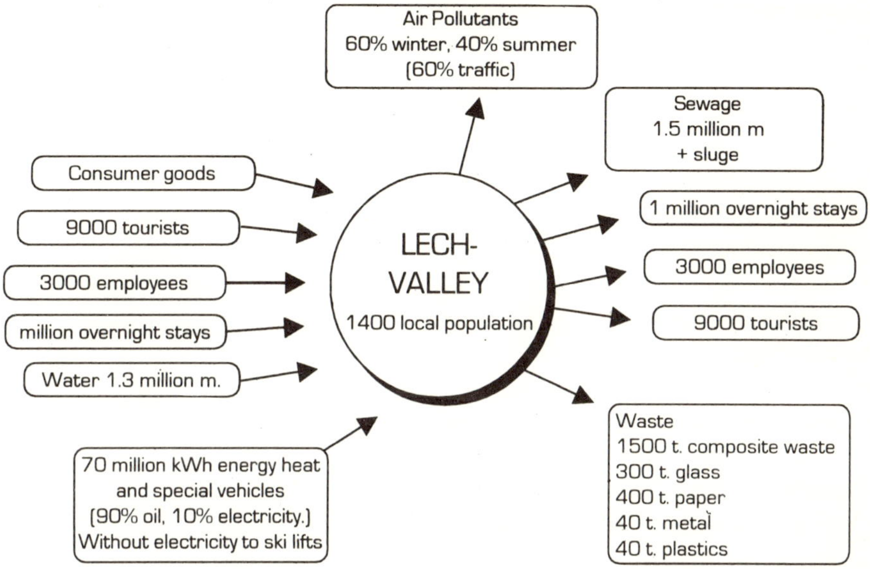

5.2.4. The Lech-Valley: Ecology oriented life and economy – restructuring a major winter sports resort

Lech-Valley is a major winter sports resort in the Alps. Its population of 1,400 and 3,000 non-local staff members are hosts to more than 1 million overnight stays per year. During the peak season tourists outnumber the local population by a ratio of seven to one. Short-term tourism on weekends also acts to intensify the pressures of tourism (cp. Fig. 3).

In view of these figures the decision was taken by the community politicians to restrict the access to the valley in order to preserve the quality of life for hosts and guests. When the sale of 17,000 ski tickets is reached, then the "entrance doors to the valley are closed".

This in turn led local decision-makers to initiate the project "Ecologically oriented life and economy in Lech". The main goal is that Lech-valley should become a tourism destination with optimum quality regarding the economy, ecology and social constraints. The concept should guarantee a sustainable development for the economy, nature and humans and should secure the natural and cultural resources for the future. The project is based on a vision for the next 20 – 50 years. On a modular design, the goals should be reached by 3 main steps:

- As a reaction to the "historical development" certain problems have to be solved immediately, for example traffic congestion and pollution.

- The medium term development should be devoted to educating hosts and guests, thereby raising their consciousness and encouraging them to think and act in a sustainable manner.
- In the long term all actions should be based on sustainability.

Action taken to date includes:

Phase 1 was dedicated to the development of an ecology - oriented development profile for the Lech-valley.

Phase 2 will embody the project in the community, tourism enterprises will work out special ecological management measures by

- workshops on improved use of energy and water, waste prevention, co-operation models with agriculture to secure agricultural income
- information campaigns
- use of schools for co-operation and the diffusion of information
- individual consultations with tourism enterprises.

The effects of these measures should be the

- implementation of ecological measures combined with positive economic effects for the enterprises
- motivation of entrepreneurs to participate in the ecological development process of the whole community
- planning and realization of community-based activities.

The first results:

- investments for a more efficient use of energy (within the next 15 years the need for energy should be reduced by 30 - 40 % with a share of renewable energy resources of 90 % - today the share is 10 %)
- the introduction of a bonus - malus payment system for the use of water (this measure will reduce the amount of water use and will save the community of Lech an investment of about 3 million $ which would be necessary in case of increasing water needs for an enlargement of the water supply and the sewage system)
- school projects increased the ecological awareness of students.

This is the first and only example in European mountain areas where a major tourism resort is redefining its development strategies in favour of a sustainable future.

5.2.5. 'Green Villages in Austria': Eco-labelling on the community scale

'Green Villages in Austria' is an association of 36 villages that produce their own marketing materials, and which acts as a self-regulatory body. In order to qualify, a village must meet certain criteria.

The village character:

- Quality of village setting: typical of the region, set around a church or village green, a close cluster of buildings etc., active measures have to be taken to improve the village appearance and attractiveness of the village center.
- Building height: maximum of three storeys.
- Architecture: good balance between old and new buildings.

Ecological minimum standards and load thresholds:

- Agriculture and forestry: typical natural landscape, proximity to a variety of protected landscapes, sensible use of fertilisers etc.
- Water: Grade 1 drinking water.
- Air quality and noise: at least 3 kms from motorways, limited through traffic on main roads etc.
- General transport structure: designated cycle paths, traffic free or traffic calmed zones, good public transport.
- Supplies and waste disposal: recycling, refuse separation, avoidance of unnecessary packaging; existence of a good direct supply network of local and regional farm produce for shops and hotels.
- Quality of leisure facilities: built with consideration for the environment, available to local residents, and child friendly.

Social and tourist minimum standards and load thresholds:

- Population size: maximum of 1,500 village inhabitants.
- Second homes: maximum of 25% of primary home owners.
- Bed capacity: proportion of inhabitants to guest beds should ideally be 1:1. Large hotels should be avoided in preference of smaller establishments.
- Village community: should be active and be involved in tourism-related decisions by way of citizen participation models.
- Tourism infrastructure: there should be a tourist information office, and minimum tourist requirements such as a grocer, baker and hairdresser, as well as good access to natural tourist amenities such as a network of path for walkers (Source: Dorfurlaub in Oesterreich).

A worldwide eco-labelling attempt for the travel and tourism industry is the initiative 'Green Globe' providing awards for outstanding performance according to WTTC (World Travel and Tourism Council) environmental guidelines and research results (for more information: http://www.fleethouse.com/wttc/wttcq.html).

In Europe there are several attempts to promote eco-labelling programs, based on the EU program "LIFE" which offers a new approach to environmental policy by balancing human activities, economic development and environmental protection and sharing of responsibility (e.g. NASC, Ireland). The purpose of eco-labelling in tourism is to give a guarantee of special environmental standards and qualities for certain tourism regions. The final aims are EU-wide recognized "Green Tourism Quality Standards", comparable to the International Quality Assurance Standards ISO 9000-9004 for industry.

5.2.6. Farm Holidays in Austria – the level of co-operating enterprises

Farm tourism plays an important role in Alpine areas in view of the significant presence of farms, the pressures on agriculture, and the importance of farming in maintaining traditional cultures and landscapes.

Until the 1970s farm holidays tended to be seen as a cheap low quality product with little potential in the market. From 1971 a number of regional and provincial farm holiday associations were formed and finally combined in the Austrian Farm Holidays Association in 1992, linking 8 provincial bodies, including 3,300 farmers out of a total of 21,000.

There is a clear division and hierarchy of tasks to be carried out at each organisational level, with an integrated co-operation concept (Embacher 1994):

Tasks of farmers as landlords:

- Product design
- Provision of good quality tourism product
- Provision of precise information for guests
- Pre-defined quality guarantee and adequate farm management

Tasks of local pools of farm tourism enterprises:

- Organise exchanges of experience amongst farmers
- Organise training, consultancy and assistance to individual farmers
- Organise advertising on a regional basis
- Assist provincial associations in the respective regions

Tasks of provincial associations:

- Organising and optimising marketing
- Organising and executing a booking system at provincial level
- Setting up regional guest circles
- Maintaining contacts with other bodies
- Exerting an influence on the supply side (promotion, training, etc.)

Tasks of federal organisations:

- Represent agritourism at the national level, promote farm holidays at the federal level, and act as a lobbying group for farm holidays
- Maintain contacts with ministries etc., and co-ordinate activities of authorities
- Co-ordinate national and international marketing
- Basic market research
- Central information office

This co-operation of small-scale enterprises – individually weak economic entities – is a practicable example of joint planning, product development and marketing, using the partnership of two major economic sectors in mountain areas for mutual benefits.

6. The Alps 2,000: Sustainable Management Measures for a European Heritage Area

	Measures up to 2,000		
	European Union	**Nation**	**Province/Regions**
PLANNING	• EU tourism action plan 2,000 • EU – Regional Policy • Co-operation and exchange of information	• National development plans – definition of areas without tourism as future potentials • Cross-border planning, development and co-operation	• Democratic, partnership-oriented regional plans • Reduction of developed areas • Pilot models for sustainable tourism • Visitor management • Exchange of best practice
RURAL AREAS	• European Regional Development Policy extended 1999 ff • Special support for sustainable farming and landscape management	• Professional training and education for an increased awareness of the importance of sustainable development (agriculture)	• Regional co-operation initiatives • Joint marketing of quality products • Holistic view of agriculture, humans and the environment
ENVIRONMENT	• Nature protection should have a European dimension	• National Parks and Nature should be strictly regulated on a national level	• Control of land-use • Strict rules for new construction • Use of local architectural styles • Creation of buffer zones around sensitive area

E C O - S T A N D A R D	• EU-ecological standards as a minimum requirement • EU (international) 'Green Tourism Quality Standards' (cp. ISO 9000-9004 for industry)	• Strict implementation and enforcement of environmental standards on noise, drinking water, waste, air, emission etc.	• Local initiatives like alternative heating and warm water preparation • Increased use of local resources • Reduction of mass tourism • Reduce potential of pollutants
T R A F F I C	• EU-transport policy	• National transport policies • Economic incentives (energy tax/road pricing) to encourage public transport	• Local pilot projects like pedestrian areas, car-free tourism villages, reduced parking areas, electro-buses, train-combined packages

Source: The EU 5th Environmental Action Programme (5EAP), supplemented and modified by Friedrich M. Zimmermann, 1996.

References

Coccossis, H./P. Nijkamp: Sustainable Tourism Development. Avebury Press, Aldershot 1995

Croall, J.: Preserve or Destroy? Tourism and the Environment. Calouste Gulbenkian Foundation, London 1995

Commission of the European Union, DG XXIII: Taking Account of Environment in Tourism Development. Brussels 1993

Commission of the European Union: The EU 5th Environmental Action Programme (5EAP). Brussels 1995

Danz, W./S. Ortner (Eds.): Die Alpenkonvention – eine Zwischenbilanz. CIPRA Deutschland e.V., Munich 1993

Embacher, H.: Marketing for Agri-Tourism in Austria: Strategy and Realisation in an Highly Developed Tourist Destination. In: Journal of Sustainable Tourism, Vol. 2, Nos 1&2, 1994, 61-76

Hopfenbeck, W./P. Zimmer: Umweltorientiertes Tourismus management. Landsberg/Lech 1993

Krippendorf, J.: Alpsegen – Alptraum. Für eine Tourismusentwicklung im Einklang mit Mensch und Natur. Bern 1986

McIntyre, G.: Sustainable Tourism Development: Guide for Local Planners. World Tourism Organisation. Madrid 1993

Messerli, P.: Mensch und Natur im alpinen Lebensraum. Risiken, Chancen, Perspektiven. Bern 1989

Olympics´94: A Showcase for Environmental Policy in Norway 1988-1994. Ministry of Environment, Norway and UNEP. Oslo 1995

Pillmann, W./S. Predi (Eds.): Strategies for Reducing the Environmental Impact of Tourism. International Society for Environmental Protection. Vienna 1992

UNEP, Prince of Wales Business Leaders Forum, Tufts University: Partnerships for Sustainable Development: the Role of Business and Industry. London 1994

Williams, A.M.,/G. Shaw/F. M. Zimmermann et. al.: Tourism, Leisure, Nature Protection and Agri-Tourism: Principles, Partnerships and Practice. = The EPE (European Partners for the Environment) Workbook Series for Implementing Sustainability in Europe. Exeter – Brussels 1996

Zimmermann, F.M.: Austria: Rapid Expansion of Winter Tourism and Problems with the Summer Season. In: G. Shaw/A. Williams (Eds.): Tourism and Economic Development. The Western European Experience. Frances Pinter, 2. Ed., London 1991, 153-172

Zimmermann, F.M.: Issues, Problems, and Future Trends in the Austrian Alps: Changes within Traditional Tourism. In: Proceedings of the Vail

Conference on "Recreation Trends and Mountain Resort Development". Simon Fraser University, Burnaby, British Columbia, Canada 1992, 160-170

Zimmermann, F.M.: Öko-sozialer Tourismus – mehr als nur ein Schlagwort? In: Erwachsenenbildung in Oesterreich, Vol. 44, Heft 2/93, Vienna 1993, 5-9

Zimmermann, F.M.: The Alpine Region: Regional Restructuring Opportunities and Constraints in a Fragile Environment. In: A. Montanari/A. Williams (Eds.): European Tourism: Regions, Spaces and Restructuring. John Wiley & Sons Ltd., London 1995, 19-40

II

Pitfalls and Policies

Kurt Luger/Franz Rest

The Mountains of Austria

Alpine Tourism at the Crossroads

Austria, the "Alpine Republic", with its 8 million inhabitants, 84,000 square kilometres, 68% mountain area, and 385 peaks over 3,000 metres, leads the world in tourism intensity. No other country reports as much per capita tourism revenue – in 1995 the figure was almost US$ 1,900. But the age of globalisation has brought tougher competition between the tourist destinations: while in 1992 Austria was still reporting 130 million overnight stays, 95 million of them foreign guests, in 1996 the figure had dwindled to only 113 million. In view of the importance of tourism for the Austrian economy, this decline necessitated a review of the industry. At the same time the country's tourism marketing strategy was brought into line with the new considerations, focusing more specifically on the relevant target groups, and a strengths and weaknesses analysis of Austria as a tourism destination was undertaken. Although public interest focuses on the economic dimension, the debate has extended to consider the ecological, cultural and social aspects of the tourism industry.

The Longlasting Tradition of Austrian Tourism in short

Austria looks back on a long-standing tradition in tourism. By the end of the 18th century, during the Age of Enlightenment and the pre-1848 period, a fashion for travelling developed among aristocrats as well as scholars and writers. A flood of travel reports document the romantic striving and longing for faraway places. Although bathing as a tourism trend had already developed in the first decades of the 19th century around the capital Vienna, in the lake district of the Salzkammergut and in some Alpine spas, and although travelling had been made easier through the extension of the railway system, it was still largely the preserve of aristocrats and their households. From the middle of the century onwards, summer holiday areas developed in the Vienna forest near the capital. Railway stations became tourist destinations. Some areas prospered, especially those in which members of the Emperor's household spent the summer. From the middle of the 19th century onwards the bourgeoisie also discovered 'summer holidays' and thus, for the first time, tourism developed on a larger scale (Brusatti 1984). In 1890 official tourism statistics were introduced by a decree of the Ministry of the Interior. Growing interest in mountaineering – the Austrian Alpine Association was founded in 1862 – and later the rise in alpine winter sports – the Austrian Ski Association was established in 1905 – encouraged further growth.

However, the outbreak of the First World War put a temporary end to the development of tourism, and it was not until the middle of the 1920s that any prosperity returned. In 1923 a national Tourist Board and other tourist organizations were set up in most provinces. With 168,598 hotel beds and 108,757 privately rented beds, Austrian tourism reached almost 20 million overnight stays in 1929, of which 42.9% were visitors from abroad. A further stimulus to the industry was provided by the construction of various cable-cars as well as the introduction of the Salzburg Festival (1920) and the Vienna Festival Weeks (1928), which are still highbrow cultural events of great attraction to foreign tourists.

The world-wide economic crisis of 1929 once more brought a decline in tourism and during the pre-war years Austrian tourism suffered from travel limitations for Germans imposed by Hitler's Germany. Following the annexation of Austria and its integration into Nazi Germany, the number of holidaymakers from the Old Reich rose dramatically, encouraged by the "Kraft durch Freude" ("strength through joy") tourist propaganda. The longer the war continued, though, the more tourism declined and Salzburg, once called "the district of good nerves", became the "district of military hospitals" (Kerschbaumer 1994 120).

Tourism and Development after 1945

After the end of the Second World War, tourism developed into an engine for economic growth and an instrument of reconstruction. In 1946, responsibility for activities relating to tourism was transferred to the department in charge of rebuilding the tourist industry under the Ministry for Trade and Reconstruction. In 1955 this was turned into the Austrian Tourism Board, supported by the State, the State Provinces and the Chamber of Commerce.

During the war, roughly a quarter of all tourist beds were completely destroyed, with the damage in the east of Austria far greater than in the west of the country. The Marshall Plan and the ERP (European Recovery Programme) made financial aid in the form of low interest loans available for building up Austrian tourism during the 1950s. The western federal provinces of Vorarlberg, Tyrol, Salzburg and Upper Austria were the first to benefit from this.

The repair of important railway lines and roads as well as the resumption of civil air traffic paved the way for a rapid development of tourism in the country. Not until 1947, when the Austrian Government decided to encourage foreign tourists, was it possible for tourists from abroad to come to Austria again, although it was necessary to get permission from the allied forces to cross the border and until 1952 a visa was required. Another problem was the shortage of food: some food was still rationed in Austria until 1953. In fact, in 1946, it was only through considerable supplies of food from the UN that an outbreak of famine could be prevented. As foreigners were entitled to five times more calories than Austrian nationals they had to be strictly separated from the local people and could only stay at specially selected hotels. Due to the absence of tourists from Eastern European countries as a result of the new political situation there, advertising for tourism concentrated on guests from Western Europe, Italy, Scandinavia and the USA (Luger/Rest 1995).

As a knock-on effect of the German 'Economic Miracle', the 1950s saw the first wave of travel and with it an enormous increase in figures in Austrian tourism. Holiday trips became affordable to an ever larger section of the population. By the end of the decade, almost 42 million overnight stays were recorded. The number of foreign travellers rose continuously, with most of them preferring the western provinces of Austria. In the winter of 1959/60, 52% of the overnight stays recorded were made by foreigners and in the summer of 1960 the figure was 60%. 44% of all overnight stays recorded in Austria in 1960 were travellers from the Federal Republic of Germany. Apart from the Germans, people from Britain, the Benelux countries, France, Italy, Switzerland and the USA spent some days holiday in Austria.

The Media as a Catalyst for Austrian Tourism

Support for the tourist trade's efforts to fill tourist-beds in Austria came from the culture industry. 'Heimatfilme' (sentimental films in idealised regional settings) and popular songs aroused nostalgic associations with Austria, and in so doing were responsible for media marketing. By 1965 122 'Heimatfilme' of different types had been filmed by the Austrian film industry. They were released in all German-speaking countries and became the most popular form of leisure-time entertainment in the new Austrian republic (in 1958 alone, 122 million box office tickets were sold). These films not only served Austria's own search for a new national identity, but also advertised for Austria in German-speaking areas. In these films the scenery, though it served only as a setting or backdrop, was the focal point of a plot which usually turned on a personal destiny; and farming life was idealised and presented from the summer holiday angle. The songs reflected personal happiness and described the beauty of the countryside

– the wine-growing villages of the river Danube valley, the mountains and lakes of the Salzkammergut etc.; a safe and perfect world among contented Tyrolean cows was staged or produced as a commodity. The Heimatfilm helped suppress the memory of the Nazi era (in the country village, so it seemed, all was still well with the world) and accompanied the gradual transformation of the most attractive rural areas of the province into a holiday paradise. The countryside became estranged from its rural cultural identity, but in so doing became a national, commercial, cultural and tourist attraction (Luger 1990 81).

The Hollywood musical The Sound of Music, starring Julie Andrews as Maria Trapp, which was filmed in and around Salzburg in 1965 on the threshold of the audio-visual age, was the most efficient and cheapest image-making campaign of all times for Austria and, in particular, for the city and countryside of Salzburg. In the first few years after the release of the film the number of Americans visiting Salzburg doubled. Three out of four tourists still give this film – which is shown frequently on TV in the USA – as the main reason for their trip to Austria or Salzburg. A special Sound of Music tour takes tourists to the film locations. The city, birthplace of Wolfgang Amadeus Mozart, not only owes its fame as a tourist attraction to the Festival, which has attracted lovers of classical music and theatre from all over the world for more than 70 years, but also to its clearly defined image within the global entertainment industry (Luger 1994 184).

Over the years Austria's tourist marketing has integrated appropriate sights, souvenirs and cultural specialities into its usable collection. Tyrolean hats, coffee-houses, dancing white horses, Viennese waltzes, New Year's Concerts, Mozart chocolates, mountain peaks – images of Austria have been turned into powerful catchwords and clichés. Even the folk music programmes broadcast on TV are popular because they apparently satisfy the longing for an unproblematic, rurally harmonious world. In these productions regional nuances and cultural idiosyncrasies are abandoned so that the films can be understood in all German-speaking areas.

Mobile Privatization – Modernization and Cultural Change

The way in which the media and tourist industry can bring about cultural change can be seen by taking a look at the 1960s, when holidays and tourism became firmly established, in a cultural sense, as part of the way of life. It was the decade of eager attempts to remove all barriers, not only in questions of social values and moral concepts, but also in the gratification of long-dreamed-of external contacts. It can be described as the decade in which the life-style of most Austrians was noticeably influenced, for the first time, by "mobile privatization" (Williams 1973). The development in almost every European country was characterised by unparalleled mobility, a great burst of kinetic energy unleashed by road, rail and air traffic. Both mental and physical distances suddenly started to shrink, and features of foreign cultures could be incorporated into one's own cultural identity. The term also refers to the dichotomy between the search for individual, private freedom and at the same time the search for identity within the constraints imposed by society. This was manifested mainly in what the consumer was buying, the way apartments were furnished, and in the family sphere. The TV became the characteristic technical acquisition of the decade, comparable with the refrigerator in the 1950s. Rising incomes, mass production and a reduction in the price of appliances, as well as a demand for more convenience and prestige goods etc. led to a rise in the number of TV households from 200,000 in 1960 to 1.4 million in 1970. This privatization can thus be described as domesticity, as withdrawal. At the same time technology now offered the possibility of hitherto unimaginable mental mobility and a chance to take part in events world-wide – something previous generations could only have dreamed of. Through this the population could participate in pushing back the horizon and could experience media-events all over the world, such as space flights, moon-landings, and the Olympic Games, and could watch how the USA bombed little Vietnam back into the stone-age.

In the same period the number of cars in Austria rose from 404,000 to 1.2 million, the minimum holiday time was extended from two to three weeks and weekly working hours were lowered successively to 40. The increase in leisure time favoured another kind of mobility and resulted in a collective burst of holidaymaking. For Austrians the embodiment of a holiday abroad was a trip to the Adriatic Coast, which had already become popular with the middle-class in the 50s and had now become affordable for the less well-off.

Whereas a sailing ship, all lit up, on top of the television set was once a symbol of the longing for faraway places, it was now possible to escape everyday life, not only in one's mind, but in reality, and, for a few weeks, to break out and come closer to one's imaginary dream horizon (Kos 1985). The individual radius of activity was extended considerably and the increased motorization of tourist traffic developed into tourism for the masses. For the Austrians this meant an increase of visitors, and with it a greater feeling of being the hosts in a receiving country. People stopped feeling static and became mobile, with lives full of comings and goings. The new means of communication, cars and highways, civil aviation and television brought the hierarchy of near and far into confusion, demanding, at the same time, the creation of identities, and an effort to absorb what was foreign. Mass cultures like tourism facilitated escape from an industrialized world, and the marketing of dreams became an industry of its own.

Austria – World Champion in Tourism

While economic development has made it possible for one half of the Austrian population to afford holiday trips, the other half experience tourism mainly from the standpoint of the hosts and are confronted with the enormous intensity of incoming tourism. Within a period of about forty years, tourism in Austria has become one of the largest sectors of the economy; and due to the spread of the industrially and economically oriented life-style model in Western Europe, the industrialization process in culture and tourism has continued with tremendous dynamic force. About twelve percent of Austria's economic output is produced by about 19,000 professional and roughly 40,000 private hosts, providing about 1.25 million guest beds. 150,000 jobs are directly linked to this figure and approximately 400,000 people receive earnings indirectly from it. In the Western provinces like Tyrol and Salzburg almost two out of three jobs are either directly or indirectly connected with tourism. Whereas up to the 1970s, the increase in the number of beds or overnight stays was the main concern, since then more emphasis has been placed on improving standards and the level of comfort. However, the considerable investments made by private hotel owners and landlords have led to an extremely serious state of debt in the tourist industry (Hartl 1996). In 1992 around 127 million overnight stays were recorded in the Alpine Republic, about three-quarters of which were made by foreign guests. Two-thirds of the foreign visitors were Germans, spending a total of approx. US$ 14.5 billion in Austria (Zins 1996). The income per capita from this sector of the economy is higher in Austria than in any other country: in 1993 it amounted to US$ 1,897. With the exception of some island republics, Austria is the most tourism-intensive country in international tourism (Smeral 1994 12).

While the summer used to be the most important season, nowadays about 75% of all snow-holidays are taken in Austria, with some 40% of the income from tourism coming from the winter months. World championships in skiing, the Olympic Games and the victories and places of honour won by Austrian skiers have made the country internationally popular as a winter sports region. Every year people are transported up the mountains about 500 million times by ski-lifts and cable-cars, a fivefold increase since 1972. Since the first drag-lift was built in 1908, the range of technically-assisted means of ascent has been continually expanded and modernized. In 1952 there were about 44 chair-lifts and 74 drag-lifts; in 1968 there were already over 2,000. Today, about 600 main cable-lines (cable-cars and multi-seat chair-lifts) are available and around 2,700 drag lifts (Luger/Rest 1995 662).

The Effects of Opening Up to Tourism

The considerable prosperity which many Austrian regions owe to tourism – some inner alpine villages would presumably no longer be populated were it not for this means of livelihood – has, however, led to changes, for example in the values and attitudes of those concerned and in their everyday culture. It has changed community life in tourist resorts as well as spoiling traditional customs and architecture. Tourism never fails to have an effect on the culture of target regions: the more intensive the contact, the more traditional systems of values are influenced; the more the tourists search for the "genuine" and "unspoiled", the greater the disruption of the host's cultural framework, because he feels obliged, to a certain extent at least, to orientate himself towards the expectations and images created by the media and publicity (Kramer 1997; Hennig 1997). The local population has to take on the role of host, synchronizing "back-stage" life with the production of tourist facilities and in some ways becoming stereotype, catalogue Austrians. Just how the interaction between local landlords and guests has developed in the course of the intensification of tourism is shown in a comparative pilot study. Whereas in the early stages of a region being discovered, the level of the host's involvement is very high and personal congeniality tends to veil the business side, as professionalism increases the local people prefer to keep their distance, nonetheless maintaining the image of friendly involvement. Not until the last stage, which can usually be observed in the traditional tourist resorts, do landlords withdraw completely and try to reduce personal involvement to a minimum (Schrutka-Rechtenstamm 1995).

In the long term this "normalization" of business relationships between host and guest may lead to a reduction in turnover, as hospitality, a relaxed atmosphere, culture and direct contact with the local people (a "home away from home") are precisely the ingredients of an Austrian holiday that are praised by satisfied guests. They form the marketable aspects of Austrian identity which, in the forms of communication in tourist advertising, are especially prominent. It is therefore necessary to develop new, sustainable ways of living with tourism – which does not always operate without conflict. As a consequence of mass tourism, people living in the tourist resorts have in recent years become increasingly tired of tourism. Surveys show that the pressure limit has already been reached in many areas, and tourist organizations have found it necessary to carry out public relations campaigns in Tyrol, Vorarlberg and Salzburg to demonstrate the advantages of tourism to the local people (Luger/Rest 1994).

Up to the 1980s the question of tourism was discussed only with regard to the economic significance of the sector, which was becoming increasingly important to the balance of payments. As a result of this importance, however, criticism of tourism became louder. Sustainability as a holistic approach to tourism was discovered, „gentle tourism" considered a new market niche, and a new concept of tourism, aiming to serve not only the tourism industry but also local people, went on the agenda in the public discussion. The tolerance levels seemed to have been reached and as a consequence of the negative effects of mass tourism, widely discussed in public, demands were made for a gentler and more environment and culture-friendly form of tourism. At the centre of the debate was the matter of traffic congestion, which had not only been caused by tourism, but also by Austria's sandwich position as a central European transit country. When transit traffic, local traffic and holiday traffic (the individualization of travelling means that now four out of five travellers use their own car) coincide, this has a negative effect on both traveller and local people: the former has to put up with long traffic jams and the latter with a serious depreciation in the quality of life (CIPRA 1996).

The Old Life as a Stage-Setting

Even in a highly modernized and industrialized western country like Austria the fear that tourism threatens the cultural identity of whole regions leads again and again to emotionally charged disputes. Intercultural contact with tourists, who usually come from urban areas, means that in the primarily rural tourist regions people have to adapt, a kind of service-culture is produced and local culture is integrated into what is offered to tourists. A kind of folklore emerges out of the culture actually lived by the local people, a process which usually implies a loss of culture. There can be no doubt that elements of the traditional civilization – the old life – have been subjected to considerable pressure to modernize and to a process of erosion, although tourism is not the only driving force (Luger 1995). On the other hand, many cultural or folklore activities considered typical of a region have only been generated thanks to the spread of tourism; alongside the revival of old, long-forgotten traditions. Evidence of this is the establishment, or rather re-establishment of numerous associations such as those for national (or local) costumes, customs and rifle clubs, whose „authenticity" has increasingly been doubted, even by tourist businesses (Kapeller 1991; Thiem 1994). Authentic customs are often only kept up by lovers of old traditions and they have little to do with the living, everyday culture of the regional or rural population.

The most noticeable changes in the everyday culture of tourist areas can be found in those places which, in the few years since the war, have turned from an economic system based on subsistence farming into a highly developed, tourist-service oriented society. At the beginning of the 1950s about one million Austrians were employed in agriculture; nowadays it is only about 180,000. More than two-thirds of the farming population have to take up some form of casual employment not connected with farming and often not in their local village. Agriculture is increasingly losing economic importance and its contribution to the national income is only about 2.3%. Alpine or mountain-farming has changed from a direct, economic form of production to ecologically relevant activities and has produced considerable early achievements for tourism through caring for the countryside (Rest 1994). The effects of this change in function towards "landscape-gardening" will change the cultural identity of many mountain farmers far more than the encounter with tourism has so far (Bauer/Rest/Schwaighofer 1994).

An identity-changing development is apparent in the present trend in farmhouse holidays and the romanticised and idealised world of farm life it presents. Inventive advertisers have even started to create an artificial Disney-Farm-World (with dwarf cattle and horses, and other small animals), in which a kind of farm life is presented that, in actual fact, no longer exists. Programmes offer activities such as bread-baking, making farm produce and even trips to mountain pastures and huts that are often no longer in use, as part of the chance to experience life on a farm. In order to be able to do this the farmer's wife must first have attended courses in baking whole-wheat bread, spinning wool and so on. The image produced is that of a pre-industrial subsistence farm, and, depending on the wishes of the guests, livestock and cultivation are shown in a variety of ways and old farming implements are demonstrated and put to use. Apart from the primary arrangements (bed and breakfast), the product also includes more and more extensive services, which makes demands round the clock on the farmer-cum-landlord. The main pressure of work falls on the farmer's wife, with the farmers themselves in charge of organizing the guests' activities and entertainment (cf. Schrutka-Rechtenstamm 1994; Rest 1995).

Change in the Landscape

Within merely a few decades a fundamental change has occurred in the landscape of many areas. On the one hand, this is due to developments in agricultural technology and the resulting changes in farming. Corn-growing disappeared from most Alpine areas after the beginning of the 60s. Highly developed tourist valleys show strong tendencies towards urbanization and have almost reached urban population density (Baetzing/Perlik 1995). The re-structuring of the countryside – tourism is often accused of "eating up" the landscape (Krippendorf 1975) – is mainly the result of the construction of various tourist infrastructures and tall buildings; but is also due to the spread of housing developments. In the same way the improvements to roads, and the increase in commuter traffic that has followed have also contributed to this change. The few examples of architecturally sophisticated hotel or tourist buildings in the Austrian Alps were built largely in the period between the wars, but, due to later re-construction or extension, they have lost most of their aesthetic quality. The over-use of the landscape and the ousting of agriculture in the competition for space with tourism present further, much-discussed problem areas.

This change in landscape is not only reflected in the architectural monotony of the Alpine-style architecture (Kos 1995a). Road and rail connections, car-parks, more than 3,000 means of conveyance for winter sports and ski-slopes have altered the aesthetic character of the countryside. Changes in structure have also brought about changes in the home. The old parlour, once the room where all those living and working on the farm could get together, has largely become a breakfast room and lounge for guests, and the farmer's family has withdrawn into a kitchen-cum-living-room (Conrad 1994). The regionally typical old buildings have become a favourite motif in tourist advertising, which has to convey its message graphically and concentrate on suggestive images which stimulate longing. Consequently, what tourists consider beautiful – the village as a pre-modern setting – often appears to be just an ugly old hut to the local people.

The changes of the last 50 years, the processes of modernization and mobilization have largely destroyed the earlier, stable, social structures. The modern age has seen the dissolution of traditional lifestyles and identities because of the speed and the permanence of the changes it has brought about. Living on a knife-edge between tradition and modernity, many people have found themselves changed by tourism into would-be city-dwellers in their minds and lifestyles, and they are trying to catch up with their perceived backwardness in relation to the cities.

Tourism at the Crossroads

Since the beginning of the 90s mountain tourism in Europe has been stagnating, and Austria's Alpine regions are no exception. While winter tourism continues to flourish, fewer and fewer tourists come to the Alps in the summer. Walking and mountain hiking seem to have gone out of fashion, but there are also other reasons for the trend.

One of the main factors is the recession in many European countries, above all in Germany. As Germans constitute about half of the holidaymakers in Austria, this has led to a considerable decrease in Austrian tourist numbers. The competition from cheap long-haul holidays, the relatively high prices in Austria, and the attraction of sun and beach destinations are also named as further reasons for the declining demand (IPK International 1996).

Despite favourable starting-offers for holidaymakers from Eastern Europe, they have not made up for the decline in tourists from Western Europe. The rising number of Austrians booking long-distance holidays or taking advantage of the cheaper summer holiday offers in Italy, Slovenia or Croatia has brought about a considerable deficit in the balance of payments.

Since the 1970s communications campaigns have been carried out by the national tourism marketing organization (Oesterreich Werbung), extensive sales strategies with specific themes, focusing on the content in the form of slogans. Phases of increasingly active forms of holiday have alternated with those of a gentler, more regenerative nature and been complemented by predominantly culture-oriented, recreational and educational tourism. "Lie in the meadow and let your soul dangle" was the first major campaign (from 1975-1978). From 1978 to 1983 the slogan was "Austria – a wander- and wonderland" and from 1984-87 the motto "Austria – country of festivals" was used in advertising, with the cultural attractions of the country placed in the forefront. "Servus in Oesterreich" ("Hello again in Austria"), the main advertising theme introduced in 1987, includes special packages such as "The Summer-Experience", "The Winter-Experience", "Sun-Skiing", "Cycling-Spring" and "Hello again in Autumn." In 1991 jubilee-tourism started its offensive with the campaign "Austria Imperialis – on the trail of the Habsburgers" marketing the glorious tradition of the old Austro-Hungarian Monarchy. For the period between the Mozart Year in 1991 and the Millennium Year of 1996 a historical-cultural product and advertising framework was worked out, based on 700 years of "dynastic heritage", to cater to the public's nostalgic interest. In 1997 a new campaign was launched: "The Mountains of Austria" is targeted at the younger generation and focuses on the attractiveness of the countryside as Austria's unique selling proposition (Luger/Rest 1995).

There is not always agreement, however, as to which target group to focus on. Between 1989 and 1993 the Austria advertisers were particularly after the young adventurer. Rafting, horse-trekking, paragliding, golf etc., were intended to attract especially the pleasure-seeking, free-spending members of an experience-hungry society, as it was thought Austria required a youthful image. Since 1994 attention has been concentrated on the older generations who have less of an urge to move and who seek rest and relaxation as a contrast to hectic everyday life.

While the national marketing organisation is responsible for creating and strengthening a positive and clearly outlined image as a multifaceted holiday-destination, the marketing organisations of the rural areas are more strongly oriented towards specific target groups and forms of tourism (e.g. adventure trips, family holidays, cultural tours, relaxation holidays) as well as the regional holiday products.

Austria's city tourism is an example of a growing sector. The capital Vienna (which ranks fourth in the league table of European city tourism after London, Paris and Rome) registered nearly 3 million visitors in 1996 and over 7 million overnight stays. Salzburg, the city of culture, registered 1.6 million overnight stays, and Innsbruck, host city of the Olympic Games in 1964 and 1976, 1.1 million.

The spas are a further major holiday product, very much in line with the international fitness and wellness trend; and the tourist numbers here include a large number of Austrians. The lake areas, on the other hand – the Carinthian lakes and the Salzkammergut – report a sharp downturn. Their long-established traditional tourism industry makes it difficult to respond to new demand structures and the ever-higher visitor expectations with regard to standard and comfort.

Mountain areas are the favoured destinations in the western parts of Austria, characterized by a combination of summer and winter tourism, and a preponderance of foreign tourists. Some ski resorts in Tyrol and Salzburg are only just below the capital in the statistics of overnight stays. The village of Saalbach/Hinterglemm in the Salzburg Alps with its population of 3,000 has 17,000 beds and has for years been registering over 2 million overnight stays annually. The lack of snow in the last few years has brought difficulties for a lot of the lower-lying ski resorts, and it was necessary to produce large quantities of artificial snow in order to prevent a decline of the winter sports market.

The final main area of demand is the recreation market in areas which mostly lie either close to the major tourist centres and take advantage of their infrastructure, or offer alternative, small-scale additional attractions. These places and regions, mainly in the hilly areas and foothills of the Alps, are regarded as the country's "tourism reserves" and as a retreat which has so far been untouched by mass tourism (Zimmermann 1991 160).

The Gentle Turn towards Humane Travelling

After turning away from leisure-time collectivism and the offer of an ideal world open to individual happiness-seekers, advertising has reacted to the needs of holidaymakers and the growing expression of environmental awareness with the idea of the summer resort. Visitor surveys show that 80% of holidaymakers think a clean environment and landscape are very important. Half of all German tourists consider an unspoiled environment as the most important holiday motive; two-thirds come to Austria to experience nature. Tourists' criticism targets excessive motor traffic in holiday resorts, the hustle and bustle in tourist areas and incipient environmental destruction (Smeral 1994).

In various regions in Austria these requirements are taken into account, more so in summer than in winter. In the most western province of Vorarlberg, the valley Kleinwalsertal, for example, has declared quality to be top priority and has directed all plans for future development towards optimum environmental protection and the interests of the local people. This has led to a restriction in capacity to a maximum of 14,000 long-term visitors and 2,000 day-visitors. Walsertal as a "leisure-time oasis" has won an environmental seal of quality which is awarded to environmentally-conscious hosts and landlords. The Arlberg mountain area provides a further example: here day tickets for the ski-lifts are allocated, a measure the upmarket ski resort Lech was forced to take in order to enable the quality tourists staying there to enjoy stress-free skiing. Other resorts have decided not to increase the number of beds; and in Tyrol and Salzburg agreements have been reached to prevent further opening up of ski-areas, at least for the time being, unless it brings an improvement in quality and considerable economic advantage. In order to propose measures for the reduction of traffic pollution, a feasibility study carried out by the Austrian Motoring Club calls for the use of public transportation such as the establishment of ski-bus routes, the extension of direct rail connections and the introduction of special holiday trains or unlimited travel tickets for

Austrian holidaymakers. There are in fact a large number of attempts to make tourism more gentle, but they have so far only produced modest results: tourist habits die hard, and the projects are as yet in their initial stages.

Problems regarding the environment are among the most important themes of our time. In Alpine regions especially, conserving ecologically sound structures is the decisive prerequisite for ensuring that living and recreational spaces are able to function. In tourism, ecological thinking means long-term economic benefit. Against such a background, consistent ecologicalization of the tourist infrastructure has become the central concern. This necessity was recognised in Salzburg earlier than in other federal provinces, and matters such as protection of the environment and ecology were made the subject of a comprehensive information campaign. A third of the total budget of Salzburg Province Tourism Marketing Organization is spent on measures to strengthen the environmental awareness of both tourists and local people (Scharfetter 1994).

An encouraging example of the line now being taken in tourism is the National Park Hohe Tauern in the mountains of Salzburg, Tyrol and Carinthia, which is implementing the concept of sustainable tourism to conserve the natural environment. Sustainable tourism implies a movement towards the establishment of a new attitude of mind, or ethics in tourism. In contrast to the still prevailing hard development in tourism towards primarily economic and technical effectiveness, the idea of sustainable development includes the call for economic productivity, for an intact environment, and for consideration to be given to the needs of those involved – those employed in the tourism industry and the local population. The aim is to maintain a balance between unspoiled countryside, an intact socio-culture of the local people, optimal relaxation and recreation for visitors, economic productivity, and optimal communication in terms of a meeting and exchange of cultures (Mueller 1994). To achieve this goal the economics and marketing of the tourism product must be brought into line with the needs of both hosts and guests, and the culture of travel must become more humane, with travellers and all parties involved in the industry at every level accepting greater responsibility for the effects of tourism.

References

Bachleitner, Reinhard: Der Berg als Konsumartikel. In: Haas/Hoffmann/Luger, 1994, pp 151-159

Baetzing, Werner/Manfred Perlik: Tourismus und Regionalentwicklung in den Alpen 1870-1990. In: Luger/ Inmann, 1995, pp 43-80

Bauer, Wolfgang/Franz Rest/Cyriak Schwaighofer (Eds.): Sind die Bauern noch zu retten? Ueber die Zukunft einer alpinen Kultur. Goldegg 1994

Brusatti, Alois: 100 Jahre oesterreichischer Fremdenverkehr. Historische Entwicklung 1884-1984. Vienna 1984

CIPRA-Commission Interntionale pur la Protection des Alpes: Mythos Alpen. Vienna 1996

Conrad, Kurt: Tourismus und alpine Baukultur. In: Poettler, Burkhard/Ulrike Kammerhofer-Aggermann (Eds.): Tourismus und Regionalkultur. Vienna 1994, pp 277-284

Haas, Hanns/Robert Hoffmann/Kurt Luger (Eds.): Weltbuehne und Naturkulisse – Zwei Jahrhunderte Salzburgtourismus. Salzburg 1994

Hartl, Franz: Finanzierung, Investition und Verschuldung im Tourismus. In: Weiermair, Klaus (Ed.): Alpine Tourism. Sustainability: Reconsidered and Redesigned. Innsbruck 1996, pp 55-71

Hennig, Christoph: Reiselust. Touristen, Tourismus und Urlaubskultur.Insel, Frankfurt 1997

IPK-International: Sommer-Urlaub Oesterreich. Study on the German Market. Munich 1996

Kapeller, Kriemhild: Tourismus und Volkskultur. Graz 1991

Kerschbaumer, Gert: Tourismus im politischen Wandel der 30er und 40er Jahre. In: Haas/Hoffmann/Luger, 1994, pp 120-128

Kos, Wolfgang: Eigenheim Oesterreich. Zu Politik, Kultur und Alltag nach 1945. Sonderzahl, Vienna 1995

Kos, Wolfgang: Imagereservoir Landschaft. Landschaftsmoden und ideologische Gemuetslagen seit 1945. In: Sieder/Steinert/Tálos, 1995a, pp 599-624

Kramer, Dieter: Aus der Region – Fuer die Region. Konzepte für einen Tourismus mit menschlichem Mass. Deuticke, Vienna-Munich 1997

Krippendorf, Jost: Die Ferienmenschen. Zuerich 1984

Luger, Kurt/Karin Inmann (Eds.): Verreiste Berge – Kultur und Tourismus im Hochgebirge. Studienverlag, Innsbruck 1995

Luger, Kurt: Mozartkugel und Musikantenstadl. Oesterreichs kulturelle Identitaet zwischen Tourismus und Kulturindustrie. In: Medien Journal, Vo. 14, 1990, pp 79-96

Luger, Kurt: Kulturen im Veraenderungsstress. In: Luger/Inmann, 1995, pp 19-42

Luger, Kurt: Salzburg als Buehne und Kulisse. Die Stadt als Schauplatz der internationalen Unterhaltungsindustrie. In: Haas/Hoffmann/Luger, 1994, pp 176-187

Luger, Kurt/Franz Rest: Mobile Privatisierung. Kultur und Tourismus in der Zweiten Republik. In: Sieder/Steinert/Tálos, 1995, pp 655-670

Luger, Kurt/Franz Rest: Vom Massentourismus zum sanften Reisen. In: Haas/Hoffmann/Luger, 1994, pp 200-210

Mueller, Hans-Ruedi: The Thorny Path to Sustainable Tourism Development. In: Journal of Sustainable Tourism, Vol. 3, 1994, pp 131-136

Rest, Franz: Kulturelle Identitaet und transkulturelle Heimat. In: Luger/Inmann, 1995, pp 81-94

Rest, Franz: Das leichtverdiente Geld. Ueber die Beziehung zwischen Fremdenverkehr und Landwirtschaft. In: Haas/Hoffmann/Luger, 1994, pp 160-168

Scharfetter, Hans: Tourismuswerbung im Wandel. Von der Reklame zur strategischen Kommunikation. In: Haas/Hoffmann/Luger, 1994, pp 145-150

Schrutka-Rechtenstamm, Adelheid: Einfluesse des Fremdenverkehrs auf die Alltagskultur im Alpenraum. In: Cantauw, Christiane (Ed.): Arbeit Freizeit Reisen. Die feinen Unterschiede im Alltag. Waxmann, Muenster-New York 1995, pp 151-160

Sieder, Reinhard/Heinz Steinert/Emmerich Tálos (Eds.): Oesterreich 1945-1995. Gesellschaft, Politik, Kultur. Verlag fuer Gesellschaftskritik, Vienna 1995

Smeral, Egon: Tourismus 2005. Entwicklsungsaspekte und Szenarien fuer die Tourismus- und Freizeitwirtschaft. Ueberreuter, Vienna 1994

Thiem, Marion: Tourismus und kulturelle Identitaet. Die Bedeutung des Tourismus für die Kultur touristischer Ziel- und Quellgebiete. Bern-Hamburg 1994

Williams, Raymond: Television, Technology, and Cultural Form. Fontana Press, Glasgow 1973

Zimmermann, Friedrich: Austria: Contrasting Tourist Seasons and Contrasting Regions. In: Williams, Allan M./Gareth Shaw (Eds.): Tourism and Economic Development. Belhaven Press, London-New York 1991, pp 153-172

Zins, Andreas: Reiseausgaben im oesterreichischen Tourismus. Oesterreichischer Wirtschaftsverlag, Vienna 1996

Kamal Banskota, Bikash Sharma

Understanding Sustainability in Mountain Tourism

Case Study of Nepal

The current report is a summarized version of two studies supported by ICIMOD, namely: Tourism for Mountain Community Development: Case Study Report on the Annapurna and Gorkha Regions of Nepal, and Mountain Tourism in Nepal: An Overview.

1. Introduction

Besides providing a home to millions of people, the Himalaya supplies resources which meet a large part of the mountain people's daily needs of life. Local demand for these resources is growing at a faster rate than the environment can provide and thus is leading to its gradual over-harvesting and hence deterioration. Local people have no option but to continue to use the resources as development has not been able to mitigate poverty and generate new opportunities in these remote areas. On the one hand poverty mitigation in the regions requires accelerated use of the resources and on the other its increasing use has accelerated its deterioration. The search for sustainable livelihood options under these conditions lies in the rational harnessing of its very natural comparative advantage. One way to harness these resources is by maximizing its non-consumptive uses through tourism promotion.

Tourism in the Himalaya has been gaining popularity and it has provided new opportunities and challenges. Tourism has been able to provide income and employment opportunities in remote and relatively inaccessible areas. Additionally, the Himalaya is known to harbor unique life-supporting ecosystems, and many endemic and threatened species whose potential value to mankind of all generations is enormous. These resources have few close substitutes. These resources also have significant economic value as well, which if properly utilized can provide a strong stimuli to mountain community development. The development of these resources needs to be conducted in a manner that does not in any way jeopardize the environment, while at the same time ensuring mountain community development as well. There have been negative impacts of tourism as well, and of the various impacts that on the environment is perhaps most serious, as it jeopardizes not only tourism but the also the livelihood of the mountain communities that depend on the mountain resources. Therefore, it is essential to understand resource use patterns of the mountain community and that of tourism in the context of the carrying capacity of the mountain environment in order to devise successful strategies for sustainable mountain tourism development.

This article is divided into six parts. The second part briefly discusses tourism in Nepal in general and mountain tourism impacts. In the third part tourism-related polices and major issues in mountain tourism are highlighted. In part four an attempt has been made to develop a framework to address carrying capacity of the mountain environment for a better understanding of mountain community and mountain tourism development. Part five present results on the application of the carrying capacity framework in the case of the Annapurna Conservation Area. Conclusions are presented in part six.

2. Tourism in Nepal

When tourism began in Nepal over three decades ago the country was relatively inaccessible, constrained by international air transport services as well as other facilities and services required by tourists. Tourist arrivals in the country have fluctuated but the trend has been an increasing one with an average growth of over 6% between 1976-1994 (Table 1). In the early years the majority of tourists visiting Nepal were from Western Europe followed by Asia, primarily Indians. However, in the more recent years tourists from Asia account for the larger share (Table 2). The growth in North American tourists has been declining over the years. Tourist arrivals peak during the dry season (October to March). The trend in tourists visiting Nepal indicates that the percentage share of pleasure groups is decreasing and the share of trekking and mountaineering groups is increasing (Table 3). Despite the increase in the overall number of tourists to Nepal, there has been virtually no growth in the length of stay per visitor, which has been roughly ten nights, when all trekking and mountaineering tourism is taken into account (Banskota and Sharma, 1995b).

The average per capita daily expenditure of tourists has remained low at about US$ 13 (1988), of which 53 percent is accounted for by food, beverages and accommodation, 16 percent by recreation, 15 percent by shopping and the remaining 16 percent on miscellaneous items (Table 4). Import leakages have been estimated to be fairly high in the tourism sector (Khadka).

The gross earnings from tourism increased from Rs. 636.8 million in 1980 to Rs. 8,251 million 1994, at current prices, with an average annual growth rate of about 17%. The share of earnings from tourism in the total value of merchandise exports has fluctuated between 35-55 percent, and its share in total foreign exchange earnings has remained fairly constant (Table 5). The average contribution of tourism earnings to GDP has increased from 2.3 percent in 1980 to about 4.2 percent in 1994.

From 1965 to 1970 about eight hotels came into operation, and currently there are about 159 hotels of different categories in the country. About 80 percent of the star hotels are concentrated in Kathmandu. The number of rooms and beds increased by over 11 percent between 1971 to 1992. The number of airlines and travel and trekking agencies has been steadily increasing. The number of international flights and destinations has shown little increase.

2.1. Mountain Trekking Areas

Nepal is a country rich in natural and cultural diversity and the country boasts the highest mountain chain in the world. Given its small size (142,000 sq.km) the biodiversity is also immense. In order to protect this biodiversity 14 protected areas covering roughly 14 percent of the country have been created (see Table 6). Trekking tourism is the most popular type of mountain tourism in Nepal, followed by mountaineering and rafting tourism.

Studies suggest that the protection has enhanced conservation. However, at the same time, since most of these areas were inhabited by people before protected areas (mostly National Parks) were created in Nepal, protection has also compelled people to bring changes in their traditional life styles. Conflicts between park authorities and local people have also emerged as development and tourism have not been able to benefit the wider communities that reside in protected areas. The main areas of conflict between the local people and parks can be grouped into the following (Shrestha et al. 1991; Stevens and Sherpa 1993; Yonzon 1993; Uprety 1985; Kharel 1993; Stevens, Gurung and Sherpa 1986; Steven, Sherpa and Sherpa, 1993; Sherpa 1988):

- controlled access to resources such as firewood, leaf litter, seasonal grazing, timber etc.;
- crop and livestock depredation by wildlife; and
- the absence of local people's participation in management of the area.

Mountain tourism is carried out in some of the national parks. There are at least a dozen areas in the mountains of Nepal that have been opened to tourists. The most popular of all these areas are the Annapurna Conservation Area (ACA), Sagarmatha National Park (SNP) and Langtang National Park (LNP). Over 50 percent of the trekkers visit the Annapurna Region (Table 7). The Annapurna region is easily accessible from Pokhara, which is about 200 km west of Kathmandu. The Sagarmatha and Langtang National Parks are, respectively, the second and third most popular regions. The SNP contains the world's highest mountain (Mt. Everest 8,884m) and therefore tourists come specifically to see it. LNP is easily accessible from Kathmandu and contains beautiful views of rich forests and the Himalaya. Although other National Parks in the mountains are equally beautiful, they are not as popular since they are not easily accessible.

2.1.1. Types of Mountain Tourists

Mountain tourists can be classified into two groups, namely free independent trekkers (FIT) and group trekkers. FITs generally carry their own backpacks but generally hire a guide/porter to assist them, and eat and sleep in local lodges or tea houses. Group trekkers (GT) join a custom self-contained scheduled trip organized by a travel or trekking agent. The full package includes all camping equipment such as sleeping bags, dining and toilet tents, cooking gear, three meals a day, guides and porters (Lama and Sherpa, 1994). Another dimension of mountain tourism is mountaineering. For peaks higher than 6,000 m, a scaling permit has to be acquired from the Ministry of Tourism, and for lower peaks from the Nepal Mountaineering Association. Rafting tourism is also getting popular, but at the present is still a small component of mountain tourism. This paper does not deal with rafting and mountaineering tourism. The recorded impacts resulting from group trekkers and FITs are discussed below.

2.1.2. Mountain Tourism Impacts

Land Use

Tourism has affected traditional land use practices and brought about changes in crops cultivated, cropping patterns, conversion of land from forestry to agricultural use, conversion of agricultural land to build lodges or tea stalls, leaving land fallow to rent as camp grounds etc. To some households in the SNP and ACA, agriculture has gradually become a second occupation to tourism-related activities (lodge operation, working as guides or kitchen boys, working in tourism-related services in Kathmandu) (Friend; Stevens, Sherpa and Sherpa).

Changes in cropping patterns or increase in the scale of cultivation of some specific crops have occurred in many parts where tourism is popular. Potato, fruit and vegetable cultivation has increased. Such crops bring quick cash returns to households, thus motivating the change (Chettri; Friend; Upadhyay).

In terms of forest land encroachment, no appreciable change has been observed within the SNP area, which may be due to land zoning and strict monitoring by park authorities (Upadhyay; Byers).[1] However, in the Ghorepani area of the Annapurna region, large patches of thick rhododendron forests have been completely wiped off within the last 10-15 years as households have encroached on the forest land to build lodges (timber demand as well as land) and to meet firewood needs. Ghorepani is an entirely new settlement, which has developed due to tourism.

Land is also left fallow to provide camp grounds for the tourists, indicating that the cash income from renting the fields is higher than from the cultivation of the traditional crops such as buckwheat or barley. In some areas many households have substituted pack animals for milking animals, as pack animals bring in higher cash returns to households by carrying tourist loads. At the same time there are indications that this tourism-induced change in livestock composition has added pressure on fodder supply and grazing land. Additionally, lodge owners have purchased buffaloes for milk, which has also put pressure on the surrounding forest for fodder supply (Brower; Upadhyay; Friend; Joiner).

Not all the changes in land use can be assumed to be negative, however Changes in cropping patterns can be seen as a positive change so long as the change helps mountain people earn a relatively better income than through traditional cultivation practices, so long as such changes do not negatively affect the environment (Banskota and Sharma 1995b).

Garbage [2]

It is estimated that an average trekking group of 15 people generates about 15 kg of non-biodegradable, non-burnable garbage in ten trekking days (Table 8). With about 70,000 trekkers visiting the mountain areas this problem appears to be serious (Lama and Sherpa; Bjonness). However, this problem is more the result of the lack of management or the lack of appropriate facilities for disposing of products that have recently been introduced in their life styles. With efforts that are currently being made, this problem should ease out gradually (Sagarmatha Pollution Control Project (SPCP)).

Pollution of water sources by siting toilets too close to or over streams or drinking water sources and use of chemical soaps for bathing or washing dishes and clothes in streams or too close to water sources, have been reported as some sources of pollution. Lack of appropriate facilities is the main problem and increased awareness among both host and tourist population will mitigate this problem over time (Lama and Sherpa; Gurung).

Forest

One of the most widely discussed topics relating to the mountain environment has been forest degradation and deforestation. Increased firewood demand by tourism and associated tourism activities in the mountains is viewed as the prime impact on forests, vegetation and wildlife. Three factors put pressure on firewood demand:

- tourists outnumber local people in some mountain areas where tourism is practiced;
- although group tourists are expected to use alternative sources of energy, FITs depend on lodges which continue to use firewood and the porters who accompany both types of tourists have to rely on firewood;
- growing seasons in the mountains are extremely short.

Thus, the demand for firewood originating from FITs and group tourists is different. Although group trekkers are self-sufficient in their needs while trekking, including fuel, the same cannot be said about their porters. Porters consume large quantities of firewood to keep themselves warm in the high altitude areas. On the other hand, FITs depend on lodges for all their needs. Lodges are known to use firewood to heat water (shower) as well as rooms also in some places. Although firewood use by tourists in national parks is illegal, and although tourists may have reduced firewood consumption, the same cannot be said about mountain tourism in other areas (Lama and Sherpa; Banskota and Sharma, 1995b; Bjonness; Gurung, 1990).

Table 9 highlights the demand for firewood by tourism in some of the protected areas. In all the three areas the seasonal demand for firewood by tourists is very high. The pressure on the forests to supply firewood is obvious. This demand has provided local people the incentive to sell firewood to the tourists.[3] This process accentuates deforestation as sustainable yield rates are already below harvest rates.

It is not only deforestation that destroys the mountain environment but also the loss in biomass and habitats. Lopping of dwarf junipers at base camps by mountaineering teams for fires has been a common phenomenon. The cumulative effect of the removal of this vegetation on the fragile slopes when coupled with a dense flow of tourists and their entourage can be devastating. Off-trail hiking and firewood collection can impact a much larger area than the immediate vicinity around the trail. This problem is further compounded by the fact that tourism in these areas occurs during off growing seasons, when the weather and soils are extremely dry (Byers and Banskota; Shrestha; Yonzon).

His Majesty's Government (HMG) has restricted the use of firewood by trekkers in most National Parks and mountain protected areas visited by tourists. But the use of firewood cannot be assumed to have stopped, due to the lack of law enforcement and monitoring as well as the lack of cheap availability of alternative sources of fuel. The mandatory use of kerosene in protected areas by group tourists has helped, but effective enforcement is still lacking. At the same time FITs continue to depend on local resources for food and accommodation, and the demand for firewood by lodges, hotels, tea houses and private homes cannot be assumed to have decreased.

Employment and Income

The impact of mountain tourism on employment can be assessed by estimating the number of jobs created in mountain areas, which is basically seasonal in nature. Employment created in urban areas due to mountain tourism is not considered in the study. In mountain areas, tourism generates jobs for porters, cooks, kitchen boys, and guides, i.e., support staff. Not all of the jobs created, however, may accrue to local people as people from other regions of the country may get the jobs, due to their comparative advantage in mountain tourism.

Groups and individual trekkers hire different numbers of support staff.[4] An average group size (group tourists) ranges from six to ten trekkers with one trekker requiring two to four support staff (Banskota and Sharma 1995b; Upadhyay 1984; Baumgartner 1978). On the other hand, FITs hire between 0.5 to 1.5 per trekker.[5]

Individual trekkers, however, generate other forms of employment as they depend on local facilities for food and accommodation. Moreover, these facilities are generally owned by local people and hence employment is directly generated in the local area (such as in SNP, LNP and Annapurna Conservation Area as well as along the trekking trial). However, this form of employment generated is seasonal, generally lasting six to seven months in a year.

The average length of staff employment during each trek is about ten days, but can vary depending on routes (Banskota and Sharma 1995b). Table 10 provides an estimate of the total direct employment generated by mountain tourism. Clearly, the employment impact of mountain tourism is substantial.[6]

An estimate of the income generated through mountain tourism employment is presented in Table 11 and is fairly substantial. Additional income is generated in the mountain areas as FITs pay for food and accommodation. Group tourists make small purchases as well in mountain areas and the income accrues to local people. When other revenues generated by mountain tourism (mountain royalty, trekking peak fee, trekking and park entrance permit fee, etc.) are accounted for, mountain tourism generates a substantial amount of income and employment. An estimate of overall income is provided in Table 12.

Trekkers could have a greater impact on income in mountain areas. At present, group trekkers and mountaineers purchase most of their food items in Kathmandu prior to treks or expeditions in addition to what they import. Many of these items – including vegetables, eggs, milk, and other perishable foods – could be produced locally. Encouraging the production of these items where tourism is active would benefit these areas even more than indicated above.

Socio-Cultural

The impact of tourism on local cultural traditions and values is difficult to assess. Not only tourists but also local people who travel for education, trade, or other purposes bring in new ideas and behavior that affect cultural practices. Changes in people's behavior, dress, lifestyle, family and social structure, and values and expectations; the decline in local support for local traditions and institutions; people's preference for tourist-related jobs over education; pollution of sacred places; and changes in traditional architecture are generally cited as instances of tourism's negative impact on culture. Economic impacts are also important in bringing cultural changes. It is difficult to assess whether such impacts are caused by tourism, economic factors, or by other factors. There are undoubtedly both positive as well as negative impacts of tourism on the sociocultural practices of mountain people (Sharma 1994; Lama and Sherpa 1994; Stevens et al. 1993b; Chettri et al. 1992; Haimendorf 1984; Upadhyay 1984).

Other Impacts

Although not directly attributable to tourism, there are other impacts that can be identified. These other impacts, resulting from mountain tourism, can be broadly grouped as a) impact on women; b) poverty alleviation; c) awareness generation (education, health and hygiene, conservation of natural and cultural sites, etc); d) development (infrastructure, settlement, cottage industry, etc.); e) socio-demographic; f) research; and g) publicity for Nepal (see Banskota and Sharma, 1995b for more detail).

3. Tourism Policy and Major Issues

3.1. Overview of Nepal's Tourism Policy

Although tourism as an important sector in the Nepalese economy was first realized in 1959, with the establishment of the Department of Tourism during the first five year plan period, it was only during the third plan period (1965-70) that the establishment of hotels and extension of aviation facilities were emphasized. The fourth plan period (1970-75) sought to enlarge the scope of tourism along with trade as an important source of increasing national income and foreign exchange earnings, but adequate and clearly formulated policies were not forthcoming.

The Nepal Tourism Master Plan (MCI 1972) was formulated during the fourth plan period. This Plan put forward a comprehensive set of policies to promote tourism in the immediate and future periods. The fifth plan (1975-80) focused on the preservation of historical, cultural and natural attractions of the kingdom to promote tourism and sought to spread tourism to other parts of the country, besides Kathmandu. The sixth plan (1980-85) set its main objective as increasing foreign currency reserves to improve the balance of payment situation of the country. The seventh plan (1985-90) emphasized retention of foreign currency earnings, creation of more employment and diversification of tourism activities. Emphasis was also given to protecting and conserving environmental, historical, religious and cultural resources and the promotion of import substitution industries.

The current eighth plan (1992-97) places emphasis on promotion of environmental, historical, and cultural assets through tourism promotion and on developing linkages between tourism and other sectors of the economy, among other things. A liberal sky policy in the domestic sector has been adopted to attract more visitors. Diversification of adventure travel destinations within Nepal, spreading benefits of tourism to local communities, and involving non-government organizations (NGO) and local people in monitoring and managing adventure sites are other notable points of the eighth plan. More recently a set of action plans for growth and promotion of tourism to establish Nepal as a premium tourist product have been prepared. A Tourism Development Board that will be represented by the private sector has already been approved by HMG, and 1998 has already been declared Visit Nepal Year.

3.2. Mountain Tourism Policy

Tourism policy has so far not been sensitive to the mountain condition and imperatives. Nor has it followed a policy-plan-action-continuum, despite various policy statements (see Banskota and Sharma, 1995b for more details).

One of the key points of every tourism policy adopted in the periodic (5 year) plans is the diversification of tourism to all potential tourist sites in a phase-wise manner. But there has been no commitment to priority setting in a time-frame. No tourism development area has been declared as yet in the mountain regions, or, for that matter, even in Kathmandu Valley. When tourists are permitted to visit, the private sector provides services and facilities to cater to tourist needs (i.e., demand driven). This is basically the way mountain tourism has developed in Nepal. Various trekking trails and side trails have been developed, modest services and facilities have been created by the local people, and camping grounds have been set up for group tourists, both through government and local efforts.

In some newly-opened trekking areas that have sensitive natural and cultural environments, visitor quotas as well as high trekking fees are used to control tourism, as in Mustang and Manaslu areas (see Table 6). The opening of new destinations or routes is seldom designed on the basis of a careful surveys and planning.

Recently, there has been growing emphasis on promoting group tourism since it is believed such tourists will have less negative impact on the environment. However, group tourism does not tend to benefit the local people directly given the poor supply side of tourism in the mountain areas. As a result, in order to minimize negative impact on the environment and bring greater benefit to the local community, HMG has decided to redirect 30 to 50 percent of the Park Entrance Conservation fee to areas from where such fees are collected. In the Annapurna Area, all fees collected are collected by ACAP and used or saved for the area's development. In SNP, part of the mountain royalty is used by the Sagarmatha Pollution Control Project, but use of the Park entrance fee has yet to be made. In other areas, this revenue sharing has yet to be made effective. Formation of user groups is an essential requirement for the revenue to flow into an area. Diverting such revenue to local areas is expected to make resources available for local development so that a wider mountain community can benefit.

3.3. Major Issues in the Context of Mountain Tourism

A clear long-term policy on what is desired from tourism in the context of mountain development has yet to emerge in Nepal. There has been no concerted effort on the part of the government to perceive the mountain areas as potentially rich in a variety of unique natural resources that are not easily available and accessible to international tourists in other parts of the world, or to see that the non-consumptive uses of these resources can be promoted through tourism development to transform the state of the mountain economy in many parts of Nepal. Tourism development has to be viewed in the context of conservation and natural resource management and mountain development, as it is the mountain resources that form the very basis of mountain tourism as well as the basis of survival of local mountain communities. This lack of realization has resulted in a demand-induced tourism growth pattern, without appropriate development and management of supply components of tourism.

The national economic interest has always been to increase foreign exchange earnings from tourism through growth in numbers, with little attention being paid to promoting quality and developing new products. Nepal's comparative advantage lies in the fact that it has the world's highest mountain ranges that almost span her entire northern areas. The Himalaya Environmental Resources (HER) have to be appreciated by policy makers, or they will not command value. As with all valuable assets, the sustainable use of HER has to be planned to benefit the Nepalese people as well as the future generations. The lives of the mountain people depend on the renewable natural resources of the mountain areas and tourism also thrives on these resources. A harmonious balance has to be struck, but first and foremost, it is essential to appreciate the value of the unique mountain assets at the policy level and treat them accordingly.

Despite the benefits that tourism has been able to bring to remote and inaccessible mountain areas, a wider mountain community has not been able to benefit. Even in areas that thrive with tourism, community development has not taken off. A major conclusion from recently conducted studies of mountain tourism in the Hindu-Kush Himalaya indicates that mountain tourism does not bring spontaneous benefits to local communities. It has to be planned and developed. This is an area that has been missing in Nepal. Especially in mountain areas that have strong scope for tourism development, community development must be integrated with tourism development. Thus for the wider mountain community to benefit from tourism, linkages between mountain community and tourism development have to be enhanced.

A major characteristic of mountain tourism development in Nepal has been that is has been demand-led, and supply-side development and management have been poor. In most mountain areas, tourism development has been geared to cater to the needs of the tourists. A great deal of negative impacts could have been minimized had supply-side development and management taken place effectively. The supply side of tourism can be broadly grouped into five major interdependent components: attraction, services, transportation, information, and promotion.

Given nearly three decades of tourism in Nepal, tourism product diversification and development has been slow. New areas are opened, but mountain development has not been forthcoming in the required manner. Although trekking tourism will continue to be the main type of mountain tourism in Nepal, new innovative products have to be designed as the tastes and preferences of international tourists are changing all the time. Developing new products will require infrastructural development as well as substantial human resource development. In other words, there is an urgent need to plan mountain tourism which encompasses community development.

Economic incentives and disincentives at the national and community level can play an important role in conserving mountain environmental resources. The main objective of using incentives is to smooth the uneven distribution of the social costs and benefits of conserving the mountain environment; these incentives are policy tools for correcting the problems resulting from market failure and misguided policies (McNeely 1988; Winpenny 1991).

Misguided intervention or inappropriate policies and market failures can be blamed for environmental deterioration and hence for the limited positive impact on the wider mountain community. Continued use of firewood in the absence of feasible substitutes, ad hoc changes in visa fees, absence of scientific pricing policy in park entrance, trekking permit and mountaineering fees, opening new areas without proper assessment of the potential value of resources, development of products and standardization, and overall planning to integrate mountain community development, poor monitoring and enforcement and the lack of organization and management to adequately deal with mountain tourism are some examples of both policy and market failures (see Banskota and Sharma 1995b for more details).

Thus, the major problem in the context of tourism in the Himalayas can be stated as "the lack of appreciation of the value of environmental resources and the lack of vision vis-à-vis mountain and tourism development." Without an appreciation of the value of environmental resources and a sense of vision for mountain development, permitting tourists to visit mountain areas cannot alone be considered as a panacea to improve the livelihood of the large majority of mountain people. A great deal of work remains to be carried out in this area, and it needs to be carried out urgently to conserve the environment in order to benefit local communities through tourism development.

Nepal's tourism is facing both internal and external challenges to regain its international competitiveness. Internally, the ability of the existing institutional framework to address new tourism product development and diversification, and environmental deterioration, through public and private sector coordination (partnership) are the main problems. Externally, Nepal faces a new and very aggressive competition in product development, promotion and marketing. Efforts are being made at the national level to address these problems through the initiation of a partnership for quality tourism project (HMG and UNDP jointly), an outcome of which has been the creation of the Tourism Development Board with larger representation of the private sector. Building institutional capacity at the local level has been one neglected aspect in promotion of mountain tourism with the exception of the Annapurna Conservation Area Project. Other projects such as the Makalu-Barun National Park and Conservation Area Project and the Sagarmatha Pollution Control Project are also achieving good results.

Given this past trend in mountain tourism development, the environment has perhaps suffered most. Unless the environmental issues are tackled, mountain tourism in Nepal may not be sustainable. The remaining section of this paper presents a framework to address sustainable mountain development where tourism can play an important role. First a conceptual framework to address carrying capacity is presented, which is then followed by a case study presentation of the Annapurna area.

4. Carrying Capacity of Mountain Areas

We desire that mountain development (community and tourism) be sustainable. Sustainable mountain development means "the management of all resources (mostly renewable) that can fulfill economic, social and aesthetic needs of mountain communities and tourists of present and future generations, while maintaining cultural integrity, essential ecological processes, biological diversity and life support systems found in the mountain environments."

4.1. Conceptual Issues on Carrying Capacity of Mountain Areas

For sustainable mountain development (community and tourism), mountain development thus has to be within the carrying capacity of the mountain environment or Himalaya Environmental Resources (HER). Understanding the carrying capacity of HER is not an easy task, however, but nevertheless it is necessary.

4.1.1. Value of HER

HER have significant economic value which if properly utilized can provide a strong mountain community development (MCD). MCD is meant to encompass all forms of development that address the needs of the local community and generate opportunities for gainful employment. Mountain tourism development (MTD), on the other hand, is meant to encompass activities that attract tourists, provide employment opportunities to local people, help them retain benefits locally and provide a strong stimulus to community development.

The value of HER to the local people is consumptive use value (e.g., firewood, timber, grass, pasture land, other forest products) which brings direct benefits to the local community and does not enter the market. HER have productive use value as well (e.g., firewood harvested to sell to tourist lodges, medicinal herbs, spices and mushrooms etc., or benefits derived from tourism by providing services). Consumptive and productive use value together make up actual value. Non-consumptive use value refers to nature's functions or services. HER also provide services without being consumed or traded. Tourists enjoy the Himalaya beauty, its nature and other intangible attributes of the mountain environment which are examples of non-consumptive uses of HER.

4.1.2. Relationship between Mountain Community and Mountain Tourism Development

The relationship between MCD and MTD in the context of Himalayan Environmental Resources, or HER, can be amplified by using Figures 1 and 2. Although the focus of a study may be on a mountain community endowed with unique HER, the value of HER extends beyond the geographical confines of the community and must be addressed accordingly. In Figure 1 three circles, representing HER, MCD, and MTD, are seen to overlap with one another. In Figure 2 an additional circle is drawn which overlaps the three circles in Figure 1.[7]

Area 1: Strictly Protected Area and Resources

In both Figures 1 and 2, area 1 is entirely HER, representing minimum levels of resources that need to be conserved or preserved for all generations to come. In other words, area 1 is interpreted to characterize the stock of HER (natural as well as well as man made) that should be conserved for all generations to come.

Areas 2 and 3: MCD and MTD Dependence on HER

With the introduction of carrying capacity, the scope for MCD and MTD tends to reduce as all forms of development in the fragile mountain environments cannot be assumed to be environment-friendly. All the needs of tourists cannot complement mountain community needs. However, these areas are within the carrying capacity of the HER and thus MCD and MTD are sustainable.

Figure 1. Relation between HER, MCD & MTD

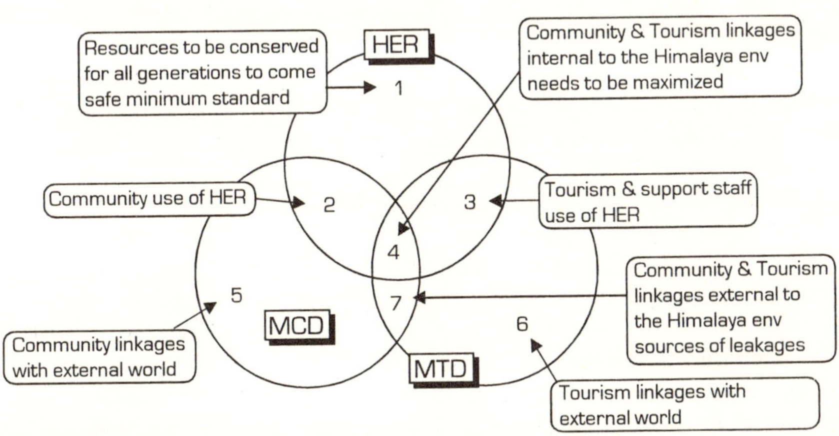

Figure 2. Carrying capacity (CC) of HER for MCD & MTD

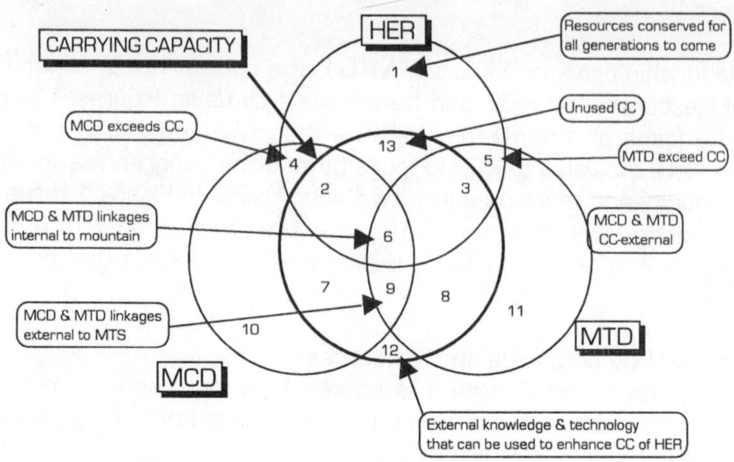

Areas 4 and 5: Exceeding the Carrying Capacity

These areas are within the MTD and HER sets, but outside the CC set, indicating that MTD and MCD in these regions are unsustainable, as the carrying capacity of the mountain environment has been exceeded. While tourism and mountain development are integrated (areas 6 and 9), they extend beyond the carrying capacity of the environment, perhaps because of encroachment upon sensitive ecosystems, the lack of appropriate technological opportunities, institutional bottlenecks and lack of improvement in human capital and other physical infrastructures, wrong investments, lack of planning, gaps in knowledge, market and policy weaknesses or failures, lack of management, and lack of coordination between different agencies. With new technology, improved infrastructure and management, etc., it is possible to exploit the potential carrying capacity while avoiding the damage that can take place in mountain areas (areas 4 and 5). It may not always be possible to completely eliminate such excesses, since there will always be gaps in knowledge. Thus, within the context of HER, each form of development has an upper limit, which needs to be realized.

Area 6: Internal Complementarity between MCD and MTD

This area represents the union of HER, MCD, and MTD and is within the CC of the HER. Here there is an integration or linkage of tourism with mountain community development. Both forward and backward linkages are established within MCD and MTD, and neither of these sectors competes for HER. Mountain-produced goods are utilized to the extent possible, import leakage is minimized, and greater opportunities for retaining benefits from both forms of development are enhanced. The complementary relationship between MCD and MTD gives rise to multiplier effects as leakages are reduced, and a larger retention of benefits within the local community is made possible. Also, since this union lies within the carrying capacity, both mountain community and tourism development are sustainable.

Area 7 and 8: Interregional Linkages of MCD and MTD

These areas are also similar to those described above (areas 5 and 6) but, with the introduction of the carrying capacity, give rise to two new areas, namely 10 and 11, which are described below. Both these areas (7 and 8) indicate intersectoral trade flows and linkages that enhance the carrying capacity. The area represents the potential contribution of external factors to the carrying capacity of the mountain environment. Many aspects of both forms of development need external inputs. For example, product and factor prices external to the mountain environment influence MCD and MTD, and hence the utilization patterns of HER, which have implications for the carrying capacity of the mountain environment. Linkages of MCD and MTD extend beyond the mountain environment, and a part of this external linkage gives rise to leakages. Thus not all benefits can be retained within the community (or the country), and some will necessarily leak out of the community (as well as the country). For sustainable MCD and MTD, this external linkage cannot be avoided and hence some leakages are inevitable, although they can be minimized. Stated differently, both these intersections represent intersectoral and international trade flows that influence the economic carrying capacity of mountain areas. Tourism is basically an international trade sector that also has to rely on resources that are external to the mountain resources.

Area 9: External Complementarity between MCD and MTD

This area is similar to area 6, except that it indicates the external complementarity linkages between MCD and MTD. The complementary nature of MCD and MTD extends beyond the mountain environment and depends on external resources as well. Many interrelated or interdependent activities of both MCD and MTD take place outside the region for their sustainability. Planning, research, and technology, as well as many activities that affect both forms of development carried on outside the mountain environment, have implications for carrying capacity. Note that this area 9 is different from 7 and 8 in that the latter areas are fairly independent, whereas area 9 is not. A part of this complementarity (area 9) is in the form of leakages from the mountain area, and being within the carrying capacity, it is necessary for sustainable mountain development (local community and tourism development) and cannot be avoided.

Areas 10 and 11: Beyond the Himalaya Environment

MCD cannot be dependent entirely on HER and MTD but will depend on external factors as well. Likewise, not all MTD can depend on local community development and HER, as many of the needs of tourists cannot be met through HER or by the mountain communities and will have to be imported. These areas represent macro-linkages of both forms of development with the external world - regional, national, and international - since sustainable development of an area, such as a mountain environment, will also depend on sustainable development at the regional or national level. Areas 10 and 11, therefore, represent those aspects of MCD and MTD that are external to the mountain environment but still very important to its development as well as its carrying capacity. In other words, these areas represent interactions of MCD and MTD with sustainable development at regional and national levels, and they are influenced by many external factors as well.

Areas 12 and 13: Potential Carrying Capacity

Both these areas stand for dimensions of carrying capacity that remain unused. In the case of area 12, the unused carrying capacity is external to the mountain environment, whereas area 13 is internal. In the case of area 13, inappropriate policies, behavior, and gaps in knowledge always result in some level of carrying capacity being left unused, and there is always scope too for internalizing external knowledge and technology (area 12) that can enhance the carrying capacity of the mountain environment. Still, it may never be possible to fully optimize carrying capacity, due to many factors. These areas (12 and 13) represent the scope for expanding the carrying capacity through research and technology, planning and management, infrastructural improvement, institutional development, and so on. Certain dimensions of the current MCD and MTD can be strengthened to eliminate parts of four and five in order to more fully utilize parts of 13, which may require external resources, knowledge, and technology (area 12).

Although it is possible to visualize other similar diagrams to describe different scenarios of mountain community and tourism development in the context of HER, the above illustration suffices to bring home the point that the best possible scenario is one where MCD and MTD complement each other to the largest extent possible and MCD and MTD are driven largely by sustainable use of HER.

5. Case Study: Carrying Capacity Assessment in Annapurna Region

Baseline information related to assessing carrying capacity is not available for the ACAP area. The method utilized to assess the three dimensions of the carrying capacity therefore relies on perceptive judgments of the visitors and host population (lodge owners and households), for which a survey was conducted. All these three groups depend on different resources in varying degrees to meet their needs. A list of variables over which investigations were carried out to understand the state of the environment, economy and social life are presented in Table 13.

Three areas were surveyed in the Annapurna region during September 1994. Ghandruk village is a popular tourist village. There are over 50 lodges that provide food and accommodation to tourists. Besides, the village contains over 200 households who depend on traditional farming activities as well. Ghorepani was the second village selected and is a new settlement consisting entirely of lodges and totally dependent on tourism. The third area selected was Ulleri village that does not have much tourism and whose households depend on farming. Altogether 50 households were surveyed, 25 in Ghandruk and 25 in Ulleri. Tourists and lodges were also surveyed in Ghandruk and Ghorepani.

5.1. Annapurna Area of the Past

Besides traditional activities such as farming and animal husbandry, tourism has become an important activity in generating income and employment in some areas of the Annapurna region. Tourism has been possible because of the unique and rich endowment of the Himalaya Environmental Resources (HER). The local community's dependence on HER for food, firewood, fodder, grazing, etc., is enormous. As tourists began visiting the area, local people responded to meet the needs of the tourists. This demand-induced tourism characterized the development of tourism in the area before the introduction of the Annapurna Conservation Area Project (ACAP). There was virtually no supply management of tourism. Lodges were being built for which tress were being cut and firewood was being extracted to meet the needs of the tourists. Forests in many parts were rapidly degrading due to the increasing pressure on HER to meet the demand of both the locals and tourists. Additionally, camp grounds, trails, villages, base camps etc. were being littered. Lodge owners were competing with one another to the extent that prices were being undercut and profits were not being reaped from their business. There were visible signs that the carrying capacity of the area was deteriorating.

This situation resembles the one described in Figure 1, where the different activities carried out had exceeded the carrying capacity of the mountain environment, i.e., situation prior to ACAP. Community and tourism (areas 2 and 3 respectively) had both intensively encroached on HER (area 1). Although links between tourism and community development existed (area 4) the links were perhaps weak and unsustainable. There was considerable leakage of income earned from tourism from the area. Large benefits were perhaps retained by tour operators (area 6) who brought tourists to the area. A wider mountain community (areas 2 and 5) remained uninvolved or had no opportunity to participate in community or tourism development, while at the same time the HER kept being overused.

It was under these circumstances that the Annapurna Conservation Area Project (ACAP) was implemented in 1986, through the King Mahendra Trust for Nature Conservation (KMTNC), to develop ways and means to improve the carrying capacity of the Annapurna region. ACAP, over the last eight years, has initiated a variety of programs through a participatory approach, where programs are identified and implemented by the local people. ACAP's objective is "to develop an innovative approach to prevent environmental degradation and loss of natural resources through the creation of a sustainable balance in needs of local people and tourism management and nature conservation" (Table 13).

5.2. Perceived Impacts

Environment

Three major steps have been taken to improve the environment in the Annapurna area, namely:

- division of the area into five land use zones;
- environmental awareness programs; and
- introduction of alternative energy and encouragement of firewood-efficient technology.

Table 14 summarizes selected impacts of the programs perceived by the host population. All households interviewed had perceived the forest conditions to have improved since the implementation of the programs. Only about 50 per cent of the households had perceived that the watershed conditions had improved. Success has also been achieved in protecting wildlife as the frequency of depredation of livestock and crop raids by wildlife was reported to be increasing. All forms of hunting and trapping are restricted in the area.

To improve the supply of forest resources, plantation programs in public and private lands have been supported by nursery development. Households' dependency on public lands for the supply of fuel wood at the present is relatively more than for fodder (Table 15). With more and more households opting for private plantation, this dependency on public lands will over time ease out, although it may never be eliminated due to the limited size of land holdings (less than 0.5 ha) of households.

Households' perception of the cleanliness and sanitation condition of their villages in general, water sources, trails, schools, scenic spots and public places, including personal health were found to have improved as indicated by a large percentage of households. Visitors also indicated that the general cleanliness situation in various places was fair to good (Table 16).

Another program initiated to improve the environment is associated with the introduction of firewood substitutes (Table 17) and firewood-efficient technologies (Table 18). Kerosene depots have been introduced to encourage households, lodges and group tourists (who camp) to use kerosene as a substitute for firewood. Kerosene use by group tourists is mandatory. An increasing number of lodges in Ghandruk have already switched to using kerosene as a substitute for firewood. Kerosene is not used by households for cooking on any large scale, as most cannot afford it.

Ghandruk has had its own micro hydro electrical plant for three years. Although the majority of households use electricity for lighting purposes only, many lodges have begun to use it in their kitchens as well. Different gadgets have been introduced to encourage lodges to use electricity and firewood more efficiently. In Ghorepani there is no electricity and kerosene use by lodges has also not picked up as in Ghandruk.[8] As such the existing level of fuel wood consumption in Ghorepani per annum is very high and is believed to be higher than the regenerative capacity of the surrounding forests.

Economic

Since poverty is a major problem of the area, economic impacts have to be judged on the basis of poverty alleviation. Poverty alleviation occurs if tourism and community development (MTD and MCTD) help generate employment and income; and help minimize tourism income leakages by strengthening the forward and backward linkages of the local economy.

First, tourism generates direct employment in lodges and tea stalls. The average employment per lodge is about 3 persons, half of which is generally taken up by females. Tea stalls are generally managed by females. In addition, most of the 45,000 tourists visiting the area hire on average two porters each for at least 10 days. With over 100 lodges and tea stalls in the three areas and including the porters, the direct employment and income impacts are quite substantial.[9] Tourism also generates induced/indirect employment in the household sector, but this impact is marginal as only about 10 per cent of the households depend partially on tourism for income generation.

Information collected from the lodge owners on their expenditure pattern, on the other hand, indicates a high import content of basic food items (Table 19), such as vegetables, rice, milk and fruit which can be produced locally. Although there is scope to minimize tourism income leakage through encouraging local production of certain items, many manufactured products will continue to be imported, and hence income leakages cannot be expected to be eliminated.

Tourism was considered to have helped reduce seasonal migration by about 20 per cent of the surveyed households. Rapid growth in land price and labor shortage in the community were some economic impacts of tourism as perceived by about 68 and 62 percent of the households, respectively. Tourism was identified as responsible for increased land prices and labor shortages. Tourism was identified as the single key factor (67%) for development of self-reliance.

Social

When asked whether the number of visitors permitted to visit the area are too many, adequate or not a problem, a small percent of the visitors (13%) perceived "too many" visitors (congestion) in the area, while another 50 per cent perceived that the number of trekkers currently permitted in the area are adequate and should not exceed the current level. Those who perceived that the current number of visitors was not a serious problem comprised less than 38 per cent. Visitors' perceptions of the density of trekkers however, varied between FITs and GT (Table 20).

Other social impacts discussed are related to visitors' perceptions of the different fees charged, prices charged by the lodges, porter wages and hospitality. The majority of the visitors surveyed (63%) perceived the prevailing trekking permit and conservation area fees to be fair. The majority of the group trekkers (57%) perceived porter wages to be low. Likewise the majority of the visitors felt that accommodation and meal prices were either low or fair. About 45 per cent of the visitors reported that the information on maps of the conservation area was helpful but inadequate.

When asked about the social life (quality of village life, family ties, situation on crime and theft, etc.) in the village, the majority of the responses were positive, i.e., a large majority (74%) of households perceived no change in their religious and cultural values and 16 percent even perceived they had improved. Regarding the preservation of cultural assets such as dance and music, 26 per cent of the households reported having experienced some improvement or promotion of local dance and music. Tourism, followed by ACAP and education, were the major factors identified as bringing the positive changes.

The conclusion that can be drawn from the results is that tourism has not brought any serious negative impacts on the social, cultural and religious values of the society in the case study area. Crime and theft appear to be the most serious negative impact brought about by tourism. But local people also perceived that other factors (lack of education, skills, population growth etc.) besides tourism were also responsible for some negative impacts on social life in the village.

5.3. Assessment of Carrying Capacity

The study indicates that tourism in remote areas can be made beneficial to local communities. In the case study area of the Annapurna region of Nepal, tourism has brought significant benefits to the local people. In addition, the different programs that have been initiated by the Annapurna Conservation Project have been able to complement the overall tourism development in the area. The results indicate that while there have been improvements in the overall carrying capacity of the area, the sustainability of such positive changes is still at a critical stage given the vulnerability of the economic carrying capacity and its close interdependence with other components of the carrying capacity.

5.3.1. Environmental

Conservation education (human capital formation) has played a major role in enhancing the environmental carrying capacity of the area, as it has brought greater awareness among the local community to adopt conservation measures such as replanting and improved management of existing forests and use of alternative energy technologies (also see Banskota and Sharma, Ghandruk Energy study, 1996). Efforts made to replant areas and improve forest management are actions that have improved the forest cover and the carrying capacities in areas 1, 2, 3, 4, 5 and 6 (see Figure 2). Two problems have been raised as requiring immediate attention. The first concerns the biomass growth and the second increasing wildlife population. Improving long-run biomass growth requires silviculture practices. ACAP has however opted to emphasize social control as silvicultural practices are expensive and require technical expertise. Second, with the wildlife population increasing, livestock depredation and crop raids have also been increasing. This issue has not been adequately dealt with so far. As increasing numbers of villagers have to bear with this problem, they are likely to take action to protect their crops and livestock through means such as trapping, poisoning, hunting and poaching. Economic losses will ultimately become important to households and indicate the interdependence between the different carrying capacities.

Efforts to improve the environmental carrying capacity of a remote and relatively inaccessible mountain area also increase the dependence of such areas on factors external to the mountain environment (characterized by areas 7, 8, 9 and 10 in Figure 2) in the form of imported kerosene, cooking gas and other gadgets.

Currently, it is the lodge owners only that have been able to adopt the new technology. Unless the technology adoption occurs on a wider scale among households, the pressure on forests for firewood will exist. The high price is a constraining factor and given the large majority of the poor and subsistence households that characterizes the area and in the absence of any specific income-generating program to improve economic carrying capacity, a wider adoption of such technology may not be forthcoming (Banskota and Sharma, 1995a). Thus unless a wider community can afford the new technology, the environmental carrying capacity will still be critical. The introduction of electricity and fuel-efficient technology are examples of how external knowledge and technology (area 12 in Figure 2) can be internalized to enhance the environmental carrying capacity of the mountain areas.

Although success in improving the environmental carrying capacity in the case study area is being achieved (but is still critical), the successes have not been widespread in the greater Annapurna region beyond the pilot area of Ghandruk. Efforts are being made to develop electricity in other areas as well. A new micro hydel plant has been recently opened in Sikles inside the Annapurna area, where limited ecotourism is conducted, and another will begin electricity production in Ghorepani next year. Although a large number of lodges will benefit from these alternative energy programs, it is unlikely that households will be able to afford the alternative energy as a substitute for firewood. The price of alternative energies will always be a limiting factor in promoting its wide-scale adoption. For many years to come, households will continue to rely on firewood as their main energy source. As plantation programs increase on both private and public lands and with improved forest management techniques, firewood supply is bound to increase and will perhaps not be scarce.

However, use of alternative energy sources is confined to lodges and most of the households even in Ghandruk continue to use firewood for cooking. In Ghorepani and Ulleri, the pressure on forests for firewood does not appear to have eased as lodges and households continue to use large quantities of firewood. Kerosene use by lodges in Ghorepani is also significantly less than in Ghandruk. Use of alternative energy and technology in other areas is also constrained by the lower levels of income. As transport cost increase, both alternative energy and technology also become expensive, which will deny many poorer households access to these alternatives.

Economic

Given the widespread poverty and poor linkage (high leakage) of tourism with the local production system, the economic carrying capacity of the area does not appear to have improved relative to the other aspects of the carrying capacity. First of all scope exists to enhance economic opportunities and minimize tourism income leakages by encouraging households to produce different agricultural and livestock products to supply to the tourist lodges. Additionally, the only form of tourism that has received attention at present is trekking tourism and new products have not developed adequately.[10] However, as 50 percent of the visitors indicated their motivation was to enjoy nature, there is scope to develop new tourism products and diversify destinations, so that more employment opportunities are generated for local people. The ecotourism trail developed in the Sikles regions is to be welcomed, but how local communities will benefit from this endeavor still remains to be seen.

Given the immense endowment of HER in the Annapurna region there is tremendous scope to develop high-value tourism products and to develop both forward and backward linkages with community development. Unless the economic carrying capacity improves by diversifying tourism products and developing tourism linkages with the community, simply increasing tourist numbers to the area is unlikely to enhance the economic carrying capacity. This is also likely to have adverse effects on households' ability to afford alternative energy sources and new technology, and on the environmental carrying capacity.

Social

Of the three carrying capacities, social carrying capacity is perhaps the most healthy. Getting local people to organize themselves and participate in various community and tourism development programs has enabled the community in the case study area to improve not only the social carrying capacity but also the overall carrying capacity.

There were no serious comments made by the visitors that indicated their experience was not as expected. With regard to congestion, about 50 percent of the visitors perceived the current volume of tourists to be comfortable. This implies that the level of experience/satisfaction of the visitors can deteriorate if more trekkers are permitted to visit the area with the same level of services and facilities provided.

It is interesting to note that local lodge owners felt that there would be few problems if tourist numbers were to double. More tourists would generate more employment and income, thus helping the economic carrying capacity to enlarge. However, at the same time, the lodges during the peak seasons are already fully booked. The demand for firewood would increase as well. Based on the trekkers' response, crowding will be experienced by a larger number of visitors if new areas are not developed.

Based on the results it may be argued that the area is reaching a point beyond which the level of experience of the visitors will perhaps begin to deteriorate if more trekkers are to use the same level of facilities and services.

6. Conclusions

A major conclusion of this study is that tourism can bring benefits to local communities in remote mountain areas such as in the Nepal Himalaya, provided complementary activities are simultaneously undertaken. The development of tourism supply components and environmental conservation should receive priority. The HER have significant economic value, both to the local community as well as to the tourists. HER provide the basis for both mountain community and tourism development and therefore development in mountain areas must be within the carrying capacity of the mountain environment.

A simple conceptual framework was developed to address the carrying capacity, which was simplified in terms of environmental, economic and social carrying capacities. None of these carrying capacities are independent, but they are highly interrelated. Improvements in one dimension of the carrying capacity also tend to reinforce the other two, if properly planned. At the same time if the interdependency is not taken into account, focusing on only one component can impact negatively the other two carrying capacities, which in turn can impinge upon the overall carrying capacity. Different variables were analyzed to assess impacts on the environment, economy and social dimensions to understand the carrying capacity in the case study area.

The results indicate that the overall carrying capacity in the case study area has improved relative to the situation prior to the ACAP project. Tourism has played an important role in bringing benefits to the local community.

Tourism in this area was popular prior to ACAP but for a variety of reasons the benefits were not being adequately realized by the local community. In the first place, the social carrying capacity was weak as the community was disorganized. Forests were unmanaged and firewood was harvested as in an open access regime. This situation, however, is changing through a simultaneous effort being made to enhance the social, environmental and economic carrying capacities of the area.

Efforts made to improve the environmental carrying capacity in Ghandruk are laudable. External knowledge and technology have played an important role in transforming some sections of the community to use alternative energy sources and new energy-efficient technology. Improved management of the forests and private plantation to increase the biomass will have to be greatly encouraged along with the development of electricity and cheaper fuel-efficient technologies in future.

The introduction of electricity and fuel-efficient technology are examples of how external knowledge and technology [area 12 in Figure 2] can be internalized to enhance the carrying capacity of the mountain areas. At the same time efforts made to replant areas and improve forest management are actions that enhance the carrying capacities in areas 1, 2, 3, 4, 5, and 6.

Although a great deal of local production activities can be promoted to meet the food needs of the tourists, this does not appear to have been adequately dealt with. As a result, the tourism link with local production activities does not appear to be strong. Improving the economic base of the area appears to have been confined to activities related to lodges, and economic growth in the household sector appears to be lagging behind. This has resulted in a great deal of tourism income leakages. This undermines the overall sustainability and carrying capacity of the area and efforts made in other areas can be seriously jeopardized. A strong link between community and tourism development is unlikely to be fostered if tourism has to depend on imported food and the local community's potential to produce food is not improved. Ways and means have to be explored to establish strong linkage of tourism with local production systems so as to minimize the leakage and enhance the multiplier effects through cross-sectoral linkages.

Poverty and conservation go hand in hand, mutually reinforcing one another. If poverty is exacerbated in mountain communities their link with the external world is seriously jeopardized and their access to new knowledge and technology is also seriously curtailed [area 12]. Although critical resources such as fuel-efficient technology and electricity help promote conservation, they would be useless if households could not afford to use them. Poverty thus becomes the main constraining factor. Income-generating activities in the ACAP region, aside from lodge operation, are seriously lacking. Lack of tourism linkage with the local economy can significantly undermine ACAP's programs in the future.

Tourist perception and reaction to congestion in critical areas need to be constantly monitored to understand the social or behavioral carrying capacity beyond which visitor experience is impaired. From this perspective, the existing areas visited by tourists, although they do not show congestion, are likely to reach beyond the acceptable or tolerable limit if more tourists are permitted to visit the same area under the current state of infrastructural facility and policy. The scope for expansion and improvement in the existing facilities and diversification of tourists in other areas need to be assessed to enhance or cope with this type of carrying capacity. Facility constraint in terms of electricity, for example in Ghandruk, is likely to adversely affect both social and biophysical carrying capacity unless tourism products and areas are diversified. It is therefore necessary for ACAP to begin developing new products and new areas and to integrate these products and areas with community development (areas 2 and 6) to not only enhance the carrying capacity of the overall region but also to avoid development that is unsustainable (areas 3 and 5) as may result through overcrowding.

An important part of the community development has been the formation of grass roots institutions. Such institutions have been formed to protect HER, and promote both MCD and MTD. Although it is extremely difficult to predict whether institutions such as those formed will be sustainable or not, these institutions are currently playing a critical role in their communities. Without local management capabilities being developed, simply pumping resources into rural areas alone is unlikely to achieve development. Human resources can be developed, but they need to be organized to promote social capital, which is equally important for sustainable development or improving the carrying capacity.

Finally, it is necessary to scrutinize the successes achieved in Ghandruk and assess the cost effectiveness of the programs. This study has not been able to address this issue. Understanding the critical success factors is essential for duplicating similar programs in other areas of ACAP as well as in other parts of Nepal. At the same time detailed documentation and investigation on the failures is also needed so that factors responsible for the failures can be identified and avoided in other programs.

Footnotes

1. Note that almost all National Parks in Nepal have human settlement.
2. Garbage includes non-biodegradable rubbish such as plastics, glass bottles, tins, foils and batteries, improperly deposited or discarded along trails, at campsites, outside trekking lodges and at the base camps by tourists, trekking staff, porters, trekking lodge staff and local residents. It also includes inadequately buried toilet pits and scattered toilet paper around campsites and trails and all other forms of garbage.
3. The daily requirement of firewood by rural households is already high, but is not considered in the discussion here, since this demand exists with or without tourism.
4. Since group treks are generally organized by trekking agencies, the hiring of porters and other support staff is generally conducted in Kathmandu by the sirdar (Banskota and Upadhyay 1991b). If supplies are transported from Kathmandu by bus or airplane, then some porters may be hired locally.
5. Generally, two individual trekkers hire one to three support staff members.
6. Note that employment generated in lodges, tea houses, and hotels and other forms of indirect employment is not considered in Table 10.
7. For a more detailed explanation refer to Banskota and Sharma (1995b).
8. This situation will change in Ghorepani as well, as it will also get electricity next year.
9. This direct employment does not include the other jobs created by tourism in hotels, travel and trekking agencies, airlines industry and other sectors outside the three areas.
10. An ecotourism circuit has only recently begun in Sickles.

Table 1: Annual Flow of Tourists to Nepal

Year	Number
1978	156123
1980	162897
1985	180989
1990	254885
1991	292995
1992	334353
1993	293567
1994	326531

Source: Nepal Tourism Statistics, Ministry of Tourism and Civil Aviation, Department of Tourism, HMG.

Table 2: Percentage Distribution of Tourist by Continents

Year	N.America	W.Europe	Asia	Australia	Others	India
1980	10.9	43.2	38.0	5.0	2.9	25.0
1984	12.5	33.8	47.2	3.2	3.3	33.2
1990	10.3	43.5	38.6	5.1	2.5	23.4
1991	8.2	37.7	47.8	3.6	2.7	31.6
1992	8.2	39.6	46.8	3.3	2.2	31.9
1993	8.6	41.6	43.9	3.4	2.5	28.4
1994	8.0	40.6	46.2	3.0	2.2	31.4

Note: Percentages may not add to 100 due to rounding errors. Indian tourists are included in Asian tourists. Source: Same as Table 1

Table 3: Proportion of Tourists by Purpose of Visit

Year	Pleasure	T&M*	Business	Official	Other	Average Stay (days)
1980	80.2	11.8	3.4	2.9	1.7	11.2
1984	70.8	15.9	5.8	5.1	2.4	11.3
1990	63.5	15.7	4.6	10.4	5.8	12.0
1991	60.5	14.4	5.0	12.7	7.1	9.3
1992	71.1	10.5	9.5	6.3	2.6	10.1
1993	58.0	23.7	6.6	5.4	6.3	12.0
1994	51.5	23.5	7.2	6.3	11.5	**na**

* Trekking & Mountaineering

na is not available. Source: Same as Table 1.

Table 4: Composition of Tourist Expenditure

	1975	1981	1988
Accommodation	33.0	29.0	26.6
Food & Beverage	23.0	22.3	26.4
Sight Seeing, Transport etc.	19.0	19.8	16.1
Handicraft, Curios	19.0	23.7	14.7
Miscellaneous	6.0	5.3	16.2
Total	100	100	100
Rs. Per Tourist/day	169	390	747
Length of stay (nights)	6.9	14.5	9.3
Rs. Per Visit	1166	5657	6975
Rs. Per Capita (74-75 price)	1166	3510	2352

Source: NRB 1990

Table 5: Tourism Earnings from Tourism

Year	Total Earnings as Percent of		As Per-cent of GDP	Earnings (millions)	
	Merchan-dise Export	Foreign Exchange Earning		Rupees	US $ (Rs. 50=$ 1)
1980	54.6	26.9	2.3	636.80	53.51
1985	26.6	19.8	1.6	735.40	40.05
1990	59.5	23.3	3.2	3121.00	106.37
1991	47.1	21.8	3.6	3587.60	77.32
1992	35.9	20.0	3.7	5016.90	100.34
1993	34.5	17.6	3.7	5966.00	119.32
1994	42.4	19.6	4.4	8251.70	165.03

Source: Economic Survey, Ministry of Finance, HMG, 1993.

Table 7: Mountain Tourism by Destination (1980-1992)

Year	S.N.P	L.N.P.	A.C.A.P.	Others	Total	S.M.T.
1980	5836	4113	14332	3179	27460	22.47
1986	9900	5250	33620	805	49575	29.49
1990	11314	7826	36361	6591	62092	31.82
1991	11862	9603	39107	5198	65770	32.80
1992	12325	9457	9457	7104	71437	31.36

Note: SNP, LNP, A.C.A.P. and SMT refer to Sagarmatha National Park, Langtang National Park and Annapurna Conservation Area Project and Share Mountain Tourism respectively.

Source: Nepal Tourism Statistics, Ministry of Tourism and Civil Aviation, Department of Tourism, HMG.

Table 8: Garbage Deposit in Mountain Environment, 1988 (in kg)

Area	Number of Trekkers	Total Deposit (Kg)
Annapurna	37902	56853
Khumbu (SNP)	11366	17049
Langtang (LNP)	8423	12635
Others	3582	5373

Source: Lama and Sherpa

Table 9: Estimate of Firewood Consumed by Tourism in Selected Protected Areas (mt)

Year	1976	1977	1980	1981	1982	1987	1988
SNP							
Group	619	692	858	747	917	1323	1671
FITs	165	184	229	199	245	353	446
LNP							
Group	217	293	466	577	514	693	955
FITs	27	36	58	71	63	85	118
ACAP							
Group	229	294	456	543	628	985	1204
FITs	131	168	261	310	359	563	688
Others							
Group	102	110	748	507	436	295	863
FITs	9	9	62	42	36	25	72
Total							
Group	1168	1390	2528	2374	2495	3295	4693
FITs	331	398	610	623	703	1025	1324
All Total:	1499	1788	3138	2997	3198	4321	6017

Source: ERL 1989; Gurung 1990; Banskota and Sharma, 1995b.

Table 10: Direct Man Days of Employment Generated by Mountain Tourism (in man-days)

Tourists		1985	1986	1987	1988
Group	High	667,480	793,160	853,480	914,920
	Low	338,740	396,580	426,740	457,460
Indiv.	High	176,550	206,700	222,425	238,425
	Low	58,850	68,900	74,137	79,475
Total	High	844,030	999,860	1075,885	1115,345
	Low	397,590	465,480	500,875	536,935

Source: Banskota and Sharma, 1995b..

Table 11: Income Generated Through Direct Employment of Porters and Support Staff in Mountain Area by Tourism: 1988

Type of Tourist		Income (Rs)
Group	High	61,299,640
	Low	30,649,820
Individual	High	15,974,475
	Low	5,324,825
All Tourists	High	77,274,115
	Low	35,974,645

Notes: The high and low income estimates provided in the above table are multiplied by the average weighted wage rate of Rs. 67 per day.
US$ 1 =Rs.50. Source: Banskota and Sharma, 1995b.

Table 12: Estimate of Income Generated by Mountain Tourism
In 1000

Year	Wages (NRs)	Food (NRs)	Mountaineering		Trek Park NRs.	Peak Fee NRs.	Total Mountain Revenue	
			Exp. NRs.	Royalty NRs.			NRs.	NRs.
1980	22.07	48.07	21.40	1.14	4.45	2.87	73971	6216
1985	25.29	51.63	14.35	2.65	3.15	2.93	12449	7074
1990	26.95	51.10	17.72	1.88	1.93	0.42	385754	13256
1991	19.51	50.26	25.38	1.45	1.28	2.12	616081	14428
1992	1992	51.95	15.82	4.74	1.34	3.26	640662	15039

Source: Banskota and Sharma 1995b.

Table 13: Variables Addressed to Assess Impacts & Carrying Capacity

Variables	Perceptive Judgement
Environmental Carrying Capacity This is generally split into a physical (size of space available for use) and biological or ecological (limit to acceptable impact on the flora, fauna, soil, water and air quality)	Cleanliness situation in villages, schools, lodges, public places, camp sites, scenic spots, etc. Situation with respect to wildlife, biomass growth, sanitation, garbage, energy use, conservation etc.
Economic Carrying Capacity Economic carrying capacity may be referred to as the ability to absorb tourism development without squeezing desirable local development	Poverty, incomes, employment, linkages, tourism growth, product diversification, trekking and conservation fees, food and accommodation prices, porter wages, etc.
Social Carrying Capacity This generally refers to the level of impact tolerable before visitor experience is impaired. It also includes impact on the host population and its culture.	Cultural & religious values, conservation of cultural & religious sites & monument, family ties, women development, community development, visitors perceptions on various issues, congestion etc.

Adapted from Banskota and Sharma, 1995a.

Table 14: Summary of Major Programs Carried out in the Annapurna Region

Conservation Related	Community Development	Tourism Management
Forest Resource Management: * area zonation * regulation of firewood use * plantation programmes * nurseries development	Health & Sanitation * community health * mother & child health care * family planning * toilet construction * cleanliness programmes	Lodge management * food preparation & lodge management * standardization of menus & prices * hospitality * hygeine & sanitation * account keeping
Conservation education * awareness programmes * targeted at children in schools * curriculum development	Infrastructure development: * bridges * trails	Trekker education: * brochure * museum * visitor information center * code of conduct
Wildlife Conservation	Adult education	Product diversification: Eco-tourism
Fuel efficient technology & alternative energy development * kerosene depot * electricity production * back boiler stoves * solar water heater * improved firewood stove * space heater	Women development: * lodge management * mother and child health care * literacy * income generation programmes	Kerosene depot management
	Electrification	Community lodge development

Source: Adapted from Banskota and Sharma, 1995a.

Table 15: Household Head's Perception of Changes in the Environment

Perception	Forests	Pastures	Wild-life	Awareness	Watersheds
Improved (%)	100	38	98	90	54

Source: Banskota and Sharma, 1995a.

Table 16: Annual Household Consumption of Firewood and Fodder and Sources of Supply

	Firewood (Kg/HH)	Fodder (Kg/LSU)	Percent met From			
			Fuelwood		Fodder	
			Public	Private	Public	Private
Ghandruk	3040	7661	77	23	54	47
Ulleri	8847	3934	89	11	39	62
			84	16	46	54
Total	6003	5797	84	16	46	54

Source: Banskota and Sharma 1995a.

Table 17: Percentage of Households Using Different Types of Energy

	Gas	Fuelwood	Kerosene	Electricity
Ghandruk	16	80	60	88
Ulleri	-	100	100	-

Source: Banskota and Sharma, 1995a.

Table 18: Percentage of Lodges Using Different Gadgets

Energy Devices	Ghorepani	Ghandruk
Improved Stoves	17	18
Back boiler heater	61	27
Solar heater	0	46
Space heater	6	9
Rice cooker	0	68
Electric jug	0	68
Kerosene	22	91
Cooking Gas	11	32

Source: Banskota and Sharma 1995a.

Table 19: Share of Local Purchase and Imports among Lodge

Items	Ghorepani		Ghandruk	
	Local %	Import %	Local %	Import%
Rice	0.00	100.00	3.18	96.82
Flour	4.12	95.88	48.41	51.59
Bread	14.71	85.29	42.42	57.58
Vegetables	85.25	14.75	79.09	21.91
Meat	75.00	25.00	81.94	18.06
Egg	0.00	100.00	1.14	98.86
Milk	0.00	100.00	21.14	78.86
Fruit	0.88	99.12	0.00	100.00
Jam/butter	0.00	100.00	0.00	100.00
Furniture	90.29	9.71	85.45	14.55
Others	5.56	94.44	0.00	100.00
Total	23.59	76.41	31.91	68.09

Source: Banskota and Sharma 1995a.

Table 20: Visitors' Perception about Information (in %)

Visitor's category	Helpful and adequate	Helpful but inadequate	Not helpful
Independent trekkers	40	53	7
Group trekkers	39	39	22
Total	39	45	15

Source: Banskota and Sharma, 1995a.

References

Banskota, K., and B. Sharma: Tourism for Mountain Community Development: Case Study Report on the Annapurna and Gorkha Regions of Nepal. Center for Resource and Environmental Studies (CREST): International Centre for Integrated Mountain Development (ICIMOD), Discussion Paper Series No. MEI 95/11 Kathmandu, Nepal, 1995a.

Banskota, K., and B. Sharma: Mountain Tourism in Nepal: An Overview. Discussion Paper Series No. MEI 95/7. International Centre for Integrated Mountain Development (ICIMOD), Kathmandu, Nepal, 1995b.

Baumgartner, Fred et al.: "Tourism and Development in Nepal: Impact of Trekking - Tourism in Hill Areas." Report on a Field Survey in Fall 1977. Zurich, Switzerland, 1978.

Bjoness, Inger-Marie: "Ecological Conflicts and Economic Dependency on Tourist Trekking in Sagarmatha (Mt. Everest) National Park (SNP), Nepal. An Alternative Approach to Park Planning." Norwegian Journal of Geography, March 1980.

Brower, Barbara: "Policy and Pastoralism in Sagarmatha National Park", unpublished Paper.

Byers, Alton C. and Kamal Banskota: „Environmental Impacts of Backcountry Tourism on Three Sides of Everest." World Heritage Twenty Years Later. World Heritage Twenty Years Later (compiled). IUCN Gland, Switzerland and Cambridge, UK. 1993. Also printed in Parks, Peaks and People. Compiled and edited by L. S. Hamilton, D. P. Bauer and H. F. Takeuchi. East-West Center Programme on Environment with Assistance from the Woodlands Mountain Institute, U. S. National Parks Service and IUCN, 1993.

Byers, Alton: "An Assessment of Landscape Change in the Khumbu Region of Nepal Using Repeat Photography." Mountain Research and Development, 1986.

Chettri, J. K., I. Neupane and B. Sharma: "Off-Farm Employment in Nepal: A Case Study of Marpha-Jomsom VDCs, Mustang District." MPE Series No. 18, International Centre for Integrated Mountain Development, 1992.

Department of Tourism (DOT): Nepal Tourism Master Plan, Kathmandu, Nepal, 1972.

Friend, Joe: "Trek Tourism, Energy and Ecologically Related Impacts within the World's Deepest Valley." Center for Environmental Studies, University of Tasmania, Hobart, Tasmania, Australia, 1983.

Gurung, Harka: "Environmental Management of Mountain Tourism in Nepal." Paper Presented at ESCAP Symposium on Tourism Promotion in Asian region. Hangzhou, China, 1990.

Haimendorf, C. Von Fuerer: The Sherpas Transformed: Social Change in the Buddhist Society of Nepal, New Delhi: Sterling Publishers, 1988.

Joiner, David: "The Effects of Trekking Tourism: A Case of Bagarchap Village, Manang District, Nepal." University of Wisconsin, College Year in Nepal Programme, 1986-87.

Khadka, K. R.: "Tourism and Economic Development in Nepal." Ph.D. Dissertation. Development and Project Planning Center, University of Bradford, 1993.

Kharel, Fandira R.: "Park-People Conflict: Langtang National Park." Master Thesis, Lincoln University, Canterbury, New Zealand, 1993.

Lama, Wendy and A. Sherpa: "Tourism Development Plan for the Makalu Base Camp Trek and the Upper Barun Valley." Revised Draft Report. Makalu-Barun Conservation Project, February, 1994.

McNeely, J. A. Economic and Biological Diversity: Developing and Using Economic Incentives to Conserve Biological Resources, IUCN, Gland, 1988.

Ministry of Commerce and Industry (MCI). "Nepal Tourism Master Plan." Department of Tourism, Kathmandu, 1972.

Sagarmatha Pollution Operation Plan. World Wildlife Fund (WWF), September 1993. Sagarmatha Pollution Control Committee.

Sharma, Pitamber: "Assessment of Critical Issues and Options in Mountain Tourism in Nepal", 1994.

Sherpa, Lhakpa Norbu. "Conserving and Managing Biological Resources in Sagarmatha National Park, Nepal." Working Paper No. 8, Environmental and Policy Institute, East-West Center, Honolulu, Hawaii, 1988 July.

Shrestha, T. B., L. N. Sherpa, K. Banskota and R. Nepali: The Makalu-Barun National Park and Conservation Area Management Plan. Department of National Parks and Wildlife Conservation, His Majesty's Government and Woodlands Mountain Institute, 1990.

Stanley F. Stevens and Mingma Norbu Sherpa: "Indigenous People and Protected Areas: New Approach to Conservation in Highland Nepal." Parks, Peaks and People. Compiled and edited by L. S. Hamilton, D. P. Bauer and H. F. Takeuchi. East-West Center Programme on Environment with Assistance from the Woodlands Mountain Institute, U. S. National Parks Service and IUCN, 1993.

Stevens, S., C. Gurung and M. N. Sherpa: "Tourism Impacts and Protected Area Management in Highland Nepal: Lessons from Sagarmatha National Park and Annapurna Conservation Area." Department of Geography and Anthropology, Louisiana State University, Baton Rouge, Louisiana, 1993.

Stevens, S., L. N. Sherpa and M. N. Sherpa: "Tourism and Local Development in Sagarmatha (Mt. Everest) National Park, Nepal." Department of Geography and Anthropology, Louisiana State University, Baton Rouge, Louisiana, 1993.

Upadhyay, M. P. "Environmental Impact on Mountain Ecosystem by Trekkers and Mountaineers: Mt. Everest Trek Route Survey Report." Nepal Institute of Development Studies (NAIS), Kathmandu, Nepal, 1984.

Winpenny, J: Values for the Environment: A Guide to Economic Appraisal. Overseas Development Institute, London, 1991.
Yonzon, Pralad: "Traditional Resource Use and Problems in Langtang National Park, Nepal." Parks, Peaks, and People. Compiled and edited by L. S. Hamilton, D. P. Bauer and H. F. Takeuchi. East-West Centre Programme on Environment with Assistance from the Woodlands Mountain Institute, U. S. National Parks Service and IUCN, 1993.

Kanak Mani Dixit

Tourism and Development

The Journalist as Critical Observer

The fine panorama of Dhaulagiri's icy flanks is owned, firstly, by the people of the Kali Gandaki valley who gaze upon it. Do they earn anything for this panorama? As yet, too little.

Tourism is an industry with enormous present and potential value for Nepal. The cultural and natural resources which sustain this industry have to be carefully maintained and nurtured so that they will continue to provide income for the country's people long into the future. Besides preserving these resources, equity has to be ensured in the distribution of the wealth created by tourism. Journalists have a critical role to play in ensuring that tourism lives up to its promise, but the Nepali media is not as yet capable of fulfilling this responsibility. (By journalists, I mean independent reporters and analysts who do objective critiques for the benefit of society at large. I do not refer to the category of "travel journalists" whose job it is to write about "destinations".)

Tourism is not the only sector in the country lacking oversight by media, however. Nepali society as a whole is as yet under-served by the press, radio and television. The reasons are the following: journalism is only a few decades old in Nepal; freedom of expression is even more recent; and the market to sustain professional media has only just begun to develop. For these reasons, subjects and issues languish for want of media attention, and this is also the reason why the numerous problems that ail tourism are not addressed by journalists.

Why Supervision Is Needed

The primary role of monitoring and regulating the tourism sector is the government's, but for various reasons the political leadership as well as the bureaucracy have not been able to be fully effective. Meanwhile, neither has the private sector achieved the level of professionalism and awareness to be a self-regulator and setter of standards in tourism. Till now, the trend has been for travel business to squeeze any tourism possibility dry, through overuse and undercutting, without giving any thought to sustainable exploitation. Entrepreneurial creativity is at a premium and there is little co-operation with a long-term perspective among the players.

Aid agencies, which have by now evolved a major money-spending role in all sectors of national life, are limited by their timidity to make catalytic interventions (as elsewhere) in the area of tourism. Not many non-governmental organisations have shown interest in the tourism sector thus far despite its potential for social good. Meanwhile, Nepal still lacks tourism watchdog activists who will agitate for or against various policies, trends and activities which are seen not to be beneficial to the people and environment.

Nepali academia, which could have been at the cutting edge of studying and analysing this most important of Nepali industries, has sadly been largely ignoring tourism. The work that has come out is mostly bland, descriptive and inconsequential, or based on dubious social-scientific methodology. Many academics have turned consultants, and therefore have a strong incentive to tailor their reports to the funding agencies' expectations, which may or may not be in line with the industry's actual needs.

While the Nepali media also suffers from the general malaise that is now part of the political, economic and social landscape nationally, journalism nevertheless is the one „estate" which has been making definite advances in the last few years of democracy and market development. While there remain problems in terms of poor calibre at the upper editorial levels and timidity of publishers who have just entered the market, one can forecast a general improvement in journalistic standards in the years ahead. As this happens, tourism, too, will get the attention it deserves, both in terms of investigative reportage and analysis.

Without doubt, there are numerous areas related to tourism which Nepali journalism will be have to look into. As they do so, reporters and writers should be guided by the obvious principles of good journalism: diligence, objectivity, fairness. They should serve as lookouts for societal and environmental good. In particular, journalists should act as observers and analysts of an industry which is not attracting the scrutiny it deserves.

The rest of this presentation will pick up on the wide range of tourism-related subjects and issues which urgently require coverage by Nepali journalists. The listing of subjects and issues has been done at random, and the intention is primarily to indicate the variety of subjects to be tackled by journalists intent on covering tourism. This rundown can also be read as a general critique of the tourism industry, tourism managers and others (in the private sector, government, NGOs, academia, etc.), always, though, with the understanding that there are some healthy trends and some good actions which also need to be covered. On the whole, however, there is no doubt that the situation of Nepali tourism in the late 1990s is one that reflects reduced expectations and diminished incomes. It need not be this way.

Oh, Lumbini! Over the course of the 1990s, a Nepal-Japan archaeological team decided to break up the Rana-period structure which housed the Mayadevi shrine, in order to burrow underneath and pinpoint the exact spot where the Sakyamuni was possibly born. This could be regarded as an act of great insensitivity, given that the structure (whatever it might have lacked architecturally) was already an icon, together with the great pipal tree growing out of a side, associated with the birthplace of the Sakyamuni. There was no discussion and debate in Nepali society as this religious and cultural site was dismantled for the edification of scientific archaeology.

Beyond archaeology, the Lumbini Development Project has allowed the development of nationalist ideology and let the power of money have its role in the development of the Lumbini site, particularly in the monastic zone. Tall concrete-poured structures mimicking ancient dagobas and stupas have been put up, the place of deep and inclusive spiritualism is being rapidly eroded, and Lumbini will inevitably develop as a raucous religious fairground rather than a retreat for quiet and contemplation. It is most likely that in the next two decades or so, the typically ugly concrete and brick tenements that are the mark of the modern Nepali urbanism will envelope the Lumbini surroundings. The languid rural space that does for the moment continue to give Lumbini some level of rustic flavour will be no more.

By and large, the Nepali media's coverage of Lumbini tends to ignore the deviant trends within the Lumbini Development Project and limits itself mostly to loud protests regarding Indian 'designs' on the site. Contentions regarding the exact location Kapilvastu, the seat of the Shakyamuni's clan, are assigned to Lumbini and allegations are made, without too much in the form of evidence, of a plot to claim that the Buddha was born in India.

Chitwan Concessions

The wild lands of the Royal Chitwan National Park remain the best preserved tropical jungle in Nepal, much of the rest of the tarai forest has been colonised by settlers since the 1950s. This national park was gazetted in the 1970s with the Tiger Tops jungle resort already within its boundary. The 1980s saw the awarding in quick succession of seven concessions within the park. It has always been the expectation that these concessions will have to move out of the national parks, among other things to remain within the internationally accepted definitions of national parks and reserves. But, three years ago the authorities went ahead and extended the licence of the concessions within the park for 17 years.

There needs to be a debate on the continued existence of the concessions within the park boundaries: as there is no doubt that the support staff, the tourists themselves, the elephants and their need for forage, and the numerous jeeps which serve the tourists, bring extreme environmental disturbance in and around the areas where they are based. On the other hand, there is some amount of environmental protection that these concessions are able to provide, by reporting poachers, providing royalties for the running of the park, etc. Given that many of the businessmen involved have already bought property outside the park boundaries, however, it seems clear that they expect that they will be asked to leave and hence have alternative plans in place.

A potentially more devastating impact on Chitwan will come as the number of so-called "free individual travelers" (FITs) develops into a flood. Already, there is a lot of light and sound pollution from across the waters of the Rapti, and with the projected rapid rise in Nepali, Indian and overseas tourists, there will be a need to severely restrict tourist access into the deep forest. Other issues related to Chitwan tourism have to do with protection of the Tikauli corridor (the Barandabhar jungle) which links this inner-tarai forest with the Mahabharat range; the need for more participation and profit-sharing by the surrounding population (including, especially, the indigenous Tharu); the effluents on the Rapti and Narayani rivers which are destined to be the most polluted major rivers of Nepal and which unfortunately are the watercourses which pass through Chitwan; etc.

"It's All In the Marketing"

Nepal, essentially, has marketed itself internationally since the day it opened up to the world in the early 1950s. There has been very little marketing effort on the part of the government and the travel businesses acting together. For the first four decades there was no need to develop 'tourism products', as this remote 'forbidden-kingdom' and 'shangri-la' attracted enough visitors to satisfy the small number of tourism business houses that existed. With the explosion of travel and trek agencies in Kathmandu, however, the trade has been divided up among many more players. The expectations of the population are also up, whereas the margins are down, due to competition and undercutting. More importantly, the opening up of other 'exotic' Himalayan destinations – Tibet, Ladakh and Bhutan – and the familiarisation with Nepal generally and the despoliation of Kathmandu in particular has led to stagnation of the sector. This means that the country, at long last, needs a marketing push.

The "Visit Nepal 1998" campaign represents the recognition by the government of the need for such a push. Unfortunately, 'selling' Nepal is going to be difficult because there is little money, even less creativity, and too much bureaucracy in government. There also seems to be little co-operative spirit among players in the private sector. Whatever is done is piecemeal, and Nepal, even as urgency for action is highlighted by the "Visit Nepal 1998" programme, has failed to make a mark in the competitive world of selling destinations.

There are, of course, numerous areas where the governmental and private sectors could have co-operated towards diversifying and marketing Nepal to sustain a healthy growth both in numbers and 'quality' of tourists. To take just one example, the country has not been able to take touristic advantage of its functioning (now constitutional) monarchy. The monarchy of Nepal has all the trappings which can make it a touristic draw, and yet the travel trade has been singularly unable to 'utilise' this resource. King Birendra's 50th birthday in 1996 and the 25th anniversary of his kingship the following year were two celebrations around which to fashion an overture for international travellers. However, the tourism managers' lukewarm attempts were not enough to make a difference.

This inability to utilise existing resources creatively to attract more tourists must be put on the lap of the travel trade itself, firstly. Numerous other possibilities which are not used include marketing and sale of mid-hill treks, climbing tourism, bed-and-breakfast tourism, rice paddy tourism, ethnic discovery of Nepal, and so on. On the whole, the lack of exposure of the tourism elite to the real nature and diversity of their country, and an inability to think collectively for the long term, has been even more debilitating than the very understandable shortcomings of government.

Trekking Tourism

The promise of trekking tourism as an industry which is more distributive of profits than other kinds of tourism has only been partially realised. The Annapurna region and the Khumbu are two areas where the local Thakalis, Manangbas, Sherpas and other locals have benefited from the advent of trekking tourists. In areas where „organised trekking" is the rule rather than „tea-house trekking", there is not enough trickle-down from the trekking camp to the village on the trail. For example, the locals on the Larkey La trek around Manasulu, or the Loba of Mustang and the nearby villages receive only a minuscule proportion of the profits from trekking. The Manasulu region, for example, receives among the richest categories of trekkers coming to Nepal, and yet other than some sale of vegetables in the lower reaches, the average gain for the local is in the form of a 25-rupee charge per tent on the local terrace, plus fields pock-marked with latrine pits.

Where the government has made the promise of sharing with the local communities a significant proportion of the royalty charged to the tourists, this has not happened. Upper Mustang, for example, was promised up to 60 percent of the hefty royalty taken from trekkers, but in the best of years it has not received more than 25 percent, channelled through the ACAP organisation. Neither were the Kathmandu-based policy-makers or tourism entrepreneurs too concerned about the politics that suddenly buffeted the tiny principality when tourism arrived with its promise of largesse. The media's inability to understand and report on the disloca-tions brought about by the sudden opening up of a closed society (such as Upper Mustang vs. Lower Mustang, Mustang royalty vs. commoner, etc.) is an extreme example of the inadequacy that generally afflicts Nepali journalism when it covers tourism.

The argument is made that trekking is a kind of recreation which should be left to regulate itself, and that the young and the impecunious from the world over should be allowed the freedom of travelling the hills of Nepal without great expense. But it is a fact that the people of the high Himalaya are custodians of the high ridges and deep valleys. Up to a point, the views that their villages command, are their 'intellectual property', which should command economic value. There is no contradiction or extraordinary greed involved in claiming on behalf of the villagers of Manasulu, for example, that they should be able to extract market value for the moun-tains and culture on view as the trekker passes through.

Presently, due to poor marketing, inadequate preparation of the villag-ers, as well as lack of information, trekking in Nepal is a buyer's market. The extreme undercutting that is the bane of hotels as well as the trekking industry has undersold Nepal's hills to the world of tourists. At the same time, the villagers of Manasulu, once again, have not yet been able to take full advantage of trekkers by providing clean and comfortable halts in traditional habitations, selling local produce and curio items, etc.

The baby boom generation of trekkers are now middle-aged. They could be attracted to do more mild versions of their treks, by travelling the midhills rather than penetrating the high valleys. This is, once again, an area that requires marketing savvy. The trekking trade has as yet been generally unable to attract trekkers for specialist attractions which include ornithological adventures, rhododendron viewing, ethno-specific treks, and so on. Due to the popular writings of extreme Himalayan climbing by world famous mountaineers, Nepal has not been able to develop fully climbing the so-called 'trekking peaks' as an activity attracting a larger volume of tourists. On the whole, trekking is limited to the two primary locales of Khumbu and Annapurna, and the trekkers continue to opt for just two attractions - Tibetan culture and high Himalayan landscape.

Kathmandu Valley's Plight and Promise

The rapid transformation and mindless urbanisation which have affected the old towns of Kathmandu Valley and their periphery have been devastating to tourism. The proportion of tourists who come specifically to see Kathmandu's Newar cultural and architectural heritage has declined precipitously. What is most saddening is that the rapid loss of Kathmandu Valley's old-world ambience has happened in all of 15 years or so, even while the hotels and travel agencies continued to take advantage of the Valley's draw as a tourism destination par excellence.

The changes seen in Kathmandu Valley have to do with political change and uncertainty, construction of highways, and spread of the market. However, it can be said that Nepal's tourism houses did not do enough to raise an alarm regarding an ancient valley which was disappearing before their eyes. Even today, the destruction of what is left of the old Kathmandu continues apace. Towns which could have vied with the restored old quarters of Europe as tourist attractions, and which could have earned vast amounts of money for the people far into the future, have lost their 'feel' all too quickly.

What is interesting, on the other hand, is the tourism trade's continuing inability to take advantage of the numerous shrines, temples and neighbourhoods that still stand in their old glory and which could constitute a touristic draw. Taking the example of Patan town, package tourists continue to be shepherded through tours which were current a quarter century ago. As part of the standard half-day tour, the tourists do a quick round of the Durbar Square, the 'Golden Temple' and Mahaboudha temple. Instead, there are enough attractions within this city of inter-connected bahals (courtyards) in terms of temples, stupas, historical sites, festivals and so on, to keep tourists here a day or two longer. What is required is good information, handy brochures, and trained guides.

Kathmandu Valley's air and water pollution and the accumulation of garbage, and the loss of agricultural space to concrete tenements has been grievous. The Bagmati river can no longer serve as any kind of touristic artefact as it has seen its bed robbed of sand and its flow turned into untreated sewage. Over in Baudha, the grand stupa is now enmeshed in a web of unsightly monastic sprawl. Up at the valley rim, the Nagarkot region is slowly becoming a tourist ghetto. Meanwhile, available hillocks are in the process of being taken over by expatriate Buddhist monasteries.

The travel trade has, by and large, limited its reaction to all this cultural and environmental downturn by responding vociferously against journalists who publicise the situation. Meanwhile, those who tend to agree that the situation is bad have responded by trying to attract tourists away from the Valley and into the surrounding hills. This, too, is misplaced policy, for the Valley continues to hold thousands of sites that will rivet the tourist's interest. All that is required is some effort at producing information and in marketing. It is a specific type of 'cultural tourist' who would want to access the Valley's specific Newar urban culture, and s/he cannot be enticed away to the hills for a trek or a resort stay. That is a fallacy which is not yet fully understood.

Perhaps the best example of the tourism trade's insensitivity to Kathmandu Valley's ancient urbanism can be seen in the 'modern' brick and cement building that has come up most glaringly right next to the pagoda temple devoted to Lord Ganesh at Kathmandu's Naxal locality. This building, truth be told, was erected by none other than the Nepal Association of Travel Agents.

Civil Aviation

The inability of Royal Nepal Airlines to lease a single wide-body twin-engine jet after two years of trying (it was still not successful by June 1997) says everything that there is to say about the state of affairs of Nepal's tourism generally. The politicisation which affects the workings of the national airline is legendary, and in the democratic era of changing governments, Royal Nepal today is worse of than it was just ten years ago, with fewer aircraft and less passenger and load capacity. Its jet fleet alone was made up of four aircraft of its own back then, whereas now it has two and occasionally leases a third. The airline has less ambition and worse management than it did a full twenty-five years ago. Royal Nepal's failure is all the more incongruous when one takes into account the possibility of its being able to cash in on the exoticism of the Himalaya and the goodwill that exists internationally for Nepal.

The privatisation of the domestic airways, which was pushed through in the fluid moments when Nepal had an interim government right after the people's movement of 1990, saw domestic air routes full of airlines and the public has benefited by and large from this situation. On the other hand, the final word on success or failure of these airlines is still not out, with many flying superannuated aircraft, and the domestic skies being too small for great leaps in business and fleet expansion. A weak government, on the other hand, has stymied development of the industry by giving licences to all comers which has led to the usual problems of having too many players.

The responsibility of monitoring the airlines, however, does not seem to have been taken seriously by the government. Thus, the fact that private airlines have continued to fly for half a decade now without the advantage of hangars, indicates the makeshift nature of the domestic civil aviation as a whole, which will hardly instil confidence among tourists. The advent of Russian helicopters brought about great positive changes as well as dislocations in Nepali civil aviation, but lack of transparency on the part of the government, the general inefficiency on the part of rotor-wing operators (including the proclivity to lease rather than own aircraft), and the media's inability to follow the complicated terrain, has meant that the public at large has been underserved.

Coming Inundation

The belief that only Westerners can be high-spending tourists has been rapidly replaced with the realisation that travellers from India can provide very useful addition to the tourism spectrum, particular during the traditional 'off season'. In fact, the discovery of Pokhara by Gujarati and Maharashtrian tourists has meant the filling of hotel rooms in that town which would otherwise have been empty. Expanding tourism from India (and the larger South Asian region in the future) also provides the possibility for the midhills of Nepal to develop resort tourism.

Western tourists come, essentially, seeking the following attractions: Newar culture of Kathmandu valley, Tibetan societies of the high Himalaya, Himalayan peaks and ranges, and the denizens of the Tarai jungle, in particular the one-horned rhinoceros and the Royal Bengal Tiger. This fact has limited the tourism scope of Nepal's midhills thus far. What the South Asian nouveau riche traveller who moves with family wants, however, is resort tourism, which is what is developing in Himachal Pradesh, Uttarakhand, and the hills of the Pakistani Punjab. Similar resorts and touristic spots are bound to develop in Nepal as well, once there is better marketing, better roads, and future economic prosperity in the adjacent regions of Bihar and Eastern Uttar Pradesh.

With the growth of the middle class in India, the Nepali midhills must look ahead to and plan for the future inundation by plains tourists driving up in their Maruti and Ambassador cars. While this new tourist tradition (of resort tourism) would be welcome, as with the Western tourist, the challenge for the tourism planner is how to maintain one's culture while taking the maximum economic advantage of the traveller.

Conclusion

The examples and issues cited above are but a handful of subjects related to tourism among thousands that need to be covered by Nepal journalists as their professionalism and publication possibilities improve. There is no doubt that the role of fair and objective media coverage will do Nepali tourism itself a world of good, even if the two sides (the media and the entrepreneur) might at times be on opposite sides. If the media acts as a watchdog, it can only be for the benefit of both the trade and the people.

Till now, Nepal has 'sold' itself in the tourism marketplace, but now it is time for government and the industry to come together to chart a path together. As they do so, however, the journalist (and also the scholar) must slip into their role as monitors and critics. Unfortunately, as yet, the Nepali media sector is not up to the task.

When the media (and academia) do come up with the required commitment to watch tourism, they must decide what their position on tourism is in the context of a developing country such as Nepal. This writer would propose that that position be framed in the following manner:

Tourism is an economic resource from which Nepalis have to extract the maximum and sustainable benefit. While doing so, they have to ensure that there is maximum possible equity in the distribution of tourism's largesse.

Ludmilla Tueting

Ke garne – What to do?

Pollution in the Kathmandu Valley

I think I'm going to Kathmandu
I think it's really where I'm going to
If I ever get out here
That's what I'm gonna do

A Bob Seger Song from the early 70s

Even before the buzzword eco-tourism came into vogue Nepal was synonymous with a "green" destination. The Kathmandu Valley used to be a place which tourists loved to explore on foot or by bicycle. Many of them rafted down to the famous Chitwan National Park which lies to the Southeast of Kathmandu along the border with India. They would ride on elephants to watch rhinos, deer and other wildlife or go on nature walks. Trekkers and mountaineers headed for the hills to walk for weeks or even months and to climb snow-capped peaks. Others simply relaxed at Phewa lake in Pokhara.

Tourists still love Chitwan and the mighty Himalaya although today's jeep safaris inside the park and so called "sky treks" by helicopter don't really match the ideals of eco-tourism. In many places toilet paper trails now lead to the mountains, climbers complain of overcrowding on some peaks and the problems of sanitation, trash disposal and deforestation resulting from tourists using scarce firewood are obvious in the most popular trekking regions. Scenic Pokhara, once a tourist haven, has gone downhill noticeably in the last few years. Unplanned urbanization, uncontrolled tourism activities, lack of conservation measures and pollution of the lake have robbed the once idyllic town of its glory.

Yet, all in all, most foreign visitors still find their expected "Shangri La" in the outlying areas. It's a different matter with Kathmandu and the Valley. Something is terribly wrong there. The casual jet-set tourist who flies in for a brief temple rally, on a nice day with a breeze, protected by the clean windows of his comfortable bus, spending the night in a five star hotel, might not notice. But all tourists who stay a bit longer do. They begin to share the feelings of many of the one million inhabitants of the Valley: "The idea of walking in the streets is quite horrible, the air is suffocating. It's too much now!". Chiranjibi Kafle, who recently quoted these furious words of a friend in "The Rising Nepal", is only one of hundreds who has written about the "incessantly deteriorating environmental condition" of Kathmandu.

"Now" he said, "the people have realized that, in the dictionary of the municipal leaders, 'healthy Kathmandu' stands for 'hazy' Kathmandu where your normal process of breathing is checked or stifled by the air pollution caused by the exhaust fumes emitted by the old vehicles. Is the new government also content with mere lip service?"

"Only after living here for some time does the full measure of life in Kathmandu become obvious, when simply going about normal everyday business becomes a feat of endurance," added Rosemary Thapa in the Sunday Dispatch. Tourists are drawing the same conclusions now. Many used to come over and over again. Each trip promised new discoveries. There was so much to see and enjoy at the same time. There are still many things to be seen and to be explored by foreigners as well as Nepalis from outside the Valley. But they don't enjoy it any more. For reaching most places for sightseeing has turned into a nightmare.

"It does not seem so difficult to figure out why tourism went down by 12 percent last year," stated Jerome Edou in a letter to the Kathmandu Post. "Investing in tourism infrastructures is probably fine but first give the visitors clear air to breathe, streets where they can walk without looking at their feet all the time or protecting their noses, and they will come, since we all agree on all the other qualities of Nepal as a great tourist destination. If nothing is done soon, a few bad review articles like the one published last year by 'Newsweek', might bring down the number of tourists by 20 to 30 percent in the next few years. Even if we tourists always have the possibility to leave the country, the people in the street and their children don't have that choice, and for them it's not holidays we are talking about, it's survival," he sadly concluded.

To compare Kathmandu with Mexico City, the most polluted city in the world, as was done in Newsweek, is premature. But "a Mexico city is in the making," experts are warning. According to The Rising Nepal, they have predicted that Kathmandu will exceed the Valley of Mexico City in pollution within the next ten or 15 years if the unbridled vehicular and sound pollution continues unabated. The papers said: "According to statistics 38 percent of the smoke-belching trucks and 55 percent of the buses which ply the narrow and congested roads are older than 15 years." Hardly any vehicle in the valley is in good technical condition. Most hated although badly needed in the absence of an efficient public transport system are the little black monsters, three-wheel "tempos", which–according to Inspector Rabindra Deuja of the City Traffic Police–today exceed 3800 in number, 2000 more than three years ago.

Apart from brick kilns and the Chobar cement plant there are, unlike in Mexico City, no huge factories in the Kathmandu Valley which pollute the air. "With a clear vision, accompanied by thought, concrete legislation, efficient management, and citizen education, Kathmandu could again become the proud and gleaming capitol of the Himalaya," believes American journalist Barbara Adams who has been living in Nepal for more than 30 years. "If the government had the will and commitment the world would applaud and tourists would continue to stream in." Already in 1992 she had warned: "Bad news travels faster than good news. Assuming that Nepal will continue to depend on tourism for foreign exchange and employment, HMG (His Majesty's Government) had better act fast to counteract the adverse publicity beginning to come this way. Not just by media blitzes, or public relations campaigns–but by intelligent planning for what it wants for and from tourism in the future."

While tourism arrivals have risen from 334,355 (1992) to 393,613 (1996), the number of hotel beds has increased disproportionately from 11,800 (1992) to 25,638 (1996), and many of them remain empty. And Nepal did start campaigning to "counter the negative publicity about the Valley's environment," as at two tourism fairs abroad. Officials claim the reports are exaggerated, but you cannot fool tourists in the long run. And they will tell their friends and relatives.

Naturally tourists don't like to spend their holidays in unhealthy places. They can cope with the traditional garbage all over the place but not with "garbage" that requires mouth masks for protection. If a survey about the health status of tourists were carried out the result would certainly be shocking, especially in the low seasons. Besides diarrhoea or giardia, mainly caused by unclean water, colds, sinusitis and bronchitis are spoiling the "most wonderful weeks of the year" of many tourists, too many. It doesn't only affect westerners but visitors from Asia as well, especially if they live in places with clean air. Like Kinley Dorjee from Thimphu, the editor of Kuensel, whose nose always starts running soon after he reaches Kathmandu.

Naturally worst off are the local inhabitants who have no chance to escape the toxic, blackish air in the streets and who are never warned by their government when the smog reaches very dangerous proportions. Burning lungs, sore throats and headache are indications. The death toll of asthma patients rises sharply during the worst times.

During the first months of the year the "weather" is just awful, locals and long term visitors say. Very often it is cloudy, the morning smog rarely lifts. The warming sun is hardly to be seen in many places in town. "Only once did I see the hills surrounding the Valley," a first time visitor from Munich said, "and that was when I flew in." An international crew of about ten photographers, models and PR-managers who had spent ten days in the Valley to do fashion pictures even developed a sort of mortal terror. While desperately searching for clear, clean air and blue skies they really thought they were in danger.

Kathmanduites might laugh about it. But to this scribe and other friends of Nepal who have been coming here regularly for 20 years or more, these are very serious signals. Never had they observed signs of paranoia amongst visitors before. Quite the contrary was the case. But now there are increasing numbers of visitors who want to cut short their stay in Kathmandu and just escape, by any means, either to the mountains, another country or home. They simply fail to understand why nobody "really seems to bother": "For sure seminars, statements and promises are not sufficient, from what we gathered by reading the papers and discussing with locals. Aren't there political workers or activists who are engaged in other issues than party politics and power?" They ask: "What are all these NGOs doing? We have never heard of any massive campaign for clean air, enforcement of laws and a healthy environment in Kathmandu. Complaining is not enough. Action is needed!". Peter from England knows "they can do it. After all, they overthrew the government and a political system, didn't they? What is it then, fatalism, lethargy or what?"

Observers also wonder where all the foreign aid money for urban development has gone. After all, a great part of it is taxpayers' money. Instead the situation is worsening. According to an editorial in The Rising Nepal "everyone seems to be in a hurry to built a matchbox-like structure made of cement and bricks which passes for a house." And big houses too, one is tempted to add, often to let to foreigners for fat monthly rents. "We have been cashing in on the natural beauty and the historical skyscape bestowed on us by mountains and monuments," the editorial went on, "and with the money that has flowed in, we have built a pathetically impersonal and ugly concrete jungle. The city is crying out for breathing space. A time may come when our children might never run freely and catch a butterfly. They will grow up thinking that rice and flour grow on trees."

As if the tourism industry and the government lived on another planet they still glorify Kathmandu as "enchanting" and "magical", as a "sanctuary of artistic skill and religious devotion, which finds its expression in the Valley's urban symphony of gentle pagoda temples, impressive stupas and exquisite art works." Or "all under the spell of mystical Nepal. Kathmandu. The very name evokes exotic temples, incense aromas and the towering Himalayas." In some advertisements Mt. Everest or Ama Dablam are pasted up right behind the hotel concerned. In the lobby of one hotel in Patan hangs a revealing painting showing the very hotel in the midst of fields with no other houses for miles around. Wishful thinking? Such advertisements in glossy brochures and travel books become increasingly counterproductive after visitors have been confronted with the reality. The majority of them are still confining their stay in Nepal to the Valley. Hotel staff, tour guides and local friends have today their own story to tell–how to comfort disappointed tourists. It's mainly up to them to clear up the mess.

Now that the golden goose is laying less eggs or is even killing itself, tourism "pundits" are desperately looking for scapegoats and new fields like "quality tourism". Once again they are blaming others for their own shortcomings. As before, the scapegoat is the "low-budget charter tour tourist" or the "back-packer", commonly mistaken for "Hippie." In the pundit's view "quality" stands for "luxury". "The type of tourist that we are getting from the west for trekking or otherwise, has changed over the last five years," resumed Amar Raj Singh in February 1995 in the Kathmandu Post, "we get more of the low-spending segments that come on discounted fares and live in budget hotels. What we dream of is the high spenders staying in five star hotels." "To make real business sense, our optimum number of tourists should be about 500,000 to 600,000 every year as opposed to last year's 280,000." Basanta Raj Mishra feels. According to The Asian Age the then president of the Nepal Chapter of the Pacific Area Travel Agents Association (PATA), and Chairman of the Temple Tiger Group which runs a resort inside Chitwan National Park, also remarked: "Worse still, most of our clients continue to be backpackers, and not people who demand comforts and are ready to pay for them." Similarly he was quoted in the Kathmandu Post as saying: "Despite a growth in the number of tourists in 1994, it has not benefited the economy, for the maximum number of tourists were Indian nationals who don't add much to the earnings."

Amar Raj Singh in his article defended the Indian tourists, who amount to almost one third of all visitors (122,512 in 1996). However, he said, their total amount of spending would equal US$ 30 million, almost one third of the total tourism revenue, adding: "The good thing about the Indian tourist is that he tends to spend money. He may pay a special rate but definitely comes and stays in comfort class. Research shows that an average Indian couple spends approximately Rs. 23,000 on a visit in Nepal. It excludes spending in the casino which no one reports."

A similar injustice has been done to so-called backpackers ever since Thamel started to develop in the mid seventies. Despite a long neglect by all tourism promoters and the municipality this "Little Kowloon" flourished, earning money for many different pockets. "Having turned into a sort of ghetto where everything tourists need is available, at least it is concentrated in one area and not spread all over Kathmandu," tourism critics say.

"If backpackers had not spent a lot of money, Thamel clearly could not have grown to the extent it has," observed a long-standing visitor, "and many of these tourists transfer income to the poor villages while on a trek".

Tourists certainly don't like to be seen merely as carriers of foreign exchange or to be discriminated in the case of individual travelers (backpackers) – all in the name of the six-letter word PROFIT. Conscious eco-tourists in particular deliberately don't stay in luxury hotels where a high amount of foreign exchange has to be spent again on imports. They don't agree with the view of the tourism aristocracy which takes money from the rich in the West, Japan or India to make rich Nepalis (or Indians) even richer. Observing Nepal's lack of civic sense, eco-tourists say: "The industry should invest more in people and in the country, not only in their own business." "Almost every malaise that afflicts modern Nepal can be explained by the lack of good education," Kanak Dixit, editor of Himal, wrote furiously in The Rising Nepal, "we happily produce carpet laborers instead of exporting airline pilots to the Gulf. We churn out graduates who have degrees in their hands but no skills. Everything that is going wrong in Nepal, one way or the other, is due to shoddy and irrelevant education. Just as we have a subsistence economy we have developed a subsistence mentality!" "And an addiction to donors and foreign aid," added Barbara Adams.

So, even more foreign companies are requested to invest in tourism ventures in the Valley. Soon, with the help of the Asian Development Bank, Kathmandu will have, according to a press release, "Nepal's first international standard five star hotel" at Boudha (Bodnath) which is estimated to cost US$ 38,71 million. The 271 room Taragaon Regency Hotel is to be managed by the multinational hotel chain Hyatt, promoted by the state-owned Taragaon Development Board and controlled by the Shrestha Group, the Yak and Yeti Hotel and the Saraf Group of India. Last year a news item said the complex will be promoted as a huge "cultural tourism center". Local critics argue: "We don't need a Disneyland in which the different communities and cultures of the country are sold on 148 ropanis of land. Decentralization that planners are so fond of praising seems to be forgotten. Why yet another luxury hotel in Kathmandu?"

Its guests will probably be the "perfect clients" to fly to Pokhara just for a day "full of adventure and sightseeing" only to be "back for cocktails and dinner in the capital" – as offered by a local private airline in the true spirit of "hard" tourism.

In October 1991 the state-owned Royal Nepal Airlines published a controversial advertisement which read: "Besides Hinduism and Buddhism, there is now a new religion on the horizon: TOURISM. Service is our pooja, tourism our religion." After protests it was withdrawn. The mentality is here to stay.

References are made to "quality tourism" now, but its quality is of a financial nature only, in other words the finest, most luxurious and expensive products, and free-spending tourists, spreading foreign exchange, spending the maximum amount of money in the shortest possible time, preferably in five star hotels. The trend to cash in on luxury eco-tourism or adventure in luxury is clearly visible in Nepal, too. But luxury is incompatible with social and environmental considerations in poor remote areas. A so-called paradise is not worthy of that description if it is accessible to too many rich people with dreams of a simple life. Experience has shown that comfortable hotels, hot showers, air conditioning etc. are needed to enable tourists to put up with nature in its pristine form.

In these days of mass tourism, the objectives of eco-tourism should not be to develop the last undiscovered corners, nor should they be confined to waste management and fashionable clean-up treks or expeditions. Instead, eco-tourism should be seen as an all-encompassing concept, part of an eco-development. It must create income for the local population and at the same time protect and preserve the natural world and cultures. In the future, eco-tourism should no longer simply use and exploit nature and the entire environment, but at the same time must actively do something to preserve them. This is quite feasible as shown for example by the well known Annapurna Conservation Area Project (ACAP) in Nepal. Adventures in luxury, on the other hand, upset delicate eco-systems in fragile mountains areas.

"Our aim is to attract rich tourists without discouraging the backpackers," says Chandra Gurung, ACAP's former director. "The low-budget tourists cannot be ignored because of the vital role they play in spreading tourism income. We can charge premium prices after we have improved the product."

But quality for tourists means clean air to breathe, clean water to drink and a clean environment. No matter how much money is pumped into tourism products, first the living quality of Kathmandu and the infrastructure in the remote areas have to be improved. Not for the sake of the tourists but for the Nepalese. As environmental policy includes public health and tourism policy, tourism should be used as a weapon by the

Nepali people to fight for better living conditions. Why not start a popular movement for a healthy, clean environment along with a fight against corruption? The first human right is the right to clean air, water and soil. Without these three basic needs being satisfied, we cannot survive.

Neither can tourism, one of the major industries in Nepal. Many tourists will be only too happy to support this struggle as, for example, in Goa (Southern India). But they may not be found among the five star tourists. They can be recruited from the pool of the so-called backpackers. Those who have come to Nepal many times are particularly motivated and supportive. And unlike common belief in Nepal, many of them are in high positions and well off. They just don't believe in showing their wealth and spending their hard-earned money in luxury hotels. A considerable number of former "hippies" (overlanders) developed a strong emotional tie to Nepal and gained a good knowledge of the country.

The other day once again friends from Europe came to see me in Kathmandu – disappointed and unable to understand why I love Nepal so much. "What on earth keeps you here?", they asked while removing their mouth masks, "Kathmandu is too filthy and stinking, the traffic too aggressive. And you can't even breath properly!".

Having been used to these complaints for a few years, I first do what I always do with new arrivals: I take them up to the roof garden of the Vajra Hotel for sunset, away from the traffic, dust and noises, watching the golden colors of the brick building of Old Kathmandu below us, enjoying the hills and the mountains (if they are to be seen). I treat them to a good local meal and take them after a few drinks of home-made Rakshi on a night stroll through the then deserted alleys of the old city. We marvel at dozens of shrines and courtyards, temples and beautiful carved windows. We listen to the night concert of the stray dogs, are presented with smiles by the ever so friendly Nepali people and try to grasp some of the old magic.

But that evening my "comfort tour" didn't work. Even Chetrapati and Asan Tole, usually pretty clean after the street vendors have left, were a sea of garbage. We literally waded through plastic gags, tins, paper, rotten vegetables and what not. Occasionally small fires in which garbage was burnt, let off a pungent stench. Drunken youngsters made offensive remarks and the dogs were a bloody nuisance. "Ke garne," "What to do?" was all I could say in the true Nepali way.

Another day for my friends in the Valley, this time a trip to Bhaktapur. Gone are the days when we used to have glorious days out cycling through the fields to this beautiful town. Even the trolley buses are better avoided nowadays, most of them are almost falling apart. What is left for the eco-tourist? Since the air in the streets is black and cycling too dangerous s/he prefers to join the vicious circle and take a car to Bhaktapur. Other local buses are like sardine tins, slow and cannot be recommended either, with windows open or broken.

Yet Bhaktapur is a highlight for all guests, the more so if they decide to stay there for a night or two or even longer. "Why can't the old part of Kathmandu be turned into a large pedestrian zone too?" they asked, "it would be so much easier than at home. All the infrastructure we don't have is there: porters, push carts, rikshaws. All goods could be delivered at any given time, free of pollution. And a lot of people would have a safe income. Why do they let cars ply right through the alleys of the Bazaar?". "I'll be glad," sighed Christine, "to get out of here tomorrow."

These impressions are the sad reality of how many tourists feel today. After their sightseeing in the Valley they usually either go on with their package tour to India, Bhutan or Tibet or go for a trek in Nepal. They might complain of congested trails, especially in the Annapurna region, but they love it. And they start to like this tiny Kingdom. All my friends can now understand why I have considered Nepal to be my second home since 1974.

But no-one likes to spend more then a night in Kathmandu. They dislike the place even more if they do. If this trend continues, and there are clear indications for this development, what will happen to the tourism industry in the Kathmandu Valley in future?

Nina Rao

India's Mountain Women kept in the Background

To understand the impact of tourism on women it is necessary to be familiar with the debate on the use of the term gender. The term gender signifies the 'system of cultural identities and social relationships between females and males' (Swain 1995) and the term is therefore significantly different from the biological difference between female and male. In third world countries indigenous and political ideologies influence the perceptions, roles and relations between men and women, which then determine their social characteristics. Most tourism development studies are optimistic about the participation of women in tourism-related activity and employment, but even this optimism is coloured by a gender bias. Most of these studies identify women as being socialised to be sensitive to the needs of others because they are coping with their reproductive roles even as they cope with earning an income, generally considered supplementary to the income of the male members of the family. There is a clear distinction not only in defining tasks as feminine but also in giving decision-making power, based on ownership and economic activity, to women. The biological-functional view predominates in such ideologies. This view takes advantage of the fact that women in third world countries, particularly in backward regions, have a significantly lower level of literacy. Lack of knowledge then legitimises a woman's place in a patriarchal value system.

The women in development approaches, which aim to enhance the participation and role of women in development projects, which is often the case with tourism in mountain regions, attempt to place women as community managers and economic producers. They fail to notice the tension that such a role involves for women who also have responsibility for nurturing, preparing and presenting items of daily life and ritual, which indicates that women do not function as leaders, but as implementers of tradition. An example is the issue of village water supply, which becomes important since tourism is a water intensive activity. In the mountains water is generally carried to the point of use. Women are supposed to be merely carriers of water since they have no technical training, and any decision on the use of water and method of its collection and carriage is decided by men; women implement such decisions. Similarly, women who have a certain economic autonomy in the informal sector lose this autonomy in the developmental process which tries to bring women into the formal economy, resulting in the introduction of male control in areas which had been a female preserve. Their mobility and location is thus determined by the indigenous and political ideology, which is gendered. Many have criticised the pressure of development approaches to bring women who operate in the informal sector into the formal sector as eurocentric, since European economies do not depend so much on the informal sector. In the case of tourism, however, the bed and breakfast business remains in the informal sector in many parts of the world, where women dominate. It is interesting to see that women do feel an erosion of their position as tourism grows and enforces international standards the world over.

Gender in Tourism

The reason for looking at the issue of women and tourism in this perspective is to recognise that gender is a significant variable in any human relationship, and much more so in the relation between a woman or women as members of a 'host' community, and tourists. As a third world activist and scholar I am interested in exploring local and global gender relations in the process of tourism activity as it takes place in an intercultural encounter. Therefore this paper will discuss the variable of gender as mediated by characteristics like class, race, ethnicity and nationality. The term "mediation" indicates that women do not form a class, as some schools of feminism postulate in the west. In Asia and in India there is a great deal of social stratification as well as some cases of pre-patriarchal relations in the eastern Himalayas, where tribal, ethnic group and racial differences also determine the status of women, and the indigenous and political ideologies reflect these differences. For example, the Khasi tribe determines inheritance through the youngest daughter of the household. Since Meghalaya has entered the mainstream of Indian social and political life, men are attempting to bring in a bill in the State Assembly to change the inheritance law to one similar to the rest of the country. The speaker of the Assembly has said that such a change will destroy Khasi culture, and the Khasi inheritance system should not be changed to the patrilineal law prevalent elsewhere.

While looking at the nature of tourism impacts on mountain women we are again moving into a complex and variegated field. Mountain areas, even within a political or administrative boundary, have cultural identities that change from one valley to another, and the status or the relations between male and female reflect such changes. Development theory recognises only common generalisations that have an impact on the lifestyle and life processes in the mountains without distinguishing cultural identities and social relationships. For example, the sexual freedom enjoyed by some women in areas of Spiti (in the North of the Western Himalayan state of Himachal Pradesh) may not be socially acceptable to women in Nepalese mountain areas, or in a specific region where tourism is to be developed. Again, sexual relations between such women and tourists or the industry that supports tourism are quite different to sex tourism as promoted in Thailand. Interestingly, once Japanese women began to emerge as a significant market the Thai sex tourism trade began to take steps to cover up the attraction of Thai brothels for Japanese men. European women, on the other hand (as reported in several studies on sex tourism in Thailand, and in interviews made by myself in the Patpong district of Bangkok in 1993) felt secure with the idea of men letting down norms with prostitutes or foreign women rather than a mistress at home.

Given that tourism is a distinct form of consumerism, being a part of leisure time and involving the exercise of a quest for an experience which can be unique and extraordinary, we can see that tourism has a political structure that reflects class and the global economic hierarchy. The receiving community responds to this quest by manipulating experiences for the visitor according to the ideological features of western culture. It is interesting to note that Caribbean women are used as an exotic marker to promote beach tourism by being photographed nude to enthuse German visitors; and such a representation is taken as meaningful for the tourists.

We know that tourism proceeds from gendered societies to gendered societies; that such gendering has taken place over time and through the interplay of economic, political, social, cultural and environmental dimensions; that control, power and equality are issues that cannot be discussed without looking at the role of class and race in constructing gender. Whilst most gender studies look at these issues within the systems of patriarchy and capitalism, in India we see the problem as one of the very survival of women, since at different economic, social and cultural levels, women are often denied the right to live. In many areas infanticide is practised; in general a girl child consumes fewer calories, has less access to medical care, and has no access to schooling. She is also unable to determine the age at which she can marry or the number and spacing of her children. In many cases she may not survive the demand for dowry. None of the income/employment oriented tourism case studies provide data to show that significant changes have occurred at major tourist destinations in any of these indicators.

Women and Employment

The increase in both family and societal violence against women has not been decreased by tourism development. On the contrary, Manali, a major tourist destination in Himachal Pradesh for both domestic and international tourists, has seen so much tourism-related violence against women in the form of sexual harassment and eve-teasing since tourist numbers began to increase, that women residents have demanded tourist police to protect them from tourists.

In most case studies relating to mountain tourism and the role of women, tourism has been looked at as a benefit in economic, socio-cultural and environmental terms. Nowhere have these studies shown that employment in tourism is not gender stereo-typed or that it does not fall outside the international division of labour where no new economic or income-earning opportunities are availed of by women. India, which received 2.4 million tourists last year and sent out 4 million tourists, is viewed not as a tourist generating market but as a tourist destination, because Asian destinations are viewed from the perspective of destinations for tourists from the major markets of the West. The developing countries have to use the tourist dollars for development, so they continue to be seen as destinations, because their populations are too poor to be participants in the international market. Tourism development has not included women as agents of development, nor as beneficiaries, but as labour at the lowest rung of tourism operations. This can be seen in the role of air hostesses with Asian air carriers, who are encouraged to please male tourists who bring in dollars, regardless of their lecherous behaviour. The emphasis on glamour in Asian countries, much more than in other countries, still determines an entry into interface jobs in tourism. The interesting aspect of tourism development is that it has exploited the productivity of women without conferring ownership rights on them. Income generation is seen as supplementary to ownership, and income alone does not confer status on those who are running a lodge or cooking and cleaning for tourists. In class as well as gender terms there is no change or personal development for women because tourists are seen as belonging to a better social category than those serving them, and their economic power perpetuates this relationship over time, since the women employed in tourism cannot become tourists to the countries from where their customers have come. Tourism retains the norms of what we have seen defined as women's work (Sinclair 1996). In a case study of women in the Garhwal region of India, Rana (EPW May 1996) has shown that despite the increasing productivity of women agriculturists their status has not improved because they do not have land rights.

Most mountain tourism in India is characterised by home stay in the private sector and by government accommodation in the formal sector. In India, the state played the role of the developer in creating western-style facilities for tourists, since we did not have an infrastructure for international tourism. Thus all Indian state governments run accommodation and transport services for tourists. In both cases there is a clear gender bias. In the former case family ownership and operation is the basis for low cost. Most of the day to day work is provided by women, belonging to the family or hired locally. The marketing and management decisions are taken by the male head of the household or other male members. Sons often have more clout than older sisters and mothers or grandmothers. In the government sector, given that the status of being a government servant is important in a country with high unemployment, and in view of the fact that in mountain regions job opportunities are even more limited, even work defined as female is done by men, like cooking, cleaning and serving. As tourism grows and the number of visitors increases, the work load of the women also increases without their personal responsibility decreasing. Policy makers, by giving incentives to hotels and foreign investors, are once again bringing the informal sector within the formal sector and denying women their space in the hill districts.

Similarly, in the handicrafts industry the number of hours worked between male and female members of the family do not give the women the right to manage and market production, nor do they have access to the income for any other uses. This indicates that even though tourism does offer opportunities for income and employment, it does not transform the fundamental relationship between male and female members of the household and the community. It is abandoned women or women-headed households where we find there has been a change in the situation, since there is no male control. The Status of Women Committee report published in 1980 indicated that 36% of households were women-headed, where the male head had either died or abandoned the family. In such households the economic decision-making is generally in the hands of the mother, but she often does not have ownership of the assets, which she holds in trust for the eldest male child. In cases where no assets are involved, women who have been deserted or abandoned or widowed can make use of their income for the improvement of the living standards of the family. In Asian countries women are involved in the retail sector, but this is also in the informal sector at pavement or local market level. No studies have followed up the use and retention of money by women from retailing activity.

We can also see that in tourism the traditional outmigration of men, their role as porters and their role in agriculture are extended to guiding, boating, riding etc. as a representation of their greater strength and social position. Women are seen as being good at routine jobs, particularly serving, where their feminine attractiveness is an advantage. In tourism services many employers select uniforms and make-up to enhance the attractiveness of female employees and demand that they encourage the flirtatious advances of the customer. Men do not have any barriers to mobility and can migrate from their home villages to access employment in tourism wherever the project is located. Young, unmarried women can have such access only when their male decision-makers allow their participation and at marriage the husband would demand their presence at home. The proportion of men and women in the workforce as well as their representation in the hierarchy of tasks is determined by gender ideologies, both local and national. Research shows that tourism, like other economic activity, only masks the determining role of gender in employment and does not bring about any radical societal change, as is often claimed by policy makers.

Tourism development, through demonstration and through changes in value systems or family systems, is said to promote modernity through the guest-host interaction, rather than promoting otherness. In this perspective it might be interesting to see that an increase in women-headed households due to the outmigration of men or the traditional male occupation of porterage leads to the transfer of economic power to a younger generation, since it is the younger males in the family who are allowed to interact with the tourists and to seek their company and also earn an extra income through such activities. These young men neglect traditional occupations which do not bring in the same amount of money, and they transform the relationship between man and nature. They also displace traditional value systems, since money income determines respect, decision-making and cultural relations between the generations. There is also the desire for urbanisation in rural societies since it is assumed that urban women have more freedom. This need not be the desired fruit of modernity. These 'benefits' are, however, the trend in western cultures. Similarly, cultural, racial and moral differences continue to play a role in the way in which marginal or subordinate racial groups (adivasis, tribal or original people), cultures and sexualities are defined and constructed as 'others' in relation to the privileged categories, like upper castes or western tourists or high-spending tourists.

There are several contestable assumptions in the pro-tourism debate. These can be briefly summarised in the following way: that male experience is universal, including the North as male and the South as female. That women are to be judged by male standards which are universal; that male biological superiority is a model that is not necessarily oppressive; that being women-centred is a divisive issue; and that both male and female experiences are mediated by other characteristics (primarily biological and socially functional) and can not be looked at as contradictory (Swain 1995). Concerned research has shown that woman-centred field work has on the other hand opened up not only the tourism debate but also the disciplines which have now been associated with social and cultural studies and brought new insights to the question of exercising the tourism option.

Economic and Social Issues

In the Himalayan region we have to take up the assumption of the modernity of the modern sector and the backwardness of the traditional sector. It is in this context that we have to locate an analysis of issues like unemployment, poverty, conflicts between castes, religious sects, tribes, regions and women. Added to this are the conditionalities of the globalisation processes that tourism demands in terms of minimum international standards. We can look at these contradictions in the following way:

1. Direct intervention by state or NGO sponsored development in the form of development plans and foreign exchange earnings for communities which have to be brought out of backwardness and poverty. In such planning the role and participation of women is considered critical to the success of the project, and the whole community is educated to allow women to play their part. Ecotourism and conservation give an important place to women, but in their gendered position. Income is the lure and most women would choose this option because as nurturers they have to find the supplementary income as a survival strategy. But in time, the fruits of this development pass out of the hands of women in the local community and into outside hands. The aspirations of the local people are thus not realised beyond the introductory phase.
2. Impoverishment leading to anti-elite conflicts, as can be seen in the expansion of tourism facilities in the hill areas which is being resisted by the local people, for example the Spiti Tourism Society which opposes the state government's proposal to build a three-star hotel in

Spiti even if it means forgoing the Rs.30crore (300 million) investment.

3. Economic poverty and distress used by comprador fundamentalist forces (fundamentalist forces funded from abroad or outside the region) who identify one major enemy, as has happened in Kashmir, with the pro-Islamic militancy movement attacking tourists and destroying the households dependent on tourism, to carry the fight against the Indian state to all fronts.
4. Competition for direct foreign investments leading to secessionist movements, as in the case of a separate state of Uttarakhand (including the hill areas of Uttar Pradesh) which has to depend on tourism for economic development. Here women would be agents of the desired changes, since tourism offers a low-paid and low-skilled employment opportunity for a region poorly endowed with resources. The power structure which has used the agency of women against the state and its repressive forces then represses the social role of women and relegates them to mere income-earners, bringing them back to the hearth from the street.
5. Unemployment and food insecurity which cause the backward regions to want to secede, with the nation state becoming too weak to intervene, as we have seen in the case of several militant movements in the North-East of India, all of which see tourism as the source of foreign exchange needed to catch up with the advanced regions of the country. Women are again the agents, since Christianity and the English language have made them open to international tourism and western culture, not only for cooking and serving, but also for agricultural support and handicraft production, which are the mainstay of tourism in such regions.

In all these cases women have played a militant role, whether political, military or economic, but they have also been subjected to gendered punishment in the form of molestation, rape and widowhood. They have also suffered from drug abuse by male family members and tourists and many have become addicted as well. This region has the highest number of drug addicts and HIV positive cases.

Environment, Society and Culture

Tourism development also raises environmental issues, and the gender perspective is important, since women are generally the fuel, water and resource gatherers in the mountains, where the cost of many of the items for cooking and cleaning are high. In Ladakh it is the women who negotiate with the army for low-cost kerosene supplies and the army quota of rum and petrol, since firewood is in short supply and the high altitude makes cooking time for non-Ladakhi food much longer. In return, women operate bars where the soldiers come to drink the rum they sell, at a higher price for the company of women, since they are separated from their families. Development planners do not consider the impact on the community of women when redesigning the planning process. They take for granted the ability of women to develop survival strategies in the most demanding situations.

In the modern period of tourism development, the discovery motif has been a dominant symbol of tourism to the east. The discovery motif represents the discovered land as an empty space on which linguistic, cultural and eventually territorial claims can be made, much like the colonisers of the past. Indian hill tourism is a British development in which a series of hill stations were developed in the four Presidency areas with the latest technology and as urban centres to cater to the needs of the English families resident in India. There was no relationship between the life and the culture of the local people and the colonialists who appropriated their land and resources.

By drawing on the motif of discovery the travel writer/tour operator can lay a claim to new knowledge, which is then processed and circulated via the binarisms that race and nationality endow on the privileged discoverer - in this case the dollar-spending tourist, primarily white, who has set the standards and norms of international tourism behaviour. This is a kind of self-inscription on to the lives of the people at the tourist destination, who are conceived of as an extension of the landscape. The gendering of tourism rests on the colonial functions of civilising, rescuing, idealising and demonising Indian subjects as the other. The Indian upper class is also co-opted into taking a similar position. Western civilisation and its native clone are superior to the backward and primitive cultures of the back regions where tourism has located its spirit of adventure. The rescue scenario states that Indian women are to be saved from their backward social institutions and their character and lives improved according to western liberalism; the woman question has been an important marker in the colonial discourse and become the distinguishing characteristic between the modern west and the backward east. It was believed that native women led devalued lives whilst their European sisters led a supposedly superior existence. Women became mute but central characters in the dialogue between western and Indian men. Modern or traditional, the qualities of virtue, fidelity and subservience were desirable in women. They were thus ideal for the service or hospitality trade as long as they were kept from mingling freely with male customers (Singh 1996). For the tourists, however, the objectives were different.

An important aspect of gender in tourism is the opportunity for sexual encounters with local women who are located in a liminal space, outside the domestic sphere and inhabiting the location of the recreational space. Contemporary tourists, not unlike their predecessors, and modern planners, in their reformist zeal, have not included the reappraisal of the status and rights of women in their new agency as community leaders in income and employment generation as well as in the process of modernisation. Who is being rescued in such an enterprise? We have seen that tourism is rescuing the male controlled and structured social and cultural relations that different production systems in the mountains have created (Stephen 1992).

If this were not the case we would not have had tourists on treks in Garhwal Himalayas photographing nude hill women for a dollar fee, since these women have the responsibility of keeping the money-order economy going without the right to earn a money income from other sources, which are denied to them by the hierarchy of tasks that apply to tourism as well. Drug peddlers have also used male control of the social role of women by paying the male head of the family to allow them a live-in hill woman as a cover for their procurement of drugs along well-established circuits in the Himalayas.

Hill women have always been projected as fair and beautiful, fit subjects of an oriental idyll, and like other native women full of pure passion for their western lovers. The post 1857 novels are replete with such stories, where these illicit liaisons are concluded by the death of the native woman. The white lover is absolved of guilt and returns to the bosom of the home cultural values (Singh 1996). Is modern tourism discovering such delights in the Himalayas too?

Conclusion

I would like to point out that tourism projects have made no difference to several indicators that determine the status of women in the hill states, as a look at the Census of India Report 1991 shows. In spite of all the inputs in the mountain regions, problems such as the declining sex ratio, adult illiteracy, number of girl children being retained in the school system, infant mortality rate and infanticide, life expectancy and birth rate, have not closed the gap between men and women. Access to health and nutrition have also not been studied. The age of marriage at 16 years (as an institution conferring status on women) has also not been strictly adhered to for girls, who have to be watched as long as they are single so that they do not bring dishonour to the family. Violence against women, such as rape of minors and dowry deaths, are on the increase.

Women's awareness about themselves and their society has also not been transformed with the development of tourism, as the role of women has remained behind the scenes, except in the field of entertainment, where culture has been transformed into folk displays by being alienated from its material conditions in society. Women now perform in the public eye as objects and carriers of local colour.

Every society identifies the use of consumer items as an indicator of social progress, for example, the use of footwear, reading a newspaper, using mill-made cloth or cosmetics. In all these areas women are still lagging behind the progress made by men. Watches, clocks and radios are also favoured items of consumption, and men are again ahead in such consumption. Traditional food is also an area where men have diverted to the changes that multiculturalism has introduced. This imbalance is reflected in language skills as well. In rural areas these are all representations of modernisation and closely identified as the privileges of the urban rich, the class to which tourists belong. Women are still excluded from the world of consumer goods that are bought in the market.

As researchers in the field of women and tourism development, we have often wondered why the field studies remain at the level of income and employment. Have we not been swayed by the predominant ideology of the sixties of tourism as a blessing? As we accept and internalise models created in completely different circumstances, are we not closing our eyes to the fundamental gender issues that confront women in mountain communities in the third world, where the environment as well as the social system is still hostile to their equal participation?

References

Apostolopoulos, Y./S. Leivadi/A. Yiannakis (Eds.): The Sociology of Tourism. Theoretical and Empirical Investigations. Routledge, London 1996

Dreze, J./A. Sen: Economic Development and Social Opportunity. Oxford University Press, Delhi 1996

Economic and Political Weekly, Vol.xxxi No.19, May 11, 1996, pp 1125

Johnson, Peter/Barry Thomas (Eds.): Perspectives on Tourism Policy. Mansell Publications Ltd., London 1993

Kinnard, V./D. Hall: Tourism: A Gender Analysis. Wiley and Sons, 1994

Pearce, D.G./R.W. Butler (Èds.): Tourism Research: Critiques and Challenges. Routledge, London 1993

Sinclair, M. Thea: Gender, Work and Tourism. Routledge, London 1997

Singh, Jyotsna G.: Colonial Narratives, Cultural Dialogues. Discoveries of India in the Language of Colonialism. Routledge, London 1996

Voase, Richard: Tourism - The Human Perspective. Hodder and Stoughton, 1995

Basit Khan

Fountains of Life?

Tourism in the Northern Areas of Pakistan

In 1898, John Muir, founder of the US conservation movement, wrote, "Thousands of tired, nerve shaken, overcivilised people are beginning to find that going to the mountains is like going home; that wilderness is a necessity; and that mountain parks and preservations are useful not only as fountains of timber and irrigating rivers, but as fountains of life." However these mountain visitors are finding that what they are trying to escape is following them up the slopes.

Mountains make up one-fifth of the world's landscape and are home to at least one-tenth of the world´s people. An additional 2 billion people depend on mountains for much of their food, hydroelectricity, timber, and mineral resources. Mountain ecosystems and environments are of crucial importance as rich and unique centres of biological and cultural diversity. Biologically their high diversity, including prolific concentrations of endemism, leaves them vulnerable to losses of whole plant or animal communities. Outside the dominant cultures of plains, most of the mountain cultures are ethnic minorities who live in abject poverty. They are also remote from centres of political or commercial power where much of their fate is determined. Mountain communities, both human and natural, therefore have unique vulnerabilities, stemming from similar characteristics, such as steepness, isolation, and marginality, that often leads to their neglect.

Degradation to mountain ecosystems is caused by three external factors. They are:

1. Due to the prevailing patterns of inequitable land ownership and population growth, many mountainous developing countries are facing growing scarcities of arable land and increasing strain on subsistence communities.
2. Due to high consumption patterns, these communities and the associated natural resources are targets of intensive resource extraction.
3. Mountain ecosystems are attractions for skiers, trekkers and mountaineers, generating a global boom in tourism and recreation which lays a heavy burden on the carrying capacity of the area.

All over the world mountain peoples face cultural assimilation, debilitating poverty, and political disempowernment. Because of their fragility and sensitivity, mountain ecosystems have become proving grounds for sustainable development. The mountain ecosystem, housing human and natural resources, is complex, very interdependent, and needs to be fully comprehended in order to bring about any change. For many solutions, revolutionary changes are required. However there are short-term measures, at the community, regional, national, and global level, that are imperative and politically achievable.

The Northern Areas cover 7.04 million ha in the extreme north of Pakistan, forming the upper limits of the Indus basin. It is dominated by jagged granite, snow-covered Hindu Kush mountains in the north-west, the Karakoram mountains in the north-east and the Great Himalayan mountain range in the central east. A pristine mountain ecosystem, which has come under threat since the opening of the Karakoram Highway, now finds itself with the dilemma of unsustainable resource exploitation and a boom in the tourism industry. This paper identifies the status of the tourism industry in the Northern Areas, the specific issues which the industry faces in order to remain sustainable, and how these issues may be addressed.

The Northern Areas

Pakistan is divided into four provinces: Sind, Balochistan, Punjab, and the North-West Frontier Province (NWFP). Two other regions, the Northern Areas (Gilgit, Hunza, Chilas, Diamer, Baltistan, and Ghizer) and Azad Jammu and Kashmir are also part of Pakistan but due to unresolved border disputes with India, the constitutional status of these areas is ill-defined.

Geographically Pakistan falls into three main regions: the mountains in the north where the Hindu Kush, Karakoram, and the Himalayan ranges meet, which mostly fall in the Northern Areas (NAs); the vast but sparsely populated plateau of Balochistan; and the Punjab and Sind Plains spread over the Indus river basin and its five tributaries. Apart from the Indus plain, Pakistan is mostly mountainous desert with arid and semi arid plateaus.

The Northern Areas, comprising the three great mountain ranges, house the world's youngest mountains. Approximately 55 million years ago, the Eurasian and Indian geological plates collided by the northward movement of the Indian plate. The Indian plate is still moving northward at an annual rate of 5 centimeters (2 inches), pushing the Eurasian plate causing the mountains to rise at rate of 7 millimeter (0.28 inches) a year. Thus Pakistan has the densest concentration of the highest mountains in the world; five peaks over 8,000 m (26,000 ft) and 101 peaks over 7,000 m (23,000 ft) above sea level. All these peaks lie within a radius of 180 kms (112 miles).

Great expanses of rocky desert, bare of vegetation, dominate the land-scape at 5,000 to 6,000 m. Over half the territory is glacier rock and scree. Its rugged beauty attracts thousands of foreign visitors each year. Mountain ranges form a natural barrier to summer monsoons, making the climate dry. Most precipitation falls as snow. The climate undergoes extremes of temperatures - dry and hot (up to 35°C) in summer and dry and cold in winter. Valley floors are at 1,200 to 1,500 m. Precipitation here is only 120 to 150 mm per year, but increases with elevation. At 3,000 m there is enough snow (equivalent to 750 mm of rainfall) to support grasses, scrub and coniferous forest. The population of the area in 1993 was 800,000 with most people living in small villages and towns in the valleys and lower foothills.

Mountaineers and trekkers are attracted to the Northern Areas from all over the world, bringing tourism and therefore foreign exchange to the area. In 1995, the total amount of royalties earned from granting permission to mountaineering expeditions alone amounted to US$ 389,751. These expeditions insured and hired approximately 4,500 porters, 58 liaison officers, and some 119 guides, cooks and high altitude porters. Despite the obvious benefits to the region, such tourism carries with it the risks which perhaps are not as beneficial as one would assume.

Tourism Resources and Types of Tourism in Northern Areas

There are different types of tourism available in the Northern Areas, which are as follows:

Mountaineering

With the highest concentration of mountains in the world and the largest mass of glaciers outside the polar zones, mountaineering is very popular in the Northern Areas. Most of the mountaineering expeditions come in the summer months (May to September). Expeditions in winter months usually have not been successful. Baltistan, Gilgit and Hunza are the key areas for such tourism.

Baltistan lies at the heart of the mountaineering activity with 60 peaks that rise to a height of over 7,000 m. The four peaks above 8,000 m include the second highest mountain in the world, K2 (8,611 m), Gasher-brum I (8,068 m), Broad Peak (8,047 m) and Gasherbrum II (8,035 m). Skardu, the capital of Baltistan, is located at the confluence of the rivers Indus and Shigar. Most expeditions begin at Skardu. Apart from some wheat and corn grown in the valley, most of the region is desert and covered by mountains.

Gilgit, termed by some British writers the fulcrum of central Asia, is a trading post in the region. Due to the Karakoram Highway, the population of the city has increased manifold. It has been transformed from a barren dusty glacial fan to one with terraced fields and irrigated croplands and orchards. Mountaineering expeditions attempting Nanga Parbat (8,125 m), the ninth highest peak in the world, and the Rakaposhi (7,788 m) in Hunza, use Gilgit to start their expeditions.

Trekking

The region abounds with a range of treks, which are unique and unlike other treks in the world. Most of these trekking paths follow the animal trails from the last village in the valley to the snout of the glacier, usually at 3,000 m. The trek then crosses over, usually, a treacherous pass, and into the next valley. These treks are spread evenly in the region, however hot spots include Hunza, Ghizer, Baltistan and the Nanga Parbat massif. Although trekking is highly concentrated in Skardu and of all the trekking areas, Skardu accounts for 82 % of trekking parties and 78 % of all trekkers.

The trekking areas in the region are divided into open and restricted zones. The open zone includes Diamer whereas the restricted zone consists of Gilgit and Skardu. A permit is needed for the restricted zone. The only closed zone is Siachin.

Skiing

There is only one Ski resort in the Northern Areas which is maintained and run by the Pakistan Air Force (PAF). This resort at Naltar is mainly used by PAF officers. However some private organisations (NGOs), such as the Adventure Foundation of Pakistan, who organise skiing activities in Pakistan, are also allowed to use the facility.

Polo

Polo is a traditional sport of the area. It is played in most of the places where space permits. Gilgit, Skardu, Khaplu, and Shandoor are areas renowned for this sport. Matches are played with traditional music. In Gilgit the Polo season starts in March/April, but the most colourful events are held in November. The Shandoor Polo tournament is the most famous Polo tournament in the country, usually attended by the President or the Prime Minister. Every year the event is growing in size resulting in environmental degradation and other socio-economic impacts.

White Water Sports

This sport is slowly gaining popularity. Three rivers, at limited reaches, may be used for white water rafting/canoeing. The Indus is manageable between Jaglot and Thakot, however some rapids should be avoided. The Hunza River, from Aliabad to Gilgit, can be rafted. In fact, some expeditions have tried this with success in the recent past. The Gilgit River from Ghizer area turns turquoise in winter months and may be suitable at some reaches for white water rafting.

Angling and Fishing

Angling and fishing for brown and rainbow trout is another tourist attraction. This fish is not endemic and was introduced during British rule. Areas known for this sport are Satpara Lake in Baltistan, many of the lakes in the Ghizer area (Handrap Valley, Shandoor Lake) and some spots around Gilgit.

Biking

This sport is gaining popularity as KKH is one of the most challenging routes for bikers in the world. The elevation at the Khunjerab Pass, the entry point to China, is approximately 16,000 ft. Bikers or other tourists are not allowed to travel inside China on their private conveyance. This restriction is another constraint for tourists traveling in the area.

Resort Tourism

Resort tourism is famous along the KKH and in Baltistan. The KKH was one of the historical routes that linked the Indian sub-continent and China for the promotion of the silk trade. The route is now a 955 km-long metalled road, connecting Islamabad to the Khunjerab Pass (to China), winding through one of the most awesome and exhilarating mountains in the region. The road is used for many purposes ranging from trade, a travel link to China, and resort tourism at Abbottabad, Chattar, Besham, Chilas, Gilgit, Hunza and Gojal. According to a survey, many travelers go to the NAs by road and use the KKH. The majority of them are from Pakistan, traveling for trade and business. Only 8 % of tourists use the route for recreation, sightseeing and religious purposes. The survey further estimated that nearly 1,500 tourists travel daily on this route. They use mostly buses, followed by trucks and then motor cars. About 43 % of them spend two to three nights, 12 % spent five to seven nights, and 10 % spend 41 to 90 nights. Many of the travelers in the last category travel by air to Gilgit.

The major problems on the route are those of congestion due to shortage of proper accommodation; a lack of essentials including food and daily utilities, resulting in inflated prices; and environmental degradation.

Cultural Tourism

Cultural tourism attracts both foreign and domestic tourists. It contributes to the economy and also plays a role in making people aware of their past and the need to preserve whatever remains of it. Although there are indigenous cultures in the Northern Areas (Shimshalis, Baltis) due to lack of promotional campaigns and the lack in the development of cultural tourism outlets, this category of tourism is not very popular in the Northern Areas.

Constraints to Mountain Tourism Development

Development of mountain tourism calls for a set of conditions and opportunities which facilitates the promotion of mountain tourism. The following constraints restrict the development of mountain tourism in the Northern Areas:

Political and Economic Stability

The number of international tourists coming to Pakistan steadily increased from 365,000 in 1983 to 495,000 in 1989 and then decreased to 352,000 in 1992. The country was in a quasi-stable political and economic state from 1983-89 (martial law period) but since 1989, when the democratic set-up started functioning and the government was weak, there has been instability both politically and economically. However, the Northern Areas have usually been peaceful and stable apart from a few instances (1988). Riots in Karachi and bomb blasts in the plains have had direct impacts on the flow of tourism and development of tourism infrastructure. Under conditions of economic instability, it may not be possible to attract foreign investment in the tourism sector.

Infrastructure Requirements

Due to the physiological constraints in a mountain area, infrastructure development is a slow process. It took 20 years for Pakistan and China to complete the construction of the KKH. Although the road is a masterpiece of engineering prowess, it is still not reliable in the rainy season. Due to the construction and blasting, the mountain slopes have become unstable and during the rainy season, numerous land slides block the road at various locations, making it unreliable for the tourists. Link roads to other areas are yet to be developed and questions about environmental degradation (habitat destruction, access to wildlife areas) are potential issues to be addressed.

The number of accommodation facilities has increased but is not sufficient in the peak season. Due to the short tourist season, inflated prices and limited number of domestic tourists, it is economically less viable for a private entrepreneur to develop such facilities. The public transport system is unreliable and needs further development. Northern Areas Transport Company (Public Sector) and some private transporters operate on the KKH. Their service is efficient but does not cater for the volume and destinations available. The area does not have railways.

Only Gilgit and Skardu are linked with air services. This is very much dependent on the weather. Therefore very few travelers use the air link.

Marketing

Marketing is a major tool for tourism development and is not developed and used effectively to promote tourism in the country. As a result, tourism potential cannot be projected effectively. Few of the foreign visitors have produced very good resource material on the tourism potential of Northern Areas. However it needs efforts at the state level to propagate the tourism potential. Pakistan has therefore become a tourist stopover or transit point instead of a tourist destination.

Community Development and Participation

Most of the tourist activity is managed and controlled by tour operators belonging to other regions of the country. These agents have not taken any interest in the development of mountain communities. Local communities in the NAs are only used on an as-and-when-required basis. Community based activities at the local level are not evident.

Distortions in Revenue Earnings and Development Allocations

Economic benefits from tourism are collected by the federal government and handed over to the national exchequer. These receipts are merged in a common pool and no criteria exist to allocate funds for development as per the revenue generated from the area. The average expenditure per mountaineer in 1992 was US$ 2,127, whereas only US$ 788 was spent in the local mountain area.

High Tourism Densities

As stated earlier, a concentration of tourists in a few areas for trekking and mountaineering is visible. Trekking is concentrated in Hunza and Skardu, while mountaineering on the Nanga Parbat is on the south-west ridge and Diamer face. The Karakoram range receives the highest number of expeditions but only attempting few peaks, although there are 108 peaks above 7000 m. This results in saturation and reaches the carrying capacity of the resource, resulting in limited development.

Lack of Data and Information

Mountain specific tourism requires some specialised information and data, which assists the tourist to plan well and enjoy the experience. Usually all data collected and research undertaken deals with the macro level perspectives. Information to the tourist for trekking in the open zone is not available, nor are there any precise data on tourist expenditure in the Northern Areas or on local communities.

Employment Opportunities

Tourism has not led to large employment and income generation in the Northern Areas. Some jobs are created especially, for porters and guides, who because of the requirements of the job need to belong to the local community. Some income also accrues to locals involved in the service sectors of hotels/restaurants, and in the transport and retail trade. Local communities in Sust and Chilas have resented the fact that one of the private entrepreneurs from down country was building tourist resorts in the area.

Tourism Season

The tourism season in Pakistan lasts from May to September. Most of the infrastructure and employment is used during this season. If winter sports are introduced, this period may be increased, causing a potential increase in tourism and effective utilisation of tourism related resources.

Issues Pertaining to Sustainability and Tourism in the Northern Areas

Sustainable tourism is the tourism and the associated infrastructure that now and in the future:

1. Operates within the natural capacities for the regeneration and future productivity of natural resources.
2. Recognises the contribution that people and communities, customs and lifestyle, make to the tourism experience.
3. Accepts that these people have an equitable share in the economic benefits of tourism.
4. Is guided by the wishes of local people and communities in the host areas.

Sustainable tourism development requires reference to the broader political, social and economic environment of the area. It is integrated into other forms of economic activity and cannot be considered in isolation. Sustainable tourism emphasizes the need to understand and respect the tourism resource base, to ensure a synergy of effort between different stakeholders, involving co-operation, partnership, monitoring and research.

Some of the specific problems which we face in the Northern Areas regarding sustainability and tourism are as follows:

Sustainable Tourism and Development Indicators

The Northern Areas have high infant mortality rates, high male-female ratios, low participation ratios for females, low literacy levels and outmigration of males in the working age group. These indicators undermine the development of the area and the community. This results in low human resource development and the trend is to look outside the area for employment and income generation. Mountaineering, trekking and resort tourism provide limited employment opportunities and for short durations. There is a definite need to improve the education and skill indices so as to promote social and economic well being. Education and training in environmental awareness and management, essential for integrated and sustainable development, must include social, cultural as well as economic issues.

Human Resource Development

Transformation of the labour force is itself a long-term process and is normally accelerated by external development. As the literacy rate is very low, labour force transformation has not taken place. The whole region is devoid of any institution which caters to the Human Resource Development of the area. This has created gaps in skilled labour as well as trained personnel for the tourism industry. As locals are not available for skilled jobs, the private entrepreneur has reason to bring work force from outside.

Government and Community Linkages

For sustainable tourism development, it is essential that the government and the communities are linked with each other for policy development and field level implementation. Most of the policies related to tourism are formulated in the federal capital with no inputs or consultation from the local communities. This needs to be improved. Hence there is an absence of participation of the community in the development of the area in tourism-related activities, and in the planning, conservation, and utilisation of resources.

Missing Links between Regional and Local Economies

Different sectors of the mountain economy are not linked together and these are also not integrated with the regional economy.

Seasonality

Presently, the NAs have a six month tourist season, hence seasonal employment generation is a major issue for sustainability. Alter-native income/employment sources may be identified so as to recover this deficiency. However, this present situation can be remedied to some extent by either promoting winter sports or ensuring that the tourist season remains outside of the harvesting period. Hence, farmers who have left their lands to join seasonal tourist-related employment, have a means of subsistence throughout the rest of the year.

Leakages in Economic Benefits

As the economy in the NAs is badly integrated, most of the economic benefits leak into the more developed areas which provide skills and services for tourist activity. The economic benefits thus accrue to these relatively better developed regions.

Infrastructure Development

The natural richness of the NAs is the raison d'être for the tourist industry to remain sustainable in the area. Infrastructure development sometimes is not consistent with maintaining environmental equilibrium. The infrastructure required for sustainable tourism inevitably disturbs the surrounding ecosystem. However, as tourism is unavoidable, it must ensure that minimal negative impact occurs to the environment in order to remain sustainable.

Gender Issues

Female literacy in the area is negligible. With the onset of a regularized tourist industry, the women in the area will be marginalised, unless education is imparted to them. This is vital if all sectors of the community are to profit from the benefits of tourism.

Cultural Issues

The culture of the NAs is predominantly conservative. All tourists venturing into the area need to be culturally sensitive to social norms and mores. Tourism needs to capitalize on the best of the local culture in order that it is marketed to attract more visitors. However, this is not to say that the locals should be exploited purely for economic gain, especially if they themselves will not benefit from this. Other parts of the world have witnessed the fabricating of 'traditional' rites in order to attract tourist revenue, and indeed authentic rites have been ignored which are of no interest to tourists. Hence there is a threat to the cultural integrity of the area.

Conclusion

Tourism cannot be avoided despite its often negative impacts to an area. Hence, in order to enhance and profit from the benefits that can be incurred, a management system for tourism must be instigated in the NAs. With global barriers opening and a greater interest in learning about diverse cultures, the influx of foreigners is inevitable. This may have negative impacts, but it is unavoidable. Hence a control and manage-ment system for tourism has to be adopted, especially as there is no government commitment to regulating this industry. Hence it is imperative that the tourism industry is worked for the benefit of local communities, the government as well as the tourist, otherwise misallocation of resources is inevitable.

With the extension of the Karakoram Highway to the Central Asian republics, the opportunities for development in the area are likely to increase. This would also result in the promotion of tourism. However, the local communities are not equipped to manage the increasing number of tourists and its resulting impacts. It is essential that the communities are trained and prepared to address these impacts. At the same time, the government also needs to take initiatives to involve the communities in developing policies and other practical steps to ensure sustainable tourism.

Malcolm J. Odell/Wendy Brewer Lama

Tea House Trekking in Nepal

The Case for Environmentally Friendly Indigenous Tourism

Introduction and Summary

Tea house trekking has become increasingly popular among visitors to Nepal's magnificent Himalaya, its farming villages, and forested hills. Tea house trekking is an adaptation of back-packing where travelers eat and sleep in simple village lodges or homes rather than camp out. Over the last 30 years this type of hiking has grown into an important rural-based industry that rivals the Kathmandu-based, organized camping trekking industry. It has transformed the economies of many hill communities, and has substantially raised household incomes for thousands of hill and mountain peoples, many of whom are among the most socio-economically deprived in Nepal. While good data are not yet available, tea house trekking accounts for revenues to local communities that the authors estimate exceed $5 million annually. When other trekkers are included, this rural industry is putting a total of $10 million (Rs. 580 million) directly into the pockets of rural mountain people. Thus it is now one of the largest, if not the largest source of cash income in many remote hill communities.

Trekking is an increasingly important sector of Nepal's tourism industry, which is the number one source of foreign exchange earnings in Nepal, totalling some US$117 million annually. Approximately 34% of all foreign (non-Indian) tourists go trekking in the hills and mountains. Tea house trekking has grown steadily in relation to group trekking, now constituting 46% (39,067) of the total number of trekkers (84,787) per year.[1]

Perhaps even more important than the numbers of arrivals or gross revenues suggest, however, is that most of the revenue generated by tea house trekking goes directly to villagers living in the mountains and hills. Unlike other forms of tourism, the real beneficiaries are people who otherwise operate largely outside the formal economy. Opportunities for earning cash income are minimal in these remote areas, far from roads and communication, reflected in their annual per capita income that may be as low as $40 - $60.[2]

Tea house trekking is now being examined and tested both within Nepal and other countries as a potential model for village-based tourism that has significant income-generating benefits for rural communities, and true local management. Tea house trekking has the potential to bring significant benefits to many of Nepal's marginalized hill and mountain peoples through locally owned and managed, small-scale development. Infrastructure investment in local lodges is relatively minimal: villagers can adapt a local home or build a modest lodge with toilet facilities for anywhere from a few hundred to a few thousand dollars.[3] The Nepali villager's staple food, dal bhaat (rice, curried lentils and vegetables) is an ideal high-carbohydrate trekking food. And the Nepalese peoples' gracious hospitality is what tourists report brings them back again and again to this tiny kingdom.

Many challenges lie ahead for tea house trekking, however, particularly in assuring that it remains locally owned, environmentally friendly, and not over-done: trekkers already complain about too many Coca-Cola signs and the occasional aggressive lodge brokers. With proper planning that strengthens local „ownership" of the product, with improvements in sanitation and service standards, and with adequate incentives to conserve the natural beauty and cultural heritage that attracts tourists, tea house trekking could become the foundation of a vigorous national program of ecologically and culturally appropriate, community-based mountain tourism that supports village development and sustainable resource conservation.

An Indigenous, Grass-Roots Tradition

Tea house trekking has been a part of Nepal's cultural history for centuries, and perhaps longer. Since pre-historic times and up to the present day, most Nepali villages could only be reached on foot over rugged trails. In many parts of Nepal today it is still common practice for travelers to walk until dusk and to share the hearth of a farming family in the nearest village. Where there were no lodges, Nepali and early foreign travelers alike stayed in "bhattis" or rest houses. A local farmer who owned land alongside a major travel route would erect a small shelter with a resting bench or two. There he or his wife would serve tea, local brew, and home-grown snacks such as roasted corn, soybeans, or beaten rice. Over time they would expand the facilities and services, or move their own home to the site, and offer full meals and rudimentary lodging in return for modest cash payments or guests' labor. Even today in many trekking lodges, porters can earn a full plate of dal bhaat and a place to sleep in exchange for bringing in a load of firewood.

During the last century, a new breed of traveler appeared, stimulating the development of Nepal's home-grown tea house trekking. Gurkha soldiers, returning from overseas postings with enhanced status, wealth, and many a tall tale, were ready customers for the hospitality, chaang (local beer), and home-cooked meals provided by village entrepreneurs. House guests as such are still a valued source of news and story-telling in remote areas.

This was the tradition of open hospitality that, beginning in the 1960s, led to tea house trekking. Today this business serves some 50,000 foreigner trekkers a year, plus a growing number of Nepali and Indian travelers who set off to find their roots or souls on pilgrimage to high altitude holy sites.

From Thakali Bhattis to Apple Pie and Solar Showers

Organized trekking as a form of pleasure rather than compulsory travel originated with the advent of Himalayan mountaineering in the 1950s. Slowly trekking caught the eyes of entrepreneurial ex-British Gurkhas who added the comforts of India's hill stations and the camp kitchens of the Everest region.

As Nepal pried open its doors to the outside world, its first foreign "trekkers" found a surprisingly well-established network of bhattis, particularly along major trade and travel routes linked with Tibet. The skilled Thakali women of the upper Kali Gandaki river valley, who had initially dished out hearty meals and playful banter to Tibetan traders, adapted quickly to the demands of foreigners. In the 1950s and '60s, explorers paved the way for the independent trekkers to come decades later. Very early among these were people such as Toni Hagen of Switzerland, who carried trekking permit Number One for the whole of Nepal, and the first American Peace Corps volunteers. Following back-packing world travelers, a wave of restless hippies arrived to test Nepal's fabled 'grass,' and seek spiritual enlightenment in its sacred valleys.

About the same time, former British Gurkha Colonel Jimmy Roberts set up the first trekking agency, catering to the more elite form of world traveler and the growing number of mountaineering expeditions. Roberts started, as he loves to tell it, with: "4 tents, 4 mats, 8 forks, 8 plates, 8 mugs, and a clapped out Land Rover." Throughout the 1970s and early 80s, organized trekking gradually expanded as ex-sirdars (head guides) of the first trekking agencies branched off to open their own businesses. These have now mushroomed to a total of more than 300 trekking agencies operating today.

The hippies came and went but trekking was here to stay. Its growth was promoted by the international marketing efforts of the trekking industry, His Majesty's Government, Department of Tourism, and word-of-mouth stories of the impressive standards of service offered both on organized treks and in the ever-improving bhattis.

Eventually the mountains, trails, and campsites of the popular trekking areas – Solu-Khumbu (Everest region), the Annapurnas, and by the mid-1970s, Langtang-Helambu–began to show the wear and tear of a surging visitor population. For every foreign trekker, there were on average 2 to 3 staff and porters, who together consumed more fuel wood in a day than a Nepali family would in a week. Villagers who had set up lodges or who worked as seasonal porters, cooks, or trekking sirdars, were indeed benefiting from trekking tourism. Little thought was being given, however, to the forests that were disappearing to build trekkers' lodges, to cook pizza and apple pie, and to heat water for hot showers. Attention was not paid to the effects of trekking on a village socio-economic system: the dislocation that occurs when its men are away from home for long periods and teenagers prefer to work as porters than to finish school.

Trekking tourism had grown up from the grass roots level with little forethought or planning. The time had come to take a careful look at how to sustain its benefits without spoiling what tourists were coming to see. In the words of the eminent Nepali scholar and leader Harka Bahadur Gurung: "Tourism is not the problem; what we need is managed tourism..."

Solu-Khumbu: Mountaineers, Schools, and Helicopters

To examine the evolutionary development from ad-hoc to managed tourism, it may be useful to look at the process as it took place in four different areas of Nepal. These each center around one of the major mountain peaks of Nepal: Everest, Annapurna, Langtang, and Makalu.

The Khumbu region adjoining Mount Everest (Sagarmatha) has been a prime mountaineering destination since the late '50s. Then it took a minimum of 45 days to walk to Everest Base Camp and back, as there were no roads beyond Banepa in Kathmandu Valley nor Dharan in east Nepal.

Trekking did not evolve in the same way in Khumbu that it did in the upper Kali Gandaki of the Annapurna region. Group trekking was introduced in Solu-Khumbu as an offshoot to mountaineering. Groups came fully equipped with all camp and cooking equipment, food, and trekkers' gear–all hauled up the trails on porters' backs.

Among the first sizeable groups of outsiders were the teams put together by Sir Edmund Hillary. They arrived in response to a request for schools that came from the Khumjung Lama and headman, Ong Chu Sherpa, who is still remembered for his astute remark to Hillary in 1960: "Our children have eyes but they are still blind."

From that remark, followed up by a lengthy petition signed by the Khumbu Sherpas and presented to Hillary by Lama Ong Chu's then 14 year old son, Kaldhen, emerged the Sherpa Schoolhouse Expeditions of 1961 and 1964. Following these well-publicized initiatives came countless other visitors from around the world who have helped to bring hospitals, bridges, electricity, telephones, and, ultimately, the national park to Khumbu. A major legacy of such „outside assistance" is the precarious Lukla airstrip, built in 1964 as a temporary field to bring in supplies. Soon Royal Nepal Airlines 19-seat aircraft were bringing six or eight flights of tourists a day. By 1995 the Khumbu region was being served by a helicopter airline owned and operated by Khumjung Sherpas. Two bakeries are turning out chocolate-filled croissants and filtered coffee cooked with locally generated hydro-electricity.

Evolving out of its roots in mountaineering, and due to the lack of permanent villages at high altitudes (above 14,500 ft), trekking in Solu-Khumbu emerged initially around organized or group trekking. The Sherpa people were quick to see an economic opportunity staring them in the face, and opened their homes to early trekkers and mountaineers. Khumbu's first lodge, built for local travelers, was opened in Namche Bazaar in the early 1960s by Tengboche Monastery and still operates today. Other visitor facilities were built following the establishment of a weekly market in Namche in 1966 to meet the needs of government officers, teachers, soldiers, and police stationed in the area. These simple tea shops were gradually turned into trekkers' restaurants and lodges, and soon stretched along the approach route through Solu, initially to serve Sherpas traveling to and from district headquarters in Salleri. By the mid-1980s these lodges were offering a full range of local and international food and increasingly comfortable accommodations, and were mostly run by local women.

From Porter and Kitchen Boy to "Host of Presidents"

P. K. Sherpa was born in Khumbu to a relatively poor Namche family. As a teenager he started carrying loads for mountaineers in Khumbu, became cook's helper, was promoted to cook, then to guide and sirdar for Mountain Travel, where he worked for 10 to 12 years. He led several expeditions to Everest, Dhaulagiri, and Annapurna, plus trekking groups to upper Mustang. In early 1980 he opened the Khumbu Hotel in Namche, which was registered as a lodge in 1985. P. K. hosted the former American President and his wife, Jimmy and Roslyn Carter, in 1985 and started a trekking service, "Nepal Himal", not long thereafter, with 'Bobby'

Chhetri and Pertemba Sherpa (three-time Everest climber). In 1991 he was awarded "Man of the Year" by the American Himalayan Foundation.

While he never completed formal education himself, he was able to educate his son in Kathmandu, Darjeeling, and Australia. His five daughters have been similarly educated in Kathmandu, the USA, and Canada, one of whom now is the dental therapist who, since 1991, has been operating "the highest dental clinic in the world" in Namche Bazaar.

In 1964, 20 trekkers visited Khumbu. By 1966 the number had risen to 65; nowadays 15,000-19,000 trekkers visit the area, staying an average of two weeks. The tide has turned and of these an increasing number of trekkers (40% in 1995 and rising steadily) are preferring tea house trekking to the more costly, less flexible organized camping.[4] Thus, with more than 6000-7000 tea house trekkers annually, it is estimated that they contribute as much as Rs. 60 million ($1 million) annually to the local economy.[5] When this amount is added to the local expenditures of camping trekkers, this more than doubles, to Rs. 140 million ($2.4 million) which represents trekkers net impact on the local economy.[6] What is more, the benefits are clearly staying in the region: Solu-Khumbu Sherpas' "homes" have become three and four storey lodges, often supporting a second home in Kathmandu and children in expensive boarding schools. Monasteries are flourishing with larger numbers of monks and nuns living in improved facilities, and surrounded by costly icons, elegant art, and elaborate decoration.

The question often arises in trekking tourism cost and benefit analyses over which type, tea house or group trekking, brings greater economic benefits to Nepal's rural populations. A number of studies conclude that independent trekkers spend an average of $10 a day on food and lodging in rural areas.[7] Local expenditure by trekking groups varies according to the region, the availability of food and supplies, and each trekking company's policy: one trekking company estimates that it spends $20 per trekker per day in the field due to the significant revenue generated as wages to locally hired porters; but on average, it is estimated that trekking companies spend $7-8 per trekker per day in trekking areas for supplementary food, incidentals and portering.[8]

In recent years, a new style of organized tea house trekking is being sold by some Kathmandu-based trekking agencies. Trekking groups book through an agent who provides them with a trained and English-speaking guide, and porters. But rather than camping out in the cold high-altitude terrain–often right next to a homey lodge filled with independent trekkers – these organized groups are eating and sleeping in the better quality tea houses. In a way, this type of "organized tea house trekking" has the potential to bring even greater economic benefits to local communities, in the form of food and lodging sales, but perhaps reduced porter employment as the minimal gear carried along may not be offset by the increased portering demands of shops and lodges, although hard data are not available and there is still considerable debate around these trade-offs.

The short-term economic gains of upmarket organized tea house trekking may indeed be greater than camping, but there may be environmental costs that have to be taken into account as well. Within Nepal's national parks, trekking groups are not allowed to cook with fuel wood; they use kerosene or gas instead. Khumbu lodges, however, have no such regulations, and regularly harvest the slow-growing high altitude shrub vegetation. Alternatively lodges carry in fuel wood from outside the park to fuel their kitchen stoves and toasty wood-heated dining rooms. Thus, the shift from group camping to lodge-stays in such high altitude areas is putting greater strain on slow-growing forests and shrub vegetation. Over the past 30-50 years, for example, there has been a clear decline in shrub species above Tengboche. Fortunately, however, recent research suggests that the overall condition of forests in the Solu-Khumbu region remains stable or may be gradually improving.[9]

Annapurna Conservation Area: Coping with Popularity

During the 1970s, the Annapurna region of central-west Nepal was recognized for its unique qualities of bio- and cultural diversity. By 1980 it had become a major tourist trekking destination, drawing thousands of trekking tourists annually. This flood led to rising concerns about the sustainability of the natural resource base, the mounting damage done by uncontrolled tourism, and the cultural impact of large numbers of outsiders on traditional mountain societies. While rooted in the tradition of the Thakali Bhattis that first served trekkers coming to the area, the growth of a trekking route around the Annapurna massif had made the area particularly attractive to visitors.

In response to the pressures on the Annapurna area, the King Mahendra Trust for Nature Conservation (KMTNC), by special arrange-ment with the Nepal Government, established the Annapurna Conservation Area. A supporting conservation and development project, the Annapurna Conservation Area Project (ACAP) was simultaneously established in 1984. ACAP was designed, not to promote trekking in the region per se, but to mitigate the negative impacts of a dramatically increasing number of visitors already coming to the area.

Among ACAP's first activities was a program to work with local tea house and lodge owners to raise conservation awareness, to develop uniform and improved tourism standards, to reduce fuel wood consumption, and to promote ecologically sound tourism development. These efforts have paid off: today all lodges in the Annapurna Sanctuary use kerosene or gas for cooking, and each village maintains a rubbish pit. Women's groups perform traditional dances for tourists to raise funds to run a child-care center, and hydro and solar energy fuel electric lights and cookers in these mountain villages.

Some 50,000 foreign tourists visit the Annapurna area annually, 51% of whom are tea house trekkers. On average, as in the Khumbu region, they spend some Rs. 500-600 ($10) per day while in the area, stay on average 10 to 14 days, generating revenues for local communities of upwards of Rs.180,000,000 ($3.1 million) annually.[10] Thus, tea house trekking has significantly contributed to an increase in living standards among ACAP villagers. The key question that remains, however, is who is benefiting?

In spite of widespread improvements in the living and village conditions, studies show that there is still great disparity in the distribution of tourism's benefits among various socio-economic groups of the region. Income data show that tourism contributes about 36% to the family income of the higher caste Gurungs, 25% to the annual income of other high- and mid-level ethnic groups, and only 3% to that of occupational castes. Except for minimal income from the sale of locally grown vegetables to trekking groups, there is little income generated outside of lodge-keeping and outside of families who own lodges.[11]

The economic benefit generated by Nepal's trekking tourism industry is significant, particularly among the rural populations. As seen in the ACAP example, however, age-old customs, village social hierarchies, and availability of investment capital often determine who gets ahead, and who gets left behind. Disparities reflect socio-economic forces rooted in Nepali society that transcend those introduced by tourism. Yet it is clear that overall tea house trekking is having a substantial impact on the local economy. Furthermore, the major beneficiaries are local people who are frequently well beyond the reach of other economic development efforts.

The Langtang-Gosainkund-Helambu Region: Hindu Pilgrims and Budget Trekkers

The Langtang-Gosainkund-Helambu area north and east of Kathmandu captured the attention of tea house trekkers beginning in the 1970s. In the early 1980s, when the first records were kept, 4,000 trekkers arrived annually. The Yolmos, Sherpas, and Tamangs – ethnic groups that generations ago migrated from Tibet – caught wind of trekking from the early mountaineers like Eric Shipton (of Shipton's Col) who explored the area in the 1950s. Trekking agencies began marketing the area, including the high altitude holy Gosainkund Lakes, in a spectacular three-week Langtang-Gosainkund-Helambu natural and cultural experience. Mid-elevation Helambu grew in popularity for its warm hospitality, charming old wooden homes, and relatively easy access – a short day's walk over the hill from Kathmandu.

Not until a string of lodges connected the entire Langtang-Gosainkund-Helambu route, however, did tea house trekking surge ahead of group trekking. Today it supports the highest ratio of independent to group trekkers among Nepal's three main mountain parks: 64% of trekkers in Langtang region are tea house trekkers, compared to 40% in Khumbu and 51% in ACAP.[12]

The hospitality availed visitors was frequently the province of mountain women who were adept at handling house-guests' needs and business demands alike, while the men were often away working as porters or guides. The people of Helambu in particular seem attuned to separation from home, evolving from a similar tradition of male seasonal migration practised in these peoples' homeland Tibet. Even today, nearly every family sends offspring to labor in India's mountain states or in Kathmandu to earn cash wages not available in the village.

By the late 1980s, the Langtang/Helambu area was receiving some 8-9,000 foreign trekkers annually, plus an additional 5-10,000 Hindu pilgrims to the holy Gosainkund Lakes. While pilgrim expenditures are generally minimal, the average foreign trekker spends 10 to 14 days in the area, and, as elsewhere in Nepal, spends some $10 per day. This now generates total annual revenues of some Rs. 40,000,000 ($0.7 million). Thus, tea house trekking in Helambu, as in other hill areas, now offers an alternative to out-migration – the possibility of earning income at home.

Daily local bus service from Kathmandu to Helambu and Langtang, a mild climate and stunning forests protected within Langtang National Park attract many of those trekkers. This includes many who cannot afford the airplane flight to Lukla (Khumbu) or the long walk around Annapurna.

As with any good business venture, others will soon follow suit. Recent socio-economic surveys in the Langtang-Gosainkund-Helambu region reveal that local people are concerned that the number of new lodges being constructed is exceeding the tourist demand. Lodge operators are undercutting each other's prices for food and lodging, and even offering free overnight stays to attract trekkers. There are few other income opportunities besides herding within the national park, where most resource-dependent activities are curtailed. Families sell their only wealth, the women's gold jewelry, and forego educating their children to construct simple lodges and tea shops to operate four to six months a year.

In response to these pressures several organizations, including the UNDP and The Mountain Institute, have initiated conservation and development programs. The Langtang Ecotourism Project, for example, is working in the Langtang-Gosainkund-Helambu region to help develop community-based ecotourism linked with conservation of the area's natural and cultural heritage. This three year program is being undertaken by The Mountain Institute, an international NGO based in the USA, in partnership with Nepal's Department of National Parks and Wildlife Conservation. Tourism Management Committees have been established in every village along the main trekking routes and are taking part in the planning and management of ecotourism. Promising results are already evident: villagers are taking an active interest in keeping trails and campsites clean, in using alternative fuel for cooking trekkers' meals, in protection of wildlife, and in community-supported cultural conservation.

Makalu-Barun: "Best Kept Secret of the Himalaya"

The Makalu-Barun National Park and Conservation Area (MBNPCA), Nepal's newest protected area, is located in eastern Nepal between Mount Everest and Makalu, west of the Arun River. The Department of National Parks and Wildlife Conservation and The Mountain Institute have been developing and promoting a program of comprehensive biodiversity conservation and community development here since the late 1980s. This includes an ecotourism program that seeks to balance the resource needs of the area's 32,000 residents and with the requirements and impacts of the 1,000-1,500 trekkers that visit the area annually – a very small number compared to the 50,000 in ACAP, the 15,000 in Khumbu, and the 9,000 in Langtang.

Trekkers to the Makalu-Barun area follow three main routes: some 400 head for Makalu Base Camp, deep within Makalu-Barun National Park. As there are no tea houses within the Park, all trekkers must be self-sufficient with food and supplies. They spend an average of 21 days in the area, and Rs. 500-600 (US$10) per day on local purchases, staff wages, food, etc..

Another 500-600 trekkers cross over Salpa La from Tumlingtar en route to Solu-Khumbu. They pass through the Makalu-Barun Conservation

Area, a buffer zone-like strip of land running along the edge of the national park. Another 400-500 trekkers enter the Mera Peak area from Lukla. There are basic lodges and tea shops in these areas. Together the total 1,000 to 1,100 visitors to MBNPCA generate an estimated Rs.12.5 million ($275,000) annually for the rural economy.

The Makalu-Barun Conservation Project's (MBCP) program for village tourism is based upon the tea house model. It has been broadened, however, to involve and train local people to convert their traditional homes into simple 'bed and breakfast' accommodations. With its links to MBCP's cultural conservation activities, the ecolodge program provides local entrepreneurs with training in health and sanitation, conservation values, and good cooking. Emphasis is placed on the use of local materials, designs, and foods, and small scale development rather than building new, expensive lodges.

Notes from a Makalu Journal:
From "Anikaal" Hungry-time to Doubled Incomes

Bung/Chheskam: Thur. 16 Jan. 97. The sun had set and my partner, Chandi, and I had just finished a lively discussion with Madansar Rai, Vice Chairman of the Bung VDC. He had just told us the welcome news that the economy of this area has improved dramatically in the past 5-10 years, largely due to the trekking tourism centered in Namche. When I was here in Bung just over 2 years ago, I was struck by the number of porters on the trail who reported that they were on their way to Namche with rice, meat, or other supplies. At that time it had occurred to me that this trade might well be adding more to the local economy than our MBCP development and training efforts plus those of HMG, CARE, and all others working in the area. Madansar confirmed that hunch, noting that incomes have perhaps doubled in this area over the past 5 or 10 years, since the 1989 MBCP Task Force had initially surveyed the region while planning the project.

Many men from the area now carry loads for trekkers and mountaineers while others buy rice for Rs. 100 per 'pathi,' carry it 8 days to Namche Bazaar where they sell it for Rs. 180 to 190 per pathi. The average man carries about 15 pathis, thus after deducting the cost of their food for the journey, each man brings home at least 800 rupees per 16 day round trip. Making a dozen such trips a year, the men frequently bring home over Rs. 9,000 a year, and have thus paid off their debts, some of which have burdened the family for a generation or more. In a village meeting the next day, we were told by one man that the happiest day of his life was the day he paid off his debts.

From Tea House to Ecolodge:
A "Clean and Natural" Model for the Future

The experiences of the Makalu-Barun Project in helping local people develop simple ecolodges from their existing homes and tea shops, and the lessons learned from the Langtang Ecotourism Project about promoting responsible tourism that motivates conservation, suggest a new and powerful model for strengthening tea house trekking throughout Nepal. The model promotes cultural conservation and the adaptation of typical local homes to trekkers' requirements. Villagers learn that simple, clean toilets and smoke-free kitchens in local design buildings - rather than costly construction, „imported" plastic chairs, and Western food - are the keys to profitability. At the same time these simple, natural adaptations support conservation of the environment and local cultural values. The MBCP and LEP programs are built around simple concepts easily understood, readily taught, and economically affordable: „Clean and Natural" - representing the core values of sustainable ecotourism.

Conclusion
The Case for Environmentally Friendly Indigenous Tourism

Tea house trekking has emerged from the hills and mountains of Nepal as an indigenous concept developed first by and for Nepalis themselves, and only later to host outsiders. Tea houses are by nature considered appropriate in scale and operations, and, if constructed and maintained properly, can be environmentally friendly. In summary, tea house trekking offers the following opportunities:

*Tea house trekking draws on local design, natural materials, and traditional foods.

*Energy and resource consumption are relatively low, particularly in contrast to modern sector tourist facilities.

*Tea house trekking has been developed by and is benefiting rural hill tribes, including the Thakalis, Sherpas, Gurungs, and Tamangs, some of whom are quite marginalized socio-economically and geo-politically. Only more recently has it been adopted by other ethnic groups. Thus it serves to equalize the ethnic peoples in some ways.

*Almost every tea house reflects the culture and environment of its owners and their community. Thus it is unique as an economic engine that has emerged from the hill tribes rather than from elite, politically and socially dominant groups that tend to dominate other sectors of Nepal's economy.

*Tea house trekking is generally a family operation, often run by women while men are off seeking cash employment elsewhere.

*Tea house earnings coupled with trekking, portering, and military service provides vital local cash incomes to supplement agricultural shortfall, particularly important since many hill areas, including those along trekking routes, have chronic food deficits.

*Tea house trekking provides substantial rural employment and generates a direct market for local commodities and services, including basic foodstuffs, fuel wood, local beer and rakshi. The limited outside goods used by or sold in tea houses are brought in by local porters who are major suppliers for virtually all hill businesses and industries.

*Tea houses and local lodges are built almost exclusively of indigenous materials, in local style, first as adaptations of local homes to take in occasional visitors, then as separate operations.

*Tea house trekking is estimated to account for annual revenues to local communities exceeding $5 million (Rs. 300 million).[13] When the local expenditure of camping trekkers is added to this figure, representing what trekkers spend in rural communities, this number exceeds $10 million. Thus it appears to be among the largest sources of cash income and foreign exchange in Nepal's rural economy.

Tea house trekking is unique in that it is derived largely from an indigenous tradition that has deep roots in Nepali culture. It returns a significant proportion of its earnings directly to the rural people, particularly women.

Properly developed and supported, as is being piloted in the Makalu, Langtang, and Annapurna areas, tea house trekking can help Nepal conserve its biological and cultural diversity – and generate significant revenues for people otherwise beyond the reach of most economic development programs.

Footnotes

1. Ministry of Tourism and Civil Aviation, 1995
2. While accepted statistics give Nepal's per capita annual income or GNP at US $180, these figures include the wealthiest sectors of the economy. Economist John Mellor, frequent advisor to donors and the Government of Nepal, has suggested that in many hill areas the figure of $40-50 may be more realistic.
3. Makalu-Barun ecotourism staff estimates. A modern relatively well-equipped lodge can be built using local construction methods and materials for US$6000 (Nrs. 3-4 lakhs) in most rural villages. Costs may be double in larger towns. Substantial improvements, including improved toilet, kitchen, and one or two neat and clean sleeping rooms can be made for a cash outlay of US$ 100-1000, depending on the standard sought and how much work is done by the family members themselves.
4. Ministry of Tourism and Civil Aviation 1995 (low figure); Sagarmatha National Park and local lodge and trekking service estimates for subsequent increases in numbers (high figure).
5. Based on trekker surveys conducted by Sagarmatha Warden, Megh Pandey, for MS thesis research, and Khumjung eco-tourism specialist, Ang Rita Sherpa. These suggest that the average trekker spends two weeks in Solu-Khumbu, spending locally approx-imately US$10 per day.
6. Total expenditures in local area by trekkers, excluding fees to Kathmandu trekking firms, imported goods, or supplies brought from outside local area.
7. Fleming 1991; Banskota 1989; MBCP 1995
8. Fleming 1991
9. The Mountain Institute's Dr. Alton Byers, has conducted soil and vegetation studies, coupled with repeat photography of Khumbu landscapes covering several decades, which indicate that there is reason to question the conventional wisdom that the Khumbu eco-system has been degraded since tourism came to the area; unpublished research report, The Mountain Institute, 1997.
10. Estimates by KMTNC staff reported to TMI and MBCP staff visiting ACAP area 1995, 1996; these estimates are consistent with studies conducted in other parks and trekking destinations in Nepal; see also Odell 1994/95.
11. Shrestha 1993
12. Ministry of Tourism and Civil Aviation 1995
13. This total of $5 million for tea house trekkers, and the grand total from

all trekkers of $10 million, is based solely on the available figures from the Everest, Annapurna, Langtang/Helambu, and Makalu areas covered in this report. Calculated another way, if the average trekker of the nation's annual total of 85,000 makes similar expenditures to those recorded for these destinations, a similar total of $10 million in local expenditure can be projected.

References

Banskota, Kamal/M. Upadhyay: A Survey of Trekking Tourists in Langtang National Park. Kathmandu, Nepal CREST 1989

Byers, Alton: Draft Research Report on Khumbu Ecosystem Dynamics and Repeat Photography, Franklin, WV: The Mountain Institute 1997

Fleming, W. B.: Tourism Report. Environmental Management and Sustainable Development in the Arun Basin. King Mahendra Trust for Nature Conservation, Kathmandu, Nepal 1991

Gurung, H.: Environmental Management of Mountain Tourism in Nepal. Paper presented at ESCAP Symposium on Tourism Promotion in the Asian Region, 12-15 November 1990, Hangzhou, China 1990

Ministry of Tourism and Civil Aviation: Annual Statistics Report 1995, Kathmandu, Nepal 1995

Odell, M.: US AID Quarterly Activity Progress Reports, July 1, 1994, September 30, 1994, October 1-December 31, 1994, January 1-March 31, 1995. Woodlands Mountain Institute, Kathmandu, Nepal 1994/5

Pandey, Megh Bahadur: International Visitor Attitudes to Sagarmatha (Mt. Everest) National Park, Nepal. Thesis presented to Lincoln University, Canterbury, New Zealand 1994.

Shrestha, S. K.: Trekking Use Patterns and Perceptions of Users and Residents Towards Trekking Tourism in the Annapurna Sanctuary Trail, Nepal. Master thesis University Pertanian, Malaysia 1993.

Axel Schrand

Social Indicators of Sustainable Tourism

The sustainable tourism discussion is characterized by a lack of application of social indicators, and the intention of this article is to raise some questions and offer some answers, approaches and solutions with regard to measuring phenomena of sustainable and non-sustainable tourism.

1. Sustainable Tourism

"Sustainable Tourism is all forms of tourism development and activity which enable a long life for that cultural activity which we call tourism, involving a sequence of economic tourism products compatible with keeping in perpetuity the protected heritage resource, be it natural, cultural or built, which gives rise to tourism." (Travis 1992 248)

Synonyms and near-synonyms of sustainable tourism are terms such as:

- Low Impact Tourism (LIT)
- Environment Based Tourism (EBT)
- Soft Tourism and Responsibility for Earth and Life Organisation (STRELO)
- small-scale tourism
- alternative tourism
- community-based tourism
- people-to-people tourism
- non-destructive tourism
- socially responsible Tourism

To create social indicators of sustainable tourism it is necessary to characterize sustainable tourism as follows:

- Tourism which is concerned with the quality of experiences
- Tourism which has social equity and community involvement
- Tourism which operates within the limits of the resource – this includes minimisation of impacts and use of energy and the use of effective waste management and recycling technologies
- Tourism which maintains the full range of recreational, educational and cultural opportunities within and across generations

- Tourism which is based upon activities or designs which reflect the character of a region
- Tourism which allows the guest to gain an understanding of the region visited and which encourages guests to be concerned about, and protective of the host community and environment
- Tourism which does not compromise the capacity of other industries or activities to be sustainable
- Tourism which is integrated into local, regional and national plans
- (Moscardo et. al. 1996 31)

2. Social Indicators and Sustainable Tourism

A social indicator is defined as:

"the operational definition or part of the operational definition of any one of the concepts central to the generation of an information system descriptive of the social system" (Carlisle 1972 12).

There are some problems in using social indicators for sustainable tourism research. Firstly, it can be difficult to find out all the indicators to measure the total tourism-induced phenomena. Secondly, the indicators constructed may not measure the tourism-induced phenomena accurately (problem of data collection and non-response). Thirdly, the data may not always be up to date, and may be lacking in continuity. Fourthly, access to data may be restricted.

Social indicators can be of use in the development of sustainable tourism in the following ways:

a) to measure the structure and change of tourism phenomena
b) to evaluate volume and direction of tourism development
c) to explain the causes and effects of tourism phenomena
d) to plan and implement sustainable tourism.

Social indicators can be applied in sustainable tourism research in a number of ways. As the basis of longitudinal studies conducted in different host communities, they can establish input and output variables of tourism-induced social impact. Within the framework of a holistic approach to tourism research, social indicators can identify transdisciplinary correlations. They can also be applied when awarding eco-labels, e.g. for accommodation, catering, transport, tour operations, and host communities. Finally, they are very useful for determining carrying capacities and developing visitor management programmes.

3. Special Indicators of Sustainable Tourism

3.1. Socio-economic Indicators

Area of Concern	**Performances indicator**
Tourism monostructure dependency on tourism	Percentage of tourism-induced income in relation to the total income of residents of the community.
Financing power of the community	Relation of tourism-induced receipts (taxes) to tourism-induced expenses (tourism infrastructure, etc.)
Expenditure of tourists	Expenditure of excursionists and overnight tourists per day.
Autocentric tourism development	Tourism-induced rate of foreign exchange outflow (Job 1996 125)
Dependency on incoming tourism	Income from incoming tourism as a proportion of the total earnings from experts (Job 1996 124)
Tourism-related employment	Percentage of residents who have employment in the tourism section (Dragicevic 1989 65)
Continuity of workshop places	Percentage of tourism-induced seasonal workshop places to the total tourism induced workshop places.
Structure of qualification	Level of education of tourism-induced workshop places.
Economic multiplier effects of tourism	Local/regional multiplier of tourists expenditure.
Occupancy in accommodation	Overnight stays per hotel bed.
Cost of living	Relative price index, index for food costs, index of housing costs (Crotts 1993 116)
Prices for private real estates	Relative price index since the beginning of tourism development.

3.2 Sociocultural Indicators

Area of Concern	Performance Indicator
Demographic structure	Distribution of sex, age, family status, of a host community increase/decrease of population, migration, state of health, religion.
Ethnicity/multicultural	
Social Inequality	Social class, life styles, of a host community education, profession /prestige, income/property
Personal safety of hosts and guests	Crime rate per hosts and guests
Values and change of values	Scale of values of a host community
Foreign infiltration by second homes in a host community	Percentage of second homes to all homes in a host community.
Human Rights at a tourism destination	Observation of the Human Rights Convention of the United Nations or Amnesty International.
Host-Guest Interaction in a host community	Percentage of guest who have contact with the hosts.
Identification with tourism development in a host community	Attitudes of residents to tourism development and to tourists (questionnaire).
Well-Being in a host community	Residents satisfaction with the "Quality of Life".

3.3 Sociospatial Indicators

Area of Concern	Performance Indicator
Tourism intensity in destination	Number of overnight spending per 100 residents in a season year.
Sociospatial density, crowding	Visitors per day/ha: mountain, forest, park, lake, beach, building, sights, facilities, catering
Population density in destination	Residents per hectares or acre in tourist destination.

3.4. Socioecological Indicators

Area of Concern	Performance Indicator
Energy consumption	+K Joule/tourist per day
Energy consumption of transport	Megajoules per person on 100 km (vehicle: train, bus, car, plane, ship)
Air Quality/Pollution	Number of days per year that local standards for air quality are not exceeded
Noise	Percentage of residents disturbed by noise (transport, leisure, sports, music, etc)
Water consumption	Use of water per overnight stay
Waste water	Tourists' daily water consumption
Waste	Waste per overnight stay
"Green Economy"	Percentage of tourism enterprises that have joined Eco-Management and Audit Schemes (EMAS) or similar schemes (Eco-Labels, EU Eco Audit, etc.)

References

Crotts, John/Holland, Stephen: Objective Indicators of the Impact of Rural Tourism Development in the State of Florida. In: Journal of Sustainable Tourism, Vol. 1, 1993, pp 112-119

Carlisle, E.: The Conceptual Structure of Social Indicators. In: Shonfield, A.(Ed.): Social Indicators and Social Policy. London 1972

Dragicevic, Miroslav/Tadej, Perla: Methodology. In: Bystrzanowski, Julian (Ed..): Tourism as a Factor of Change. A Sociocultural Study. Vienna 1989, pp 61-68

Job, Hubert: Modell zur Evaluation der Nachhaltigkeit im Tourismus. In: Erdkunde Nr.50/1996, pp 112-132

Moscardo, Gianna/Morrison, Alastair/Pearce, Philip: Specialist Accommodation an Ecologically-Sustainable Tourism. In: Journal of Sustainable Tourism, Vol. 4, 1996, pp 29-52

Travis, A.S.: Sustainable Concepts an Innovations in City-Tourism and in Eco-Tourism. In: Pillmann,W./Predl, S. (Eds.): Strategies for Reducing the Impact of Tourism. Vienna 1992

Malcolm J. Odell

The Challenge of Global Conservation

Protected Area Management, Ecotourism, and Local People

This article provides a brief and selective overview of the challenge of global conservation with a focus on participatory protected area management and ecotourism that involve rather than exclude local people. Many of the examples in the paper are drawn from my own experience and that of The Mountain Institute (TMI) in Nepal. Particular thanks are due to TMI's major partner in its work in Nepal, the Department of National Parks and Wildlife Conservation (DNPWC) who can be credited for their manifold and impressive programs for Parks and People, for conservation of endangered species including the Royal Bengal Tiger, Asian One-Horned Rhino, and long-snouted Gharial alligator as well as for their innovative park and protected area management programs across the mountains and plains of Nepal.

The article begins with a brief historical overview which is followed by a review of the emergence of environmental issues on the international agenda including the belated attention to mountains and the special need for incentives for local people. The paper concludes with some of my own personal reflections on tourism, environmental conservation, and local development from my experience in Africa, and here in Nepal since I first came in 1962. A number of conclusions are presented suggesting that a critical ingredient in the challenge of global conservation is to both involve and provide economic returns for local people. Community forestry and buffer zone management programs have been effective means to this end, as has community-based ecotourism, arguably the most powerful source for sustainable revenues for mountain people.

Historical Perspective on the Global Challenge

Philosophers have long placed high value on the environment: Henry David Thoreau is only one of many who have looked to the environment for inspiration and healing and his statement "In wildness is the preservation of the world" has become a favourite slogan in the world's environmental community. The Holy Bible reflects this value, noting that "I lift up mine eyes unto the hills, from whence cometh my help." Buddhism holds all life as sacred, a theme reflected in the ancient scripts and theology of most of the world's religions. Clive Punting's A Green History of the World[1] demonstrates that the Roman empire, Sumarian, Egyptian, pre-Colombian,

Easter Island, and many other civilizations at first prospered by exploiting the earth's resources but that this pattern led ultimately to their decline and eventual collapse.

The concept of setting aside protected areas led to the establishment of the world's first National Park, Yellowstone, in 1872. This action, however, set a pattern that has persisted for over 100 years – a process of chasing the people out to protect nature, and allowing them back in again mainly as tourists and researchers.

Often neglected in the review of conservation is the wisdom of indigenous leaders whose insights into the importance of the natural environment to their own civilizations has tempered the world's oversimplified view that the presence of man is antithetical to conservation. A native American, Chief Seattle, articulated the folly of separating man from nature when he proclaimed that one day all the fish will be gone, the hills bare of trees for homes, the land bare of crops, and that his people would be lost because they cannot eat money.

Among the most visionary of traditional leaders was the Maori Chief, Te-heu-heu Tukino, of New Zealand. When faced with the arriving white man's land hunger, he could see that the future of his ancestral lands was in jeopardy. In his words, "Tongariro is the mountain, Taupo is the sea, Tuwharetoa (Tu-fa-re-to-a) is the tribe, Te-heu-heu is the man." He thus drew the connection between man and mountain, and took the bold step of donating an extensive tract of land for Tongariro National Park including at its heart the sacred Mt. Tongariro of his tribe. The land, in the words of his New Zealand colleagues, was "gifted by a man with the wisdom to see the way the world was going and the generosity to share his heritage with the small but growing number of settlers who were able to appreciate Tongariro for what it is, not for what it could be turned into." Thus Tongariro became New Zealand's first National Park, 1887, just a few years after Yellowstone.

Awakening to the Mounting Environmental Global Crisis during the late 20th C.

During the latter part of the 20th century interest in conservation began to shift from setting aside green areas for protection and recreation to concern for the future of the planet. Dennis and Danielle Meadows' report for the Club of Rome, The Limits of Growth, used computer modeling to project population growth, resource utilization, and food production and warned world leaders of an impending crisis where the world could, quite simply, run out of food and energy if major changes were not made. Rachel Carson's popular book, Silent Spring, painted a picture of a world without wildlife due to growing pesticide use and its impact as a poison that posed a serious threat to many of the world's species of flora and fauna. Concern grew for the earth's ozone layer and tropical rain forests that were being destroyed as developing nations sought to raise themselves out of poverty. With growing popular and political pressure, the environment moved onto the international agenda. The process on the international stage began, perhaps, with the United Nations Conference on the Human Environment in Stockholm (1972), and received additional attention at the first Rio de Janeiro conference. Following the stimulus of these initiatives, IUCN took the lead in working with UNEP and WWF to develop the first World Conservation Strategy in 1980. This was followed by a number of other important international meetings, conferences, and commissions which led, among others, to the Brundtland Commission's Our Common Future (1984), to IUCN, UNEP, and WWF's second world conservation strategy, Caring for the Earth: A Strategy for Sustainable Living (1991) and the Earth Summit's Agenda 21 and Rio Declaration (1992).

Lest we think these global meetings and publications amounted to just junkets and talk, because of their general lack of binding commitments, a number of tangible results have flowed from them, including the commitment and mobilization of billions of dollars in funding for action programs, such as the Global Environmental Facility (GEF) of the World Bank and UNDP which is supporting numerous environmental protection and conservation initiatives in nations around the world. Most of the world's governments and donors have also put the environment on their agendas for funding and action and a global network of non-government organizations (NGOs) has sprung up to address a growing number of environmental concerns from global warming and the ozone layer to the protection and salvation of individual species of flora and fauna like the Bengal tiger, spotted owl, or Nepali gharial (long-snouted Asian alligator).

A further outcome of these international forums has been a parallel program of meetings related directly to parks and protected areas including the World Congress on National Parks and Protected Areas which has met every 10 years since 1962. This important conference has proved to be a useful focal point for protected area management and dissemination of new strategies including an increasing recognition of the vital role that local people can and must play in conservation and development. It has thus contributed to a successful shift in the focus of conservation toward including rather than excluding the human dimension.

Belated Attention to the World's Mountains

Once given short shrift, the world's mountains are now recognized for their critical contributions to the earth's people and ecosystems. Mountains make up 1/5 of the earth's landscape, provide homes for 10% of the world's people, are sacred places for 1 billion people, and the primary source of up to 80% of the world's fresh surface water. As recognition of the role of mountains, The Earth Summit led to FAO commissioning The Mountain Institute (TMI), of Franklin, WV, USA, to convene The Mountain Forum, a collaborative effort by international non-government organizations (NGOs), to prepare a follow-on initiative focusing specifically on mountain systems, essentially picking up where Chapter 13 of the Agenda 21 left off. Rio's "Chap. 13, Managing Fragile Ecosystems: Sustainable Mountain Development" played an important role in putting mountains clearly on the international agenda. However, the conveners recognized that this, too, was inadequate and asked TMI to help bring together mountain NGOs, first on TMI's Spruce Knob in the mountains of West Virginia (July 1994), and then in Lima, Peru (February 1995) with a mandate to develop a NGO consensus on an action plan and create an ongoing forum of mountain NGOs.

From The Mountain Forum came several important lessons from and for mountain protected areas, including:

Cultural Diversity

The need for protecting mountain communities and their property rights, for supporting conflict resolution, for empowering local people, and paying special attention to the sacred, spiritual, and symbolic significance of the mountains and for providing both conceptual and concrete links between mountain people and their natural environment.

Ecotourism

The subject of this book, is more explicitly explored in separate chapters. Ecotourism may be generating the largest proportion of income for conservation in mountain areas and is providing a major incentive for the promotion of environmental values in mountain areas.

Community Management of Protected Areas

Historically, today, and the future, traditional people have been and are likely to continue to be remarkably responsible caretakers for mountain systems. For hundreds, perhaps thousands of years mountain people have protected their environments, managed them sustainably, and despite severe economic pressures, have forgone short-term gain for the sake of their descendants. Gloomy predictions concerning the deforestation of mountains, as well as recent cries of alarm that mountain people have been destroying their environment have usually proven to be exaggerations, or downright wrong. Data from ICIMOD (International Center for Integrated Mountain Development in Kathmandu) shows that forest cover is actually stable or even improving in the Himalayas, where only a few years ago scholars and scientists were predicting massive soil and forest losses due to man. Dipendra Purush Dhakal, the former Secretary of Nepal's Ministry of Forests and Soil Conservation, stated that "Whatever we have today is because of the stewardship of our mountain people". Thus, it is not unexpected that world environmental leaders have rediscovered the vital importance of putting the management of mountain protected areas into the hands of local people, who have the most to gain from conservation and the most to lose by degradation and whose record for sustainable management is remarkably solid.

Providing a Return to Local People: A Fundamental Issue

Local people have generally done an impressive job in conserving their environment, in spite of frequent and severe poverty. They cannot be expected to continue to do so in the face of mounting population and economic pressures without improving their livelihoods. Thus programs to promote sustainable incomes in mountain regions are paramount. Some examples of success in this regard include several from Nepal:

Community Forests

Nepal's globally recognized program of promoting the hand-over of once nationalized forests to local Community Forest User Groups (CFUGs) is generating important new revenues for communities, as well as helping provide them with sustainable supplies of fuel wood and fodder. Through improved management and the sustainable development and utilization of non-timber forest products, such as cardamom, lokta (bark used for traditional hand-made Nepali paper), allo (stinging nettle fiber used to make fabric) and medicinal and aromatic herbs, mountain people are obtaining direct and immediate benefit from their forests. Lokta production is a big business in Nepal, providing, for example, UNICEF with a major source of material for its fund-raising products. Similarly, one allo production program is generating Rs. 650,000 in new incomes for its 300 women members, while in the neighboring Terai near Nepal's Royal Chitwan National Park, local people are managing their community forest so well that they have not only met all their fuel wood and fodder needs but are attracting significant numbers of wildlife and hosting tourists for extra income, thus effectively expanding the protected area beyond park boundaries. Nepal now has almost 5,000 community forests controlling over 300,000 ha. of forest land, and annual earnings approaching Rs. 10,000, representing savings now in the hands of rural communities that total nearly Rs. 50 million (US$1 million). Projections of feasible revenues indicate that revenues per CFUG could rise to Rs. 100,000 and thus become a major source of support for community development.

Buffer Zones and Conservation Areas

Establishment of areas adjoining protected areas, such as those sponsored under Nepal's People & Parks Program, Makalu-Barun Conservation Project, and Annapurna Conservation Area Project, is now providing revenues to local communities from Park fees as well as from income-generating activities. These programs use participatory conservation strategies to raise awareness among local people, train local people as guides, hire local people as scouts, and recently have proposed the training of local hunters (Shikaris) as indigenous naturalists and guides for photographic "safaris." Success in these ventures is indicated by local people actually rounding up poachers and exploiters of NTFP in Makalu-Barun, the nation's first National Park and Conservation Area which seeks to put long-term management in the hands of the local people rather than soldiers or armed forest guards.

Ecotourism

This industry now provides what appears to be the single greatest income generation opportunities for local communities, substantially contributing to poverty alleviation. Ecotourism has a growing reputation for contributing directly to environmental conservation (viz. Austria, Switzerland, Peru, Sikkim, Tibet, and Nepal). Perhaps even more important is ecotourism's record for generating significant revenues at the local level, putting cash incomes directly into the hands of those who have the most to gain from protection efforts and the most to lose if they fail. Tourism is now Nepal's greatest source of foreign exchange and the modest Tea House Trekking business that is flourishing along walking trails is plowing some $10 million annually into the pockets of local entrepreneurs.

Elsewhere in the world similar patterns are emerging. In southern Africa game ranching has now become a big business and is growing exponentially as tourists and hunters pay top prices both to see and to hunt game animals. Botswana's policy of providing communities with licenses and the right to direct revenues for culling excess animals has contributed to dramatic increases in elephant numbers, the virtual elimination of poaching, and strong community support for conservation.

Peruvian, Tibetan, and Sikkimese villagers under a series of TMI programs are learning from Nepal's successes, replicating programs in participatory community conservation and ecotourism that are beginning to generate important revenues for their people while promoting sustainable resource utilization.

Directions for the Future

From the shifts that have taken place in the global environmental arena from protection to conservation and from excluding toward including people have come new roles for those involved. Governments and NGOs have all had to find new ways to take account of human needs. National and international NGOs are now looking to form partnerships with governments and the private sector rather than consider them enemies. All parties have had to find new and more effective means to reach out to and directly involve local people.

Research on the global challenge of the environment, once the domain of scientists, is also seeing a shift toward involving local people. A new discipline of Participatory Research & Monitoring (PM&E) is utilizing indigenous knowledge systems and observation skills for developing indicators of success that come from the community level. Drawing on the now proven methodology of Participatory Rural Appraisal (PRA) which put the analytical process in the hands of even illiterate villagers with very beneficial results, CFUGs are engaging in this type of data collection and analysis in Nepal. This process shows considerable promise for the future.

Some Personal Reflections

The challenge of global conservation comes down to summing up how individual people all across the globe make individual decisions that have an impact on their natural environment. In the course of my 35 year international career I have had the opportunity to work particularly closely with local people in Africa and Asia and to come to some understanding about how they make such decisions on a daily basis. In Botswana, which is home to the Kalahari desert in Southern Africa, as in Nepal where I worked in the 1960s and once again during the 1990s, some interesting decisions involved local people and ecotourism.

During my 5 years in Botswana in the late 1970s, I was involved in helping shift government strategies, then focused heavily on halting desertification, from excluding local people to working with them. When I returned there in 1993 I found that the government commitment to active decentralization was real. Communities had been given steadily increasing control over range and wildlife management and direct access to the resulting revenues. This included the licensed hunting of big game under culling quotas established by a combination of rigorous scientific and participatory research - annual aerial censuses ground-truthed by local communities. Hunting licenses are given to the communities in or adjoining the wildlife areas and the communities can decide to use those licenses themselves or to sell them to others, including big game hunters from wealthy nations. Such licenses even include the African elephant, whose numbers are in real jeopardy farther north in Kenya and Tanzania. In Botswana, elephant numbers have grown to some 80,000 animals and regular culling is necessary to avoid destruction of the jungle habitat. Using or selling their licenses (the top price to foreign big game hunters approaches $10,000), the local communities are doing very well and vigorously protect their animals from outsiders, including rounding up or chasing away poachers. Just a few hundred miles away, elsewhere in Africa, centralization rules and local people are often excluded from access to protected areas, let alone involved in managing them. In these areas, poachers are slaughtering elephants and other endangered wildlife illegally, while corruption, civil unrest, and poverty are rampant. Controlled hunting under the aegis of local communities which are responsible for managing wildlife appears to be considerably more successful, and sustainable, than bans on hunting in areas where the power of local communities is limited.

In the Solu-Khumbu region of Nepal, in the shadow of Mount Everest, I have watched the evolution and development of community-based ecotourism over the past 30 years. James Fisher, another analyst with long experience in the area, has drawn several lessons from the changes that have taken place in Solu-Khumbu during the past three decades. Among these are that a combination of high quality education coupled with ecotourism has made Khumbu prosperous, without seriously undermining cultural and religious values. I can attest to his conclusions by the fact that during the latter part of a recent and busy trekking season, numerous Sherpas left their lucrative trade behind and, at considerable personal expense, traveled to Siliguri, India, for a rare visit by the Dalai Lama. Many others have invested significant portions of their trekking incomes in adding elegant Buddhist chapels to their homes. When I lived in Solu and then in Khumbu between 1964 and 1967 the area was among the poorest in all Nepal, and I never saw meat or vegetables for 6 months at a time. At that time, despite the fame of Everest, no more than 50 to 60 trekkers visited annually, a fact to which I can personally attest since most of them stayed at my home, what is now a well equipped, modern tourist lodge hosts perhaps 50 visitors in one busy night. When I returned to Solu Khumbu in 1994/95 I not only found the prosperity you all have heard about, but an extraordinary increase in wildlife. In the first 2 days of my recent visit I saw more wildlife than in the 2 years I lived there: Himalayan tahr, musk deer, pheasant and more. Forests, too, seemed in remarkably good shape, especially after all the tales of gloom that I had heard. TMI research and repeat photography, together with satellite imagery confirm that the forest cover is at least stable, and while there certainly are degraded pockets, is improving in many areas. While commercialism is clearly evident in the Khumbu region, as it is globally, local culture is remarkably intact. This pattern is not just to show off, but is rooted in the deeply held convictions of the modern-day Buddhists. Monasteries are more numerous and in better condition than before and most homes have simple if beautiful private chapels, used for family worship and meditation rather than for visitors. Ecotourism can pay substantial benefits and need not undermine local culture.

In Conclusion

Drawing on the perspectives of history, the lessons of current initiatives, and my own and Mountain Institute experiences, it is evident that a critical ingredient in the challenge of global conservation is to both involve and provide economic returns for local people. Community forestry and buffer zone management programs have been effective means to this end, as has community-based ecotourism, arguably the most powerful source of sustainable revenues for mountain people. Mountain tourism is an achievable goal in countries like Nepal and is showing considerable potential in other Himalayan areas, including Sikkim and Tibet. The potentially negative impacts of tourism are capable of being addressed through sound management and the direct involvement of local people, an area where Nepal is a world leader. Yet at the same time the world is watching and there is still a lot of work to be done to achieve this reality. In the context of Nepal, that is a challenge that, as in the past, will need the continuing involvement of government and non-government partners and, most important, a central role for local people.

Footnote

[1] Punting, C.: A Green History of the World. The Environment and the Collapse of Great Civilizations. London 1991

Les Clark

Planning for Mountain Tourism

Our perspective on planning for sustainable mountain tourism is the perspective of an international consultancy firm which specialises in planning for nature, cultural and adventure tourism. We are from New Zealand, a country which, like Nepal and Austria, has had nature and beautiful environments as part of its tourism product for as long as it has had tourism. We have had the pleasure of working in Nepal and Tibet with people from Government and multinational agencies, the tourism private sector and NGOs. We have also worked in tourism and conservation planning elsewhere throughout Asia and the Pacific.

What I am going to present is a number of rather simple planning principles, drawn from our experience, which we hope may usefully add to the debate at this conference. These principles are merely ideas about how we think planning for tourism should be approached.

We take a rather practical approach to tourism planning. We apply theory, but try not to be driven by it. If we have a special technique, it may be the idea that the best planning solutions are often found when people who understand local needs and planning issues get together in creative debate with people who have practical experience in the ways similar needs and issues have been addressed elsewhere. We try to create these creative situations. We choose planners with broad experience and encourage them to see themselves not as bearers of the right answers, but rather as sounding boards of experience against which locals can bounce their problems and ideas. We have found this approach effective in the mountains of Nepal.

This article will take a positive approach to developing mountain tourism. It is absolutely necessary to be concerned about the need to plan for limits and controls on mountain tourism – and we are. However, our work is usually associated with planning for tourism where little exists, often in an integrated conservation and development context, where the development of tourism is a trade-off to achieve conservation ends. We therefore tend to put as much emphasis on planning for sustainable commercial benefits as on the sustainable management of impacts. Although I personally came into tourism planning from a background in conservation planning, I am now a real convert to the idea that planning for sustainable tourism requires planning with, not against, the whole tourism industry in all its commercial aspects.

Our positive attitude also reflects that we believe tourism is one of the most successful development tools in integrated conservation and development planning for mountain environments. Furthermore, we believe Nepal has most of the best examples in Asia of tourism's success in this regard. In Nepal, there are many people living within mountainous protected areas who have become quite wealthy through tourism. Nepal is also an international leader in the methodologies for implementing mountain tourism development projects. The King Mahendra Trust for Nature Conservation's (KMTNC) Annapurna Conservation Area Project (ACAP) village tourism development models and their variations developed by other agencies throughout the national parks and conservation areas of Nepal are internationally renown. Nepal is even at state of the art in the area of partnerships between Government and NGOs and in using government tourism revenues to support conservation. To me, one of the great tragedies of Nepal's mountain tourism is that despite all this success, the international image of what tourism has done in the mountains of Nepal is resoundingly negative.

In summary, the aims of this article are to share some practical principles of planning for mountain tourism with fellow practitioners and I have begun with an acknowledgement that, in many respects, whose who are working in this field in Nepal are working at the state-of-the-art.

Principle 1: Define the goals of tourism

Our first principle is that the planning process for mountain tourism should be driven by clearly defined goals, preferably goals which involve the integration of development and conservation.

This sounds very obvious, but in our experience, planning does not always start with goals. Mountain tourism, like nature tourism, is susceptible to idealism. Notions of correct procedures for planning or notions of correct styles of tourism sometimes drive planning. We regularly remind our clients that "participatory planning" or "eco-tourism" are not goals in themselves. Using such labels does not excuse us from the need to judge our planning methods and the tourism activities we create against specific development or conservation goals.

Over the past decade, many conferences have set about defining „eco tourism" as if defining it will make a difference. Whichever of the various definitions you prefer, the term ecotourism has been widely adopted and it is useful. But, as tourism planners, we do not see ecotourism as something to pursue for its own sake. At best, it may be an important element in a country's tourism product mix. It should not be planned for in isolation.

Incidentally, if a label is necessary, we like the term "quality tourism" as used in Nepal. And what is "quality tourism"? In our definition it is tourism which best serves to achieve local goals. It is tourism that a community has chosen, and planned for, rather than just put up with when it arrives. This once again reinforces the notion that the starting point for tourism planning should be a clear definition of goals.

Principle 2: Take a wide planning perspective

The second principle is that a wide perspective is necessary in order to plan successful tourism. Put simply, you cannot plan tourism solely at village level. If tourists cannot reach the village, tourism will not succeed, therefore the national transport system needs to be part of village planning. If nobody comes to the country wanting village tourism, tourism will not succeed, therefore national level marketing strategies may need to be part of village tourism planning.

Tourism is made up of many parts, all of which need to be planned together, and planned at different scales all at once. At least in tourism, the notion of large scale "masterplans" is not the antithesis of appropriate scale village planning, but rather a necessary tool for it. An integrated, overall picture of tourism at a large scale is important for even the smallest of projects.

Indeed, the essence of tourism development planning could be said to be identifying the patterns of tourism of an area, now and in future, and then seeking ways to influence those patterns to achieve your desired goals.

Ideally tourism planning should start at a national, or even regional level. Having a clear, national level development concept and a framework of development strategies makes all tourism planning easier. It also makes government decision-making easier and it promotes cohesion within the industry, particularly cohesion between product developers and tourism promoters.

In this aspect of tourism, Nepal is not a leader. Although tourism masterplans for some individual mountain areas have been prepared in the past, there are few active national level development plans. HMG is acting to create the mechanism for such broad scale planning with the recent passing of an Act to establish a Nepal Tourism Board. One of the priorities of the new Board might be to build on the existing national tourism policy and the old national marketing plan and to develop some new, broad strategic plans, including one for mountain tourism.

The Government of the Tibet Autonomous Region, also with help from UNDP, is currently engaged in a tourism master planning exercise for Qomolangma Nature Preserve (QNP) which runs along the Tibet side of Nepal's northern border from Langtang National Park through to Makalu Barun National Park and Conservation Area. QNP wishes to develop tourism to address the Nature Preserve's twin goals of conservation and poverty alleviation. Their first step has been to initiate an overall tourism masterplan as a broad framework within which individual tourism development projects can be set. This is an excellent example of taking a wide planning perspective first, before getting down to detail.

Principle 3: Assess resources with markets in mind

Our third principle is that tourism resources need to be assessed with tourism markets in mind. This again sounds obvious, but it is probably the most common source of failure of tourism businesses. Tourism business mistakes regularly result from mismatches between products and the market demand. And after all, before tourism can benefit anyone, first it must be commercially successful.

In our experience, good planning solutions often come from a systematic attempt to look at tourism resources through the eyes of different markets. A recent mountain tourism example was in Sabah, Malaysia. Mount Kinabalu in Sabah is the highest mountain in Southeast Asia, outside the Himalayas. Working on a tourism masterplan there, we had to address the fact that the summit trail of Mount Kinabalu is suffering crowding problems. The technique of looking through the eyes of different markets led the planning team to realise that the market was broadly divided into two segments, one which was achievement oriented and whose primary aim was to climb to the top, and another which wanted a mountain nature walk. The planning solution was to create a separate new walking trail, catering specifically for the second segment, which does not go to the summit.

The practical application of this principle can be straightforward. Before assessing the tourism potential of an area, talk to as many tourism operators as you can and ask them to describe the tourists they cater for. Make a list of say, five or six tourist market segments likely to visit the general area. Try to describe each segment in as much detail as possible. Try also to estimate the relative size of each of these segments and find out which are growing and which are decreasing. Then make up a checklist and whenever you are making an assessment of tourism potential, assess the potential for each segment individually.

This is a useful discipline to help the members of planning team break out of the habit of judging resources with their own values only. The preliminary field assessments for the Qomolangma Nature Preserve Tourism Masterplan, mentioned above, used this approach.

Principle 4: Prepare local tourism development plans

Our fourth principle is that simple, local area development plans can be very effective. There are some good examples of tourism plans in the mountains of Nepal and many examples of good participatory approaches to strategic decision-making, but the actual drawing up of plans to guide the physical development of tourism is generally not a strength. This is an area where there is a lot of potential for innovative work in Nepal.

From our experience in other countries, we have come to appreciate how effective simple diagram plans can be. We use the term "tourism concept plans", but they are essentially just diagrams showing zones of development, linkages between the zones and as much information as possible on the guidelines and criteria for development. They are less rigid than a development design plan and more illustrative than just a list of rules. They set out, in as simple and as graphic a manner as possible, a desired development direction. At their most simple level these concept plans can look like the resource maps produced by a Participatory Rural Appraisal (PRA) exercise and indeed they might be arrived at in similar way.

Usually, it is not necessary to prepare tourism concept plans everywhere, but rather only in "key areas" where tourists will congregate or where fragile resources are involved. A tourism development strategy for a mountain national park, for example, might include concept plans for walking trails and for key tourist villages.

If developed with the maximum possible community participation, and in a manner which carefully integrates tourism with other development sectors, this type of local plan can be an important tool. They are particularly useful for explaining foreseeable potential negative impacts and for making explicit any carrying capacity limits.

Principle 5: Resource managers are needed on-site

The fifth principle is that all the careful planning in the world will not avoid problems occurring with tourism in fragile mountain environments. We do to let an opportunity go by without stressing it is vital that there be professional resource managers on-site, watching for problems and dealing with them before they get out of hand. This is a principle that Nepal is generally well aware of.

One way or another, there need to be people on the ground who know about the resources that mountain tourism relies on, understand the principles of natural resource management and understand how the tourism industry works. Such people may be in national park management agencies, in tourism departments, in key local authority positions, or in local NGOs, wherever the opportunities exist to influence resource use and development. It is sometimes unfashionable to advocate this, but we believe governments need to lead in this area, and lead strongly.

Nepal has a proud history in national park and conservation area management. New Zealanders are proud of the small part we have played in this history. There are probably more people in Nepal's Department of National Parks and Wildlife Conservation who know how to deal with tourism in protected areas than in most other countries of Asia. The challenge is to build systems where this expertise can be brought to bear in the field to good effect.

Principle 6: Partnerships are the key to management

The sixth principle is a matter of organisational strategy. Central governments should not attempt to shoulder all the load of planning and management of tourism. On the other hand, we believe the right answer is not to simply turn tourism resources over to the private sector to develop as they see fit. Nor is the answer to vest control in local government or NGOs, nor is there any other simple organisational solution.

Around the world now, leading tourism countries are managing tourism through partnerships. In particular, these are partnerships between the public sector and private sectors and in many cases they involve local communities, NGOs and special interest groups. The common rationale for these partnerships is to break the cycle of everyone blaming someone else for the problems of tourism. There are organisations deliberately created to take responsibility for doing something about the problems.

As mentioned before, HMG is in the process of creating a new Nepal Tourism Board which will be such a partnership of the public and private sectors at the national level. This has great potential for setting Nepal on a path of seeking out what "quality tourism" means for Nepal.

Partnerships for quality tourism can exist at other levels as well. Around the world there are now many examples of ad hoc bodies, in the form of boards or committees, created especially for the purpose of taking responsibility for managing and controlling an aspect of tourism. Other mechanisms for achieving partnerships including national park concession systems or, in some countries, consortiums of public sector organisations and private operators to take responsibility for key development zones.

One of the best examples of such a partnership at a local level is the Sagarmatha Pollution Control Committee (SPCC). Set up with guidance from the World Wildlife Fund (WWF), the SPCC combined the authority of national park managers, village development committees, local NGOs and and Tengboche Monastery to create a "body to take responsibility" for tourism problems. HMG's recognition of SPCC, as ACAP is recognised in Mustang, as a vehicle for returning government revenues from tourism back to local areas is an excellent model by world standards. This ranks only with Nepal's brave steps to use pricing as a mechanism to control tourist numbers in remote mountain areas as another example of an aspect of mountain tourism in which Nepal is an international leader.

Principle 7: Regional co-operation

The seventh principle extends the idea of collective sharing of responsibility a step further into the notion of regional partnerships. I mentioned above that tourism master planning is happening on the Tibet side of Nepal's northern border. This raises the prospect of trans boundary tourism planning.

For the last year, the six countries of the Mekong Region have been working together on various projects including: a package of joint destination marketing activities; a regional tourism forum to get industry people talking to each other; a training programme for resource managers; joint training courses in basic tourism skills; management plans for shared resources (in this case the Mekong itself); and recently, models for village tourism. This regional initiative has now developed considerable momentum.

While regional co-operation in tourism between the countries of South Asia has a chequered history, we believe there is good potential for co-operation between Nepal and Tibet based on the mountain tourism. Nepal tourism's private sector is already heavily involved in Tibet and a lot of joint marketing takes place. NGOs are active both sides of the border. Recently, there was an exchange of visits by officials in tourism and conservation from both countries. Co-operation between Nepal and Tibet in planning and managing mountain tourism brings the prospect of creating a whole which is greater than the sum of the parts.

Conclusion

I am sure there are many other, equally worthy principles that I have missed. I would like to now conclude this paper with the suggestion that perhaps this conference can take a lead in recognising that, in some aspects at least, Nepal is a leader in techniques for developing mountain tourism. We might also recognise the damage that a constant barrage of negative news about Nepal's mountain tourism has done to Nepal's market image abroad. Now is a good time to start emphasising the positive and highlighting good examples of where tourism is working to achieve development and conservation goals.

We might help to break the cycle of needing to stress the negative in order to impress donors and justify projects. From a donor's perspective, seeking out good examples has a practical development application because stories of success create the desire to copy them. This is now demonstrated in the mountains of Nepal by the relative popularity of lodge owner training programmes. Let us make it fashionable in development circles to put emphasis on seeking out and replicating the success stories of Nepal's mountain tourism.

Renton de Alwis

Globalisation of Ecotourism

Some Marketing Concepts

The global scenario for tourism

Travel and tourism today is the world's largest industry. According to the figures of the World Tourism Organisation (WTO) and the World Travel and Tourism Council (WTTC), in 1996, there were more than 560 million global travellers generating a total global income of over 3.6 trillion US dollars. There were 255 million employed in our industry, which is 1 in every 9 of the world's total workforce. Our industry globally generated a consumption value of US$ 2.1 trillion, accounting for a 10.7% share of the total. The industry also contributed to 10.4% of the world's total tax revenues, amounting to US$ 766 billion. Global travel industry growth has been averaging 3-4 % during the last decade. In Asia, where its economies are growing at rapid speeds, travel growth has averaged 6-8% and is continuing to grow with much vigour.

Tourism offers immense opportunities to all touched by it. It is no longer, an elitist activity as perceived by many. It is an activity which is a basic human right and its benefits extend to those that run tourism enterprises as well as those who live in the remotest parts of the world where tourists visit. Tourism today is not a mere human pursuit fulfilling our desire to see other cultures and places. It is an organised business movement through which the quality of lives of many millions improve. It generates dollars with which conservation programmes are undertaken and community development projects are initiated.

Tourism is also a movement that can unify people and better human understanding. When we enter a phase of an information technology led, ideas and creativity dominated civilisation, tourism acts as a lever to buffer the shocks, the vast changes unfolding before us so fast. In a world that is moving towards globalising communications, business and commerce, tourism works towards keeping the humanisation of this new civilisation alive.

Why call tourism names ?

With the growth of the economic and socio-political importance of tourism, the activity has been given many tags. Apart from those involved directly in the business of tourism i.e. providing products and services to the visitors, most other fringe industries have sprung up to take advantage of the new wealth that is created though the industry. The rapid growth of the business of concern for the environment has also touched the tourism industry in many ways. Ecotourism and several other similar branding tags have today become buzz terms.

According to Robertson Collins, a tourism veteran, conservationist and former Chairman of USICOMOS, there is danger in calling tourism 'names'. Referring to the example of 'Ecotourism' he stated " Most of those who tag tourism 'ecotourism', after a while begin to believe that all they do is ecologically and people friendly. The customer who buys into an ecoto-urism labelled product also satisfies his or her conscience that they are not causing any damage to nature or to the people they visit. While the intent is noble, this causes complacency and can create negative impacts. On the other hand, it makes others who are external to the 'ecotourism' labelled business think that they need not be eco-friendly".

"In my mind, all tourism should be eco friendly, all tourism should be sustainable, all tourism should benefit the people whose lives it touches. All tourism should be good."

"If we must call tourism a name to illustrate what it should be, let us call it 'Good Tourism'," he states.

'Ecotourism' today, is big business. Products with an eco label are able to command higher prices in the market place. Similarly, there is also substantial funding for 'ecotourism' proponents by donors and well meaning agencies, making it a lucrative consultancy based business as well. This situation has unfortunately led to the creation of the popular perception that 'tourism is bad' and 'ecotourism is good'. It also supports a popularised perception that 'tourism is a business activity for making money' while 'ecotourism is a noble activity and is not all about money'.

Gloablisation of ecotourism and its merits

The globalisation of ecotourism was the result of the twinning of two major forces: The rapid growth of global tourism and its revenue generating potential, and the new born awareness of the western world of the need to conserve the environment and minimise the threat of global warming. Accompanying these was also the decreasing importance of the phase of western colonialism in Asia and the rest of the developing world, and the increasing thrust towards self reliant social and economic growth of Asia. In a world where 30 percent of the world's population still consume 70 percent of its resources, the search-light was focused once again on the 'excesses' of the developing countries, while the overconsumption and waste of resources still continue in most of the developed world.

In spite of the backdrop of the development of this movement, 'ecotourism', in my mind, serves the purpose of sensitising communities to the need to conserve the resources they use and to looking at deriving greater benefits from tourism for themselves. I also believe that using it as a pure branding strategy alone for selling 'bad' tourism products at higher prices results in more damage than good.

According to the Ecotourism Society's definition of ecotourism (1993), it is "Responsible travel to natural areas which conserves the environment and improves the welfare of local people".

Market changes and 'ecotourism'

What is interesting about the interest in 'ecotourism' today is the fact that it is market driven. Although many still like to believe that it is a supply driven 'do gooder' movement, the reality is that the demand from the customer for an environment and people friendly tourism product is what gave the movement its marketing relevance. Today, the customer is willing to pay to take what he or she believes is an 'ecologically sensitive' tour. The success of several key tourism operators who switched to offering ecotourism labelled products in the eighties and the birth of several eco friendly upmarket accommodation facilities, proved that the customer demand was ripe for the movement. In today's tourism market place there are several important changes that have taken place. The most important among them is the enormity of the numbers that travel the world over. The new-found affluence in the developing world has added at least a few hundred million new visitors and has resulted in continuous growth as illustrated in the introduction to this paper. The other important change is the shift away from group travel to independent travel. In the 1970's and early 80's most travel by new entrants to tourism was in groups, where all saw the same and shared the same experience. This is fast changing with the new traveller who has become more independent and seeks customised tours to new destinations and more exotic places within destination countries. This change in travel demand has resulted in tourism's impact reaching beyond the resorts of earlier years to many natural and culturally exotic areas.

The tourist of today in general is also more discerning than before. Most tourists of today want to learn more about the places they visit and involve themselves with activities that allow them to better absorb the life styles of the people they meet. Tourism today is not a mere 'look see' activity. For most, it is also an intense learning experience.

The markets of today are more segmented than ever before. While our target markets of the past were mostly generating country oriented, today one could find markets for niche or segmented products across geographical boundaries. For example a group whose interest is ornithology can include several nationalities from several countries. This is true for diabetics, 'to be weds' or the pilgrimage travellers. Affinity groups are today easier to reach as market segments, also as a result of the information technology tools such as the internet and other networks.

The internet has become a strong marketing tool for most niche marketers. On the Internet's World Wide Web, representation for 'ecotourism' and adventure based activities is significantly higher than for 'other' tourism activities. Several Internet user surveys have revealed that tourism is one of the largest user accessed areas on the WWW. They also have revealed adventure based activities and 'ecotourism' to be much sought after areas.

This allows marketers of such products easier and cost effective access to markets and enables them to develop alliances and partnerships.

There is also the ability to share information and experiences of tourism operators today on the internet. This leads to improving and enhancing the quality of overall marketing functions. For example, the existence of many 'forums' on the internet for 'ecotourism' and related affinity groups has resulted in cross boundary and cross cultural sharing of experiences as never before. Research carried out on markets are available on the Net and searches for ecotourism operators and related subjects on its Search Engines bring tens of thousands of references to the fore.

Another sound development that has arisen as a result of the environment and community based tourism operations (ecotourism), is the realisation of the need to integrate the development of the product with the market. In the past, there were many organisations that carried out 'community development activities' in areas where tourism already existed or had potential, but did not relate the work to market demand. In most cases, emphasis was placed only on improving the quality of the product and on distributing benefits to the community at large. The long term sustainability of such efforts was not possible, as there was no effort to ensure that the demand for the enhanced products was expanded or created. It is today realised that there is an equally important function in ensuring that the product development is done to suit the needs of the customer and the market for the product and that all business starts with the customer and ends with the customer.

There is also the aspect of obtaining the right value for the products sold. In Nepal, although there are unique nature and culture based tourism products, the market positioning of the tours to Nepal is at the lower end. The reason for this is threefold.

1. Intense price-based competition as a result of too many operators chasing too few tourists
2. Lack of quality standards and
3. The vicious cycle of a low quality - low profit - no quality improvements/ declining quality - low profit trap.

This is illustrated in the fact that a trekking package that was offered at US$ 80 per day or above in the1980's, today can be had by a tourist for US$ 18 or less. Together with the concern for developing 'ecotourism', must also come the awareness for having the right yield from tourism for the destination and its operators.

Tourism and ecotourism are primarily business

We must not forget that tourism, whatever label it is given, is a business. A business must make profit deserving of its efforts and what's on offer. It is only then that we could raise the living standards of people, alleviate uncertainty in their lives and promote the conservation of resources they use. Conservation is after all 'the postponement of present use to the future'. No sane human being will postpone the use of resources to the future if he or she does not have a reasonable degree of certainty about what the future holds for him or her and the family.

Narendra Bajracharya, Yogendra Shakya

New Challenges and Perspectives for the Tourism Industry

Global Scenario

The World Tourism Organization in its 1996/97 report states that 255 million people are employed in the tourism-related industries, which is one in every nine people employed in the world, making it the world's number one industry and larger than the oil, automobile or weapons industries. Tourism also contributed US$ 653 billion to the international economy in the form of different tourism-related taxes. There is an annual growth of 4% in the world tourism market.

However, the picture is less rosy in the case of Asia. Despite its unique attractions, Asia had only 70 millions visitors in 1996/97. South Asian countries only have 5-6% tourism growth, whereas South East Asian and the Pacific Rim countries enjoy the bigger piece of pie with a growth rate of 10-11%. Although one fifth of the world's population lives in Asia, it has been able to attract only 0.5% of the world's travelers.

Nepalese Context

Nepal was an unknown tourism destination until the 1950s. Before then, Nepal was not even open for foreigners except for some Britishers who came from then British India with permission from the government to carry out scientific research, botanical surveys, etc. The royal visit of King George V in 1911 and the Prince of Wales in 1921 for their famous big game shoots in the Terai was considered as the benchmark in bringing foreigners into the country.

However, the influx of tourists began only after the popular revolution of 1951 which overthrew the then Rana rulers from power. In the early days, most of the tourists were attracted by the mighty Himalayas and the lure of mysticism, Tantrism, and cultural heritage such as temples and monuments. In the 1960s tourism in Nepal flourished only through the travelling fraternity of so-called hippies who put Nepal on the world tourism map, although it did not give the country a good image. In the 1970s with the beginning of the jet era in the country, backpackers and budget tourists started travelling to Nepal. As a result, trekking tourism began to flourish and cultural tourism was introduced, encouraged by the improvement in the infrastructure, with airports, roads, communication networks, etc. allowing tourism to grow in the country.

Tourism Master Plan

The first tourism master plan for Nepal was brought out only in 1972 and later reviewed in 1984 and 1990. The tourism master plan pointed the direction of tourism growth in the country with the decentralized pattern of development so that the effect of tourism could be felt even at grass root level and could be used to alleviate poverty. Due to the implementation of this planned approach, tourism activities were expanded and tourist arrivals grew steadily at a rate of about 8% annually. In the past two decades, tourism contributed almost 4% to the GDP of the Nepalese economy. The gross revenue is also increasing close to 12% on average: US$ 117 million in 1996.

Nevertheless, there is no reason to be optimistic about the way the growth is taking place in the tourism industry in Nepal. It has become one of the most competitive markets. It has to face tough competition not only within the region but also globally. New destinations, products, and concepts are being introduced with millions of dollars of investments all over the world to quench the appetite of the tourists; however, the results can only be viewed with mixed feelings.

Developments in hi-tech communication systems, changes in lifestyles and a greater experience in the tourist-generating countries have resulted in tourists being more choosy, calculating more keenly, and becoming more and more concerned about getting value for money. People save for a long time just to be able to travel to this part of the world. Young tourists seeking adventure tourism are growing fewer and fewer, as they are not economically in a position to visit distant destinations such as Nepal. A look at the present tourist pattern of arrivals listed by age groups shows that more than 60% of Nepal's tourists are over 30 years old. Today's tourism is financially based on middle age or "silver age" people. Nepal's image as an adventure destination is slowly fading away. Looking at the trend of the tourists and their tastes, Nepal must change its image and products to be able to sell itself in the competitive market. It must offer a new product based on environment-friendly sustainable tourism.

Nowadays travelers are relatively environmentally concerned. Not only do they feel responsible for the tourism activities of the sending country, but there is increasing awareness of tourism's effect on the host country's culture, heritage, socio-economic relationship and way of life. Nepal still has the image of a paradise "Shangri-la", however ill-informed that may be. Development activity itself has become a challenge which, if it cannot be maintained, will tarnish its image. Hence any form of environmental degradation activities such as vehicle emission, dust, smoke pollution, garbage and traffic mismanagement-management, will adversely affect its quality tourism products and have a negative impact on the tourism industry. If Nepal wants to remain in the tourism market, the present problems in this area need to be addressed with proper long-term planning.

In search of new image and tourism products, other countries such as Laos, Vietnam, Cambodia, Tibet/China have started offering themselves as adventure tourism destinations. Thus Nepal faces stiff competition in the Asian market. Even Thailand is trying to change its image from a night life to an adventure tourism destination. Nepal no longer enjoys the monopoly of Asian adventure holidays.

Entertainment and Events - New Trends in Tourism

Trends in tourism are changing. Although the first tourists to Nepal were Westerners, Nepal should no longer concentrate its entire effort on the western market alone, but must also look to its neighbouring countries. Despite their recent economic turmoil, Asian countries must still be considered as great potential tourism markets, as many Asians now travel abroad - but closer to home. Therefore, Nepal should also focus its promotional activities on Asia. Asian travellers may be adventurous too, but they would like to mix soft adventure with fun, since they mostly travel with their families or in groups. The new challenge is how to cater to this new market.

Another challenge that Nepal is facing in today's tourism industry is the changing attitude of its people. The political upheavals of 1990 along with open media and satellite television have changed the horizon of the people. They are no longer naive and isolated. They are more exposed to the international media. They have become more self-centred and demanding. The Nepalese, whether living either in the Kathmandu Valley or somewhere in the remote mountains, have started to demand their rights and benefits from tourism. Interested parties might create obstacles, call for strikes, and even collect local taxes. Everyone wants a piece of the tourism pie. Gone are the days when the smile of the innocent Nepalese people was available for free - today even street kids ask for money for posing for snapshots.

The image of Nepal as a "cheap destination" is another slap in the face for the tourism industry in Nepal. Old editions of travel and guide books which have not been updated give false impressions of the country.

In Search of Tourism Policy

Nepal should not be a cheap destination, nor, on the other hand should it be expensive either. At present, due to the policy of the Nepalese government, hotels, travel and trekking agencies are mushrooming without any vision or control. There is much more supply than demand. This has resulted in unwanted cut-throat competition. At present most of the tourism activities are concentrated within very limited geographical pockets. Even within Kathmandu, tourism activities are virtually confined within certain areas such as Thamel. There are about 600 registered hotels in Nepal, and perhaps the same number or more which are not registered. The registered hotels provide about 22,000 beds, which could accommodate more than a million tourists in the country. In 1996 there was a total of only 393,613 tourists to Nepal. 60% of the hotels in Nepal are based in Kathmandu and 70% of them are concentrated in the city core. Due to the excessive concentration of these hotels in some pocket areas, basic infrastructure such as roads, sewerage, and water have been over-used, causing many problems for tourists and residents alike.

Many problems of Kathmandu can be reduced if new areas are opened for tourism ventures. The government should give more incentives/tax breaks for the entrepreneurs who would like to venture their businesses in new areas. There is also an urgent need for careful city planning. Otherwise Kathmandu, the gateway to "Shangri-la", will rapidly lose its charm and attraction to the tourists - many of whom have begun to look for other similar destinations.

The people, the government and the tourism entrepreneurs have started to think about tourism's cost-benefit ratio: what a tourist spends in relation to what he consumes in terms of environmental impact, socio-cultural impact, and effect on the local economy. If the earning per tourist does not meet expectations, then all those concerned will start ignoring the tourism sector. Therefore the bottom line of the entire tourism scenario in Nepal should be quality tourism as opposed to budget tourism. Nepal must look for quality and not quantity at the cost of its environment.

III

The Uphill Climb: Concrete Steps

Siddhartha B. Bajracharya

Tourism Development and Management in the Annapurna Area

The Annapurna region is the most popular trekking destination in Nepal, attracting about 60% of the total number of trekkers visiting the country. It is visited by over 48,000 foreign trekkers (excluding Indians) every year. This region is endowed with and enriched by varied natural and cultural attractions. The unique mix of ecosystems includes sub-tropical low land oak, rhododendron and bamboo forests; high alpine meadows; and desert plateaus. Within a distance of 120 kms, the altitude varies from less than 1,000 m to 8,091 m in height, which is the height of Mt. Annapurna I, the 10th highest peak in the world. This sharp altitudinal gradient has made this region one the most fragile, spectacular and interesting places in the world. It harbours several unique flora and fauna in its natural habitat. There are around 474 species of birds, 101 species of mammals and 1,226 species of plants (BCDP report, ACAP 1993). This region also serves as an excellent habitat for rare and endangered mammals such as the snow-leopard (Panthera uncia), musk deer (Moschus moschiferus), blue sheep (Pseudois nayaur), red panda (Ailurus fulgens) besides being home to five of the six pheasants found in Nepal (World Pheasant Association, 1986). The Mustang and Manang areas of Annapurna region are very rich in Gompas, chortens and temples. Foreigners are attracted by colorful religious life centered around the Gompas (monasteries) of these areas.

Trekkers in the Annapurna Area

Year	Trekker's Number	Changes in %
1989	36,594	
1990	35,811	-2.2
1991	38,513	+7.5
1992	44,453	+13.4
1993	43,140	-3.0
1994	45,725	+5.7
1995	47,582	+3.9
1996	49,788	+4.4

Tourism in this area was induced by the foreign tourists more than two decades ago. The local people at that time were neither prepared nor had the basic facilities to cater to the flow of tourists. The 120,000 people of various ethnic and religious backgrounds living in this area survive on subsistence agriculture, and are to a great extent dependent on the management of the natural environment. The dependency relationship is very critical to the local population here, who live in marginal highlands where the soil is of poor quality, as terracing of the steep slopes has led to top soil erosion. There is the added fact that altitude reduces the resiliency of the ecosystems. Therefore, the environmental damage done here is often irreversible.

Besides the fragility of the mountain environment of the Annapurna region, there are other factors like poverty, a high illiteracy rate, poor health and sanitation conditions, high energy requirements, population growth, overgrazing of animals etc. which are a great threat to this region. In addition, the increase of trekking tourism in the last two decades has further disturbed the delicate ecological balance of the area. The tourists' needs are much greater than the local standards. It was estimated that each tourist brings along on an average at least one support staff as a porter, guide or kitchen staff. Thus, the area receives 90,000 outsiders, almost equalling the local residents in number. About 60% of the tourists come during the four months of March – April and October – November. Their visits are mainly concentrated on a few places. Thus, due to the concentration of the tourists by seasons and at certain localities, popular destinations suffer heavy damage, losing vast tracts of forests as well as littering some of the most beautiful places. Furthermore, the sudden influx of trekking tourism, which in most cases depends upon the same natural resources as do the local people, generates a constant conflict between the two over the use of the resources. In the ACAP region there are around 700 lodges which have signboards, not including farm-house guest rooms which have great potential to absorb more tourists.

In view of these multifaceted problems, it became highly pertinent to view these issues holistically, addressing the numerous contributing factors in turn. It was realized from the inception of the project that unless the local people were brought into the mainstream of conservation, the measures taken to conserve the natural and cultural heritage of the region would not be successful. It was imperative to design an integrated management strategy which aims at incorporating tourism management, resource conservation and community development, to benefit both the local community and international visitors. In the activities thereby undertaken, the people's participation was crucial. This was an innovative and bold approach tried for the first time in Nepal's protected area management systems. The concept emphasized the integration of conservation and development in a holistic manner, with flexibility in its program implementation.

Annapurna Conservation Area Project

By the early 1980's, both national and international development planners and conservationists had realized that without proper manage-ment measures and monitoring systems in the area, tourism in the Annapurna region would not become sustainable in the long run. The adverse effects of tourism, together with the environmental and development issues in the Annapurna region had started to draw national and international attention. Policy makers and development planners were pressurized to find a management scheme which could address these issues without depriving the local community of the development and economic opportunities brought in by tourism. His Majesty King Birendra of Nepal issued a directive in 1985 to investigate the possibility of giving a protected status to the Annapurna region. The directive clearly stated the necessity for the preparation of a management plan that would help to strike a balance between the basic needs of the local inhabitants, tourism development, and nature conservation. This Royal directive was issued to Nepal's leading environmental organization the King Mahendra Trust for Nature Conservation (KMTNC). The Trust thereby launched the Annapurna Conservation Area Project (ACAP) in 1986. The ACAP covers 7,629 sq. km of the area, forming the largest protected area in Nepal which was officially gazetted in July 1992. The Conservation Area Management Regulation was formally legalized by the Government and promulgated in the Nepal Gazette on December 1996 which enables the project to conserve natural resources for sustainable development through active participation of local communities.

ACAP's Principles

The ACAP was the first initiative in Nepal's protected area management where the people's role in conservation was recognized as that of partners and the stewards of natural resources. To achieve this, the project has adopted three guiding principles:

People's Participation

The project considers the local people as the main beneficiaries, and it believes in involving the local people from the inception in the planning, designing, decision making and implementation of the programs to their future management. The local people are empowered to take responsibilities to manage the area through local institutions.

Sustainability

For the sustainability of the Project, His Majesty's Government of Nepal for the first time allowed ACAP to collect the user's fee levied on all the visitors going to the Annapurna region which has recently been raised from Rs. 650 to 1,000 per trekker per visit. The entry fee is directly being used to create an endowment fund for conservation activities in the future. At present, around sixty percent of the total income from the entry fee is also being directly utilized in the conservation activities in the region. Sustainability also refers to the availability of trained personnel in and from the region, utilizing both formal and informal expertise. Both of these aspects are incorporated in any community development and conservation programs implemented by ACAP through the local people.

The role of a facilitator

ACAP considers itself as lami (matchmaker), in other words the facilitator who brings outside resources to meet the needs of the local people. The project acts as a catalyst to motivate, mobilize, and encourage the local people to take action. Thus ACAP builds closer working relationships with various line agencies to match their experiences, expertise and resources with the local needs.

Project Activities

The programs of ACAP are operated according to these principles. These programs can be enumerated as:

Natural Resources Conservation

Deals with the sustainable use and management of the natural resources, particularly the forests. It focuses on reforestation, management of the existing forest resources, setting up forest nurseries and the introduction of appropriate alternative energy mechanisms such as micro-hydro electricity, solar-water heaters and improved cooking stoves. For the conservation and the protection of the overall natural resources, local level Conservation Area Management Committees (CAMC) are constituted.

Sustainable Rural Development

Focuses on improving the quality of life of the local people mainly through agricultural development, infrastructure improvement, health and sanitation improvement and women's development programs.

Conservation Education and Extension

ACAP believes that unless the users of the resources, both locals and outsiders, are made aware, sustainable development cannot be achieved. Thus, conservation education is considered the backbone for the success of the project. The program includes awareness generation through school activities and curriculum development, training, audio-visuals and extension programs, networking with line agencies, public campaigns, study tours and home visits.

Research and Training

The project places emphasis on developing the capacities and capabilities of the local people, so that they become efficient managers of the resources. The focus of the training programs is on leadership and management training along with skill development. As detailed study and evaluation of the programs along with the in-depth knowledge of the region's biodiversity is essential for sustainable management and planning, research and surveys form another important component.

Tourism Management Activities

The characteristic features of the Annapurna region are – inaccessibility, fragility, and high diversity. Overcoming these constraints without unduly impinging on the natural resources poses the foremost challenge to the development of this region through tourism. Attempts have been made to limit the negative impacts of tourism and increase the local economic benefit from tourism by directly involving the local community. And by such means, to conserve the natural environment which both attracts tourists and provides local people with livelihood, enabling them to benefit from tourism. Experience from the past few years has affirmed that if tourism is properly managed, it can bring great benefit to the local people. But involvement of the local community in conservation and tourism management is more difficult to implement in practice than just to preach. In order to involve the local community effectively and confidently in conservation and ecotourism development, they should be provided with: education, and training, responsibility for tourism management, and proper incentives.

In the Annapurna region, the influx of tourism is concentrated only in limited areas, which has produced an adverse effect both on the environment and in the local community. These problems have been addressed by developing an ecotourism management program together with the local communities. Ecotourism is a response that seeks to reduce the negative environmental and cultural impacts of mass or traditional tourism. The Adventure Travel Society defines it as "environmentally responsible travel to experience the natural area and culture of a region while promoting conservation and economically contributing to local communities." Thus the prime aim is to promote or manage tourism with minimum undesirable environmental and socio-cultural impacts, to cater to visitors of different interests, and at the same time to raise the living standards of the local people. To minimize the tourism pressure concentrated only in one particular region, new eco-friendly trekking routes are being explored, designed, developed and managed in the Annapurna area. The aim is to educate both the local community and foreign tourists on the environment, and to promote conservation strategies. On these routes, campsites are placed at appropriate distances rather than haphazardly, thereby controlling the number of trekkers in the area. Lodge development, trekking trail improvement, water supply, alternative energy sources, sanitation and solid waste management, and education for both the trekkers and the local population are among the other programs. Ultimately, the aim is to develop the area to become a model for sustainable tourism management in Nepal. The influx of tourism in the area provides opportunities of employment but the scheme must be based upon a framework designed to meet the spirit of ecotourism. Ecotourism as a strategy for promoting conservation and economic development of remote and inaccessible areas has been adopted ever since the establishment of the Annapurna Conservation Area Project in 1986.

To successfully manage and develop sustainable tourism, the following activities play an important role:

Lodge Management Committees

Management committees for lodges are formed by the local lodge owners for the management of tourism-related activities in the area. All the lodge owners of a particular area or location will be members of that committee. Among all the members they select a chairperson and a secretary to run their day to day activities. They organize regular meetings where various issues are discussed. They also develop policies regarding tourism. They are responsible for improving the conditions of the lodges, standardizing their rates and preparing the menus. They also implement the "kerosene only" policy in the areas where there is acute shortage of fuelwood. In co-ordination with the local community, different eco-friendly camping sites are being developed in the different appropriate regions. Basic facilities like drinking water, garbage disposal sites, toilets, and small kitchen and porter shelters are built in the camping sites.

Capacity Building through Training and Extension

The lodge owners, who are from the local community, are provided with training aimed at improving their lodges, the quality of food offered, menu-costing, garbage disposal, sanitation and hygiene. Short-term training is also provided to the youth groups to mobilize them in ecotourism development. Among these, ecologically sensitive guide training to the local youths, and basic English language training should be mentioned here. The program introduces fuel wood saving devices such as solar-water heaters, kerosene, and micro-hydro electricity. Besides, the local people living along the tourists trekking routes are made aware of the impacts of tourism through „tourism awareness camps". In these extension programs, various approaches like audio-visuals, street theaters, posters, mass meetings etc. are used. The project also launches village clean-up and toilet building campaigns by bringing together the local people, students from schools and women's groups.

In the Annapurna region, the majority of the economically active and permanent residents are women. But due to factors like illiteracy, lack of exposure to the outside world and traditional habits, these women have been hindered in fully participating in the tourism industry. ACAP, together with the assistance of the UNDP/ILO and His Majesty's Government of Nepal, has designed a training program specifically targeting women. This training program enables women to develop entrepreneurial skills and benefit from the tourism industry by actively participating in it .

Alternative Energy (Fuel)

To cope with growing pressure on the natural forest areas, the provision of alternative energy or fuel is required. New appropriate techniques to reduce fuel wood demand or to supplement wood as fuel have been devised. Practiced methods focus either on fuel wood saving devices or the provision of appropriate energy alternatives to fuel wood. In highly fragile areas, tourists have been forbidden to use fuel wood. This rule should also be applied to the porters to significantly reduce fuel wood use. Indigenous fast-growing tree species are being planted to increase the sustainable supply of fuel wood. The aim is to create a new balance whereby fuel wood is given an appropriate cost.

Kerosene is one of the practical alternatives to fuel wood for tourists and their support staffs. 15 kerosene depots have been established in various key ACAP areas for regular supply. All these depots are monitored by local Kerosene Depot Management Committees. But kerosene is not a viable long-term remedy because it is imported from other countries. Technological problems related to poor stove reliability and efficiency also occur.

Appropriate devices like back-boiler water heaters, solar water heaters, bio gas, improved cooking stoves etc. can replace traditional fuel wood stoves to reduce the use of fuel wood.

Micro-hydro electricity is the best alternative to fuel wood in the region. The profusion of water resources provides great hydro-electricity possibilities. Micro-hydro electricity has the advantage of being an environmentally sound, nationally produced, cost-efficient means of energy production. Four community-owned micro hydro plants have been established in the region. Three community-owned micro-hydro schemes are presently under construction. All these power plants generate sufficient power for cooking, heating and lighting purposes.

Transportation

The infrastructure is extremely limited in the area, and with it the transportation facilities. The nearest large town, Pokhara, is 5 – 7 hours walk from the Conservation Area boundary. There are airfields at Pokhara, Jomsom, and Humde, Manang. While the road construction is gradually facilitating access to the southern edge of the Conservation Area, virtually all the movement in and around the area takes place on footpaths. To facilitate the movement all round the year, ACAP has been helping local initiatives to either repair and maintain or construct footpaths and bridges.

Sanitation

During the early influx of tourism in the region, toilets and garbage disposal system were virtually non-existent. Local communities and lodge owners were encouraged to construct, maintain and utilize the latrines. Education and training on safe disposal of biodegradable and non-biodegradable garbage has been regularly conducted in the region. This has been supplemented by village clean-up campaigns participated in by students, local communities, village leaders, women's groups and even trekking tourists. The impact of these efforts can be seen largely today in these regions. However, the recent increase in the use of plastic wrappers and plastic bottles (especially mineral water bottles) is becoming a new threat to the area. The project is looking for a solution to these new threats.

Information and Awareness to the Visitors

Brochures, minimum impact codes, reports and information centers have been made available to both national and international visitors. Prior to their arrival and during the trek in the Annapurna region, these information services inform tourists about the sensitivity of the fragile environment, and about plans, strategies, and action programs. There are 15 tourist information centers located in the main entry areas. Signboards are being posted at various strategic points to facilitate the movement of the locals and outsiders. For additional information regarding the project, the Himalayas, culture etc., a resource library has been established in ACAP Headquarters in Pokhara.

Ecolodge

The number of foreign tourists visiting the region is increasing at an average annual rate of 4%. With this increase, the number of lodges is also increasing in the region. The minimization of the environmental impact of this development is very crucial for the region. Through various activities like tourism awareness camps, conservation extension etc., the lodge owners have been encouraged to establish more environment-friendly lodges. ACAP has also developed criteria for eco-lodges of the region. The criteria for an eco-lodge (experimental phase) is as follows:

- Use of alternative energy (electricity, solar energy, kerosene, gas etc.)
- Improved toilet and septic tank
- Rubbish pit for the disposal of garbage
- Cleanliness and hygienic standards in and around the lodge
- Use of boiled and filtered water or water purifying tablets
- Good drainage system
- First aid kit
- Active participation in conservation activities

Those fulfilling the above criteria will be given the seal "Eco-friendly lodge of Annapurna area."

Communication Service

All ACAP field stations are equipped with wireless systems, which assist in maintaining communication between all the stations in the ACAP region, as well as with the cities of Pokhara and Kathmandu. The project provides necessary help in the emergency rescue of trekkers who have met with accidents and illness by communicating with the agencies concerned. The project has also mediated with HMG's Telecommunication Department to install telephones in main trekking areas. Telephone services are now available in the key spots of the trekking route like Bisishahar, Manang area, Jomsom, Gorepani, Ghandruk etc.

Revenue Collection

His Majesty's Government of Nepal has authorized ACAP, under the auspices of the KMTNC, to collect the Conservation Area Entry Fee from all the visitors and use the revenue to protect the environment and provide basic needs of the local communities. The Entry Fee has recently been raised from Rs. 650 to 1000 (US $ 17.54) per tourist per entry. The major portion of the revenue has been utilized within the villages of the area for conservation and development activities.

Conclusion

The destruction of the balance of the local environment, particularly the forests, is often associated with mountain tourism. However, in the Annapurna region, though it receives about 60% of the trekking tourists coming to Nepal, this has not been the case. In fact, ACAP's integrated and holistic approach through people's participation has resulted in restoring the environment of the region. ACAP's new approach of developing ecotourism in the region is an important step forward in tourism management. The involvement of the local communities in ecotourism through education, training, responsibilities and incentives has proved to be crucial for management.

References

Bajracharya, S.B.: Annapurna Conservation Area Project – Overview of eight years experience. Paper presented at the conference on the occasion of the 10th anniversary of the King Mahendra Trust for Nature Conservation (KMTNC), 1995.

Biodiversity Conservation Data Project Team (BCDP) 1994. Annapurna Conservation Area, Biodiversity Conservation Data Project – Final report vol. I-III. KMTNC, Kathmandu,.

Gurung, C.P.: Annapurna Conservation Area Project Nepal. In Eber, Shirley (ed): Beyond the Green Horizon: Principles of sustainable tourism. A discussion paper commissioned from Tourism Concern by WWF UK, 1992, pp.37-39.

Gurung, C.P.: Linking Conservation to Community Development – Annapurna Conservation Area Project (ACAP) Approach to Protected Area Management. Paper presented at the Regional Seminar on Community Development and Conservation of Forest Biodiversity through Community Forestry, organized by RECOFTC, Bangkok, October 26th – 28th 1994.

Gurung, C.P.: Investment in Conservation – Future for the Sustainable Tourism, A Casestudy of the Upper Mustang Conservation and Development Project, ACAP, Nepal. Paper presented to the PATA 43rd annual conference held in Seoul, Korea, 17th – 21st April 1994.

Gurung, D.: 1994 – Impact and Implication of Tourism on Nepalese Women – A case study of the Annapurna conservation Area Project. A research report submitted to the ICIMOD.

KMTNC/ACAP: Ecotourism Development and Circuit Trekking Project. Progress Report July 15th 1993 to July 1994.

Sharma, P.: Notes on Tourism Carrying Capacity. Paper presented to the first review meeting of the Mountain Tourism for Local Community Development Project, August 1994.

Shrestha, T.B.: Mountain Tourism and Environment. A discussion paper presented to the first review meeting of the Mountain Tourism for Local Community Development Project, August 1994.

Shrestha, T. B. Siddhartha B., Bajracharya: Ecotourism in Manaslu Area. A paper presented during Sub-Regional Conference on Culture, Environment and Indigenous Knowledge held in Jomsom, Nepal 1997

Zac Goldsmith

"Ecotourism": Old Wine - New Bottles?

Tourism creates over-dependence and economic vulnerability. The implementation of an economic policy which sees ecological and societal stability as a resource to be packaged and sold for short term material gain, has led to the abandoning of traditionally more sustainable means of survival. The addition of the word 'Eco' to the word 'Tourism' has so far proven cosmetic. Tourism today is incompatible with life tomorrow. If as an industry it is to be made consistent with ecological and human principles, then we must examine it thoroughly, both the pros and cons, and must be prepared to re-think what may well be a fundamentally flawed process. This paper begins with a broad discussion of some of the cultural and environmental impacts of tourism in Ladakh and elsewhere, based on our experiences at the Ladakh Project, its umbrella organisation the International Society for Ecology and Culture (ISEC), and the Ladakh Ecological Development Group (LEDeG) which we helped to found in 1983. It goes on to discuss tourism as part of a policy which emphasises economic specialisation and within the context of the process of economic development, and ends with a description of what the Ladakh Project and LEDeG are doing, how, why, and with what effect—in the hope that they will in some way provide a replicable model for other regions to follow.

The Cultural Threat

Tourism is the world's largest industry[1]. It has grown almost exponentially over the past few decades, is supported by a $3 trillion infrastructure[2] and is continuing to expand at a 15-30% annual growth rate in so-called 'Ecotourism' alone[3]. Because there is virtually no place on earth as yet unvisited by tourists, we can assume (and I hope generally agree) that the impact has been enormous. In addition, the very fact that there is a need for a conference of this sort, suggests that this impact is one which has been largely negative. What we have to do, therefore, is to look very closely, and very broadly at the problems which arise from such an industry, and more importantly, to look for ways in which tourism can be changed.

If we look historically at any human culture, it is clear that no society can exist in static isolation. In Ladakh, for example, a place largely unvisited until recently by curious outsiders because of its harsh environment and inaccessible passes, the culture has by no means remained uninfluenced. As a place of pilgrimage, and as an important trading route, traditions have been altered, and the people have absorbed change at a human, manageable pace, and above all on their terms. Today, however, change - in the form of tourism and other economic pressures - is coming rapidly, threatening cultural and individual identities while creating dependence on a global economy beyond local control. It is vital that we look at the broad implications of such change, considering both the social and environmental impact.

Surrounded by Mexico, Guatemala and Honduras, Belize is one country among many which has experienced some of the problems of mass-tourism. Island after island off the coast has been consumed by what has become an almost cancer-like industry. Tourists have descended upon the islanders, have brought about an end to an agricultural way of life, have polluted and destroyed some of the last remaining live coral reefs, and have created the 'need' for the building of hotels and bars, in which some of the luckier locals now work. Others have quite naturally turned to drugs and crime. The place, having been rendered unattractive to outsiders, is simply abandoned by the surviving tourist businesses. What hope can there be for a once self-sufficient society after agricultural land has been polluted or developed; after the death of sensitive coral reefs, and consequently any hope for a revival of the coastal economy; after generations of acquired agricultural knowledge has been washed away in a matter of years; and after all hope of revival of the tourist industry has also been washed away? Very little.

The same is true of the islands of Bali, Phuket, Barbados, Hawaii, of places like Goa, Marbella and Chiang Mai etc.: the list goes on. In their search for the ultimate, 'virgin' lands, tourists are abandoning 'the beaten track'. First comes the adventurer, who generally respects the place and is keen to learn the language and traditions of the host country, and then, when it is 'discovered' within a wider circle, its name and photographs plastered in magazines and journals, posters and post cards, a cultural invasion takes place. Eventually the culture is considered 'spoiled' and is abandoned. As the Rethinking Tourism Project has explained:

"Tourism further threatens indigenous cultures as foreign values and ideologies are introduced. Sometimes traditional art and rituals become marketing commodities through tourism, losing their relevance to the local community. Local populations are displaced by tourism development with a resultant break in family and economic patterns. Indigenous peoples often leave traditional activities to work in hotels and restaurants, adversely affecting traditionally more sustainable economic sectors and increasing reliance upon fluctuating, foreign-based tourist economies. Tourism development encourages young people to migrate from their homes to 'service cities' close to resorts, tourist destinations, and other urban centres. Indigenous women are at a serious risk as they exchange traditional roles for service jobs, which in turn affect family and community relationships. They are also most likely to be recruited as prostitutes to serve the tourist market." [4]

Simply to add the word 'eco' to the word 'tourism' therefore is not enough. Hundreds of millions of pounds are being pumped into what is known as tourism development, and region after region is being restructured according to criteria set out by institutions like the World Bank, who between 1969 and '79 poured $450 million into tourism-related projects [5]. Whether 'eco' or not, the patterns of the process are virtually indistinguishable. In order, for example, to create Belize's Cockscomb national park, an area of indescribable beauty, the indigenous people were a few years ago forcibly removed and resettled onto marginal lands where they were expected to forget their age old culture and traditions and begin again from scratch. Their lives once tied intricately to the land, their economy shaped around those resources locally attainable, they are now in a position of having to cater to the tourists either through posing or selling trinkets. With a newly created need for money, they must now buy all those things which could once have been taken for granted. No one visiting them in their slums would be able to guess that they were once the proud and healthy inhabitants of Cockscomb national park. Indeed, under the Eco-tourism banner, according to Anita Pleumaron:

"In Namibia, bushmen either had to leave a 6,000 square kilometre nature reserve in Eastern Bushmanland or pose as a tourist attraction. In Botswana, the Basarwa people in the central Kalahari Desert were resettled to make way for an eco-tourist project, while in the Okavango delta, local people have been prevented from planting, hunting and gathering wood on land set aside for eco-tourists. In Rwanda, residents of land designated for "gorilla tourism" have been branded "poachers". In Uganda's Kibale Forest, forest dwellers have been threatened with eviction to make way for 'chimpanzee tourists'." [6]

A list of similar examples could continue indefinitely. Genuine cultural exchange can clearly not take place if the locals are led to view tourists as nothing more than sources of cash or trouble. It has been claimed that, for example, it costs $4.6million to run the national parks in Nepal, four fifths of which goes on "employing troops to keep villagers ... out of the parks".[7] The situation is worsening rapidly, so that the local response to tourism is fast becoming one of violence. Whether it be in Goa, where hatred towards tourists is intensifying, or Egypt where random shootings have driven out all but a few of the tourists, it is becoming clear that this form of cultural and environmental prostitution is leading to disaster. Even Belize, which until a few years ago was an almost totally crimeless society, is now considered to be a dangerous place to visit, with a thriving crack trade, and a machete murder epidemic.

Specialisation, monoculture and dependence

Tourism is not an isolated or separate economy - it is inextricably linked to other sectors of the economy, all of which are based on an underlying premise of comparative advantage. In the modern world, economic growth is synonymous with this principle - formulated by Adam Smith and David Ricardo in the early nineteenth century. Essentially, this has led to a blind dogma which assumes that societies will benefit by specialising in those areas in which they have a supposed 'comparative advantage'. For relatively 'untouched' cultures, that means tourism. The less developed, i.e. industrialised they are, the more attractive they become to the urbanised masses hungry for natural beauty, clean air, peace and cultural vibrancy, i.e. all that they have lost. For these cultures, tourism is nothing short of prostitution, as they 'Disnify' themselves for profit. This specialisation is not only soul-destroying, it is also responsible for pulling people away from a more diversified and self-reliant economy. The locals abandon their fields and their families for cash in the tourist industry - something which is reinforced by the fact that tourists tend to coincide their visits with the warm, i.e. agricultural season. In addition tourists abound in such large numbers that food and other basic needs have to be imported, thus undermining local agriculture further.

If, as an industry, tourism is to be made compatible with the maintenance of cultural and ecological balance, a massive public awareness campaign must be initiated, both in North and South. Outsiders need primarily to know something about the culture which they are visiting, and basic assumptions they may carry with them from the West must be questioned. Ladakh, for example, has suffered tremendously from the effects of well- meaning outsiders who had been led to believe that their own culture and way of living was superior. Save the Children on arrival set out to 'save' the children without really considering what it was the children needed to be saved from. They handed out large amounts of free wheat and rice, and consequently contributed directly to the beginnings of the collapse of Ladakhi agriculture. Others have set up voluntary educational organisations on the grounds that Ladakhis are somehow 'uneducated'. What this means is that Ladakhis have not yet been trained to be Westerners, with urban consumer values and tastes. Today, children as young as three or four are being taught the English alphabet with charts on which each letter represents a western industrial gadget. At a conference recently in Ladakh, one doctor from Karnataka, who has been living and working with indigenous tribal people in Bangalore, gave an example of a tribal boy who was able not only to name 350 local plants, but was also able to describe their medicinal qualities. Is he 'uneducated'?

According to conventional economic accounting, Ladakh is one of the poorest countries on earth. Virtually no money changes hands there. Per capita income is, or at least was until recently, virtually non-existent, and unemployment in the modern sense is extremely high. However, on closer inspection, Ladakh emerges as one of the more balanced of societies. According to a wide range of doctors, farmers, scientists, veterinarians and nutritionists who worked together in Ladakh for many years, the general health of the people as well as the cattle is substantially higher than would be found in the UK[8]. So much barley is grown each year that over half of the yield is used to make local beer [9]. There is no record of there ever having been food shortage in the region, and if researchers were to measure human life-expectancy from the age of two years until death, Ladakhis, it would appear, out-live average individuals in virtually every country in Europe. On top of all this - in a culture which respects the roles of each individual, whether it be a small girl feeding the Dzos, or an old man looking after his grandchildren, "unemployment" simply does not exist. Crime and violence, too, are almost non-existent.

One very dangerous assumption that seems to have invaded the minds of so many people is the idea that bringing societies into the global/monetary economy is by its nature a good thing. It is an assumption whose roots lie in the myth that all societies have been suffering from miserable poverty since the beginning of time, waiting for modernity to scrape them up and build for them a 'civilization'. However, the transformation of an environment-specific economy to one which is disconnected from the natural world is a process which has in many ways only led to mass impoverishment. While there are aspects of the West from which places like Ladakh can learn, the norm has been an either all or nothing situation. Region after region is consequently tumbling into the same web that has consumed the slum dwellers of Calcutta, Mexico city, Sao Paulo...

What is it that we are measuring when we describe an economy as being healthy? We know, for example, that the Exxon Valdez oil spill in the US spurred a significant rise in America's GDP, that the Kobe earthquake disaster in Japan also boosted the Japanese economy. Clearly these events were not desirable, and yet our economic indicators measured them as positive economic factors. The path we are currently taking is quite clearly unsustainable. Already according to a 1996 worldwatch report ("Climate of Hope: New Strategies for Stabilising the World's Atmosphere") there are 80 countries suffering from chronic water shortages[10]. In England, where the average person born today can expect to watch television for 11 solid years before dying[11], cases of mental illness in children under the age of 10 has doubled in the past 5 years[12]. And yet, while infectious disease deaths are rising fast worldwide, while unemployment and the gap between rich and poor are also increasing within (and between) countries worldwide, the 500 corporations that control 70% of world trade currently employ only 0.05 % of the world's people[13]. These are global trends, and represent barely a fraction of the problems which actually exist.

The exportation of the unsustainable Western system to other cultures is called "development". No matter where it is happening, it involves the restructuring of cultures and economies until they are almost indistinguishable from each other. It should not be described as an 'American' system, or a 'European' system; only as something abstract in front of which notions of culture or family are merely obstacles. It is a model which is incompatible with the way things are in traditional societies like, for example, Ladakh. When a country embraces this economic model, people lose the ability to survive in their own environment without external, artificial life support systems. The inhabitants of Ladakh's capital, Leh, for example, are no longer able to grow food at 14,000 feet. The knowledge of these locally adapted skills has been educated out of the young so that now their skills are limited to services in the global economy. According to Anita Pleumaron: "The development of 'underdeveloped areas' required more than capital input and technology transfer. Cultures too had to be reconciled with economic competition and integration. Tourism provided a means to achieve both. Dispatching large numbers of people from the

North to the South was also seen as a way of helping instill modern values in traditional societies."[14]

Seeing tourists with large amounts of money and free time leads Ladakhis to see the West as a sort of paradise, in which work is unnecessary and money is endless. Yet while it is true that many Westerners do earn perhaps twenty times more money than many Ladakhis, there is no need in Ladakh to buy most things. Their every basic need from water to food, from family to housing, is available locally. Money need not pass hands.

Tourist attitudes, however, are changing. People visit places like Ladakh out of genuine interest and respect. There they will witness a little of what they themselves lack. The danger, however, has shifted more towards the centrally controlled media: television, radio, newspapers etc. Tourists now, through lack of understanding, are reinforcing rather than shaping Ladakhi attitudes towards the West. Indeed, the media, and to a very great extent schools, have collectively painted a picture of the Western world which is based on fantasy. It is a world which does not exist. What is happening, therefore, is that artificial, false images are causing Ladakhis, and people the world over, to see themselves as inferior, as backward. Even in the US, while more and more people are dropping out of society altogether, where unemployment is reaching record heights, and while suicide is become a major problem, these images are necessary to propagate the myth that success for anyone is just around the corner.

Sonam Wangchuk, director of the Students Educational and Cultural Movement of Ladakh has pointed out:

"Once a people's self-confidence and pride is destroyed, then you don't need an external enemy (like China in Tibet) to destroy other aspects of culture like language, dress, and social values. The people who feel inferior work hard to destroy these things themselves."[15]

So, the situation has reached a stage at which even if tourism as an industry were to collapse, these powerful images, generated from the global economic system, would continue to consume all that has allowed Ladakh to become what it has become. Tourists therefore now have a responsibility which, if their impact is to be made positive, they must fulfil.

Helena Norberg-Hodge founded the Ladakh Project in 1978, bringing counter-development'—that is information about the full social and environmental costs of economic growth in the Western world. Ladakhis, like so many other people, are being pushed to adopt a model about which they know very little. Their knowledge of the Western economic model is limited and the only sources of information they have access to are quite clearly one-sided. In their rush to achieve what they believe other industrialised countries have achieved, they have been led to ignore all possible consequences. People are having to discover these negative side-effects as they take grip on the region. Much of the work for this organisation therefore concerns public education, with the goal being to put people in a position from which they will, as a society, be able to make these fundamental decisions in the full knowledge of what it is they are choosing.

The Ladakh Project

In 1983, the Ladakh Project helped to found the Ladakh Ecological Development Group (LEDeG), an indigenous organisation, which today has over 160 full-time employees working in over 100 villages. The group has been introducing technologies appropriate to the ecology, culture and economy of Ladakh, for example solar power, ram pumps, small hydro installations, solar cookers and trombe walls which are both easily maintainable and locally available in terms of most of the resources needed to put them together. The aim is to make accessible to people the aspects of modernity which they now demand, without forcing them to sacrifice their economic independence. They need not reshape their lifestyles around technologies which must be brought in from hundreds of miles away at great cost, or around vast hydroelectric constructions over which they will never have any control. Also as a means of avoiding, or at least slowing down urban migration while city life is still seen as vastly superior, the Ecology center has initiated a handicrafts programmes. Ladakhis are able to sell to tourists, among other things, clothes made during the eight least active months of the year, the idea being to reduce the newly created 'need' to leave the land in search of largely non-existent jobs in the city.

In preparation for the long term, however, public awareness campaigns on as large a scale as possible are the priority. Recently, we helped to build what has become an alliance of over 2000 rural Ladakhi women. Through village meetings, festivals and radio, they have already become a respected and significant factor in the public education process. Working closely with them is the Amchi association, made up of 120 traditional doctors, all of whom are involved in rethinking the development process which is responsible for introducing many modern illnesses and consequently the need for modern medicine. Their aim is to restore the conditions in which their generations of accumulated medicinal knowledge can survive and prosper. Ladakh has also won the right to a Hill council which has the final say on most important decisions affecting Ladakh. Three of their four directors are former directors of LEDeG. It has in fact been described as the world's only genuinely green government, and it has made clear its intention to save and restore traditional agriculture, which it has described as the backbone of Ladakhi society.

Common to all the leaders of these movements is first hand experience of the West. Because of the difficulties in contradicting the powerful and fantastical images mentioned above, the Ladakh project set up a fund with which we could give leaders the opportunity to experience the Western way for themselves. We organised for them to be taken to Europe. They were introduced to elderly residents of exclusive old people's homes, where people can be described as waiting to die, their lives void of meaning and responsibility, their families dispersed, their chairs positioned in front of their only source of company: the TV. They toured the slums and spoke with the homeless. 'Reality tours' also included visits to other NGOs, in order for Ladakhis to understand that we in the West have experienced for some time the model which they are taking on, and we are in increasing numbers trying to change it. A few years ago, The Ladakh Project produced a comic book, "A Journey To New York", in which a young Ladakhi boy is given a ticket to the US only to have his overly glamorous images of modern urban life dismantled. Those who return from the West almost always do so in the belief that Ladakh must not slide down the same path, that their own 'backward' region will one day serve to inspire and lead others towards a sustainable future.

The Ladakh Project, besides providing support for many of its offshoot organisations has devoted itself largely to educating tourists. On a daily basis throughout the tourist season, roughly 60-70 tourists visit the Ecology center to watch our video, "Ancient Futures, Learning From Ladakh". Some of the problems of conventional development, and others experienced within the industrialised West, in contrast with a beautiful picture of traditional life, serve to de-romanticise modern industrial society. The video, and Helena Norberg-Hodge's book on which it is based, have been translated into over 29 languages, including Navajo Indian, Portuguese, Czechoslovakian, and more recently Korean. The tourist response to "Ancient Futures" has been tremendous, and it is always followed by a lively discussion on some of the broader issues raised within the video. Besides learning from Ladakh the principles of small scale and sustainable economics, we also explore ways in which tourists could help reverse, rather than contribute to the destruction of host communities. Recently, we have organised a 'Farm Project', which is being initiated in collaboration with the Women's Alliance. The aim is to give Western volunteers the opportunity to work on a Ladakhi farm for a month or more during the agricultural season. The volunteers have the rare opportunity to experience first-hand a human-scale culture in which the sense of community is still strong and the connection to the land is still deep. The most important benefit for the Ladakhis could be seen in the faces of children beaming with pride in their own local knowledge when Westerners asked for help in milking a cow or damming an irrigation channel. Indeed, the very fact that Westerners are prepared to work for a year in order to be able to do what the locals have been led to see as the lowest possible occupation, is an effective means of raising the status of farming - and rural life in general - especially among the young.

The problems faced by Ladakhis, however, are deep and far-reaching. No single step will bring about total solution. What is needed is a change in direction at all levels of society. Our alternative technology programmes and the handicrafts projects were designed as a means of slowing down rash urban migration, by giving people access to desired and useful technologies, giving them the ability to raise cash for their families - without being forced to drastically compromise their way of life. The Hill Council, too, has been instrumental in trying to slow down the rate of uncontrolled change in Ladakhi culture. One plan, for example, is for the school holidays (which today are given during the coldest months of the year) to coincide with the growing and harvesting seasons, thus bringing about an end to what has amounted to generation segregation. Combined, they have made quite a difference, but these steps can only slow down the process of breakdown, and unless supplemented with a general educational, counter-development scheme, they would prove useless. Their value lies more in buying time to allow for a change in attitude, before people are sucked off the land and into the city, before their vast reservoir of agricultural knowledge is lost forever. This was the reason for the initiation of perhaps the most important side of our work. The hugely effective 'Reality Tour' project, the enormously popular and now influential Women's Alliance of Ladakh, and more recently the Farm Project, have helped bring about a greater understanding, but due to the nature of the problem, and due to the awesome power of those who seek consciously or unconsciously to mislead Ladakh, this has been our most difficult task.

The Farm Project has had its problems, of course, ranging from language difficulties to altitude sickness, which can be severe, and because of the inferiority which many Ladakhis feel towards tourists, many were embarrassed to ask for anything more than superficial help on the farm. Other problems existed for Westerners staying with families which had already been heavily influenced by modernity. Some ended up living in the homes of alcoholics, for example. One Israeli woman found it difficult to adapt to the idea that all the females of the house should visit the toilet together, and even harder that they should share beds in a relatively roomy house. The effect of the programme, however, was enormously beneficial, and the Women's Alliance will push for an expansion of the project.

More difficult, but at the same time successful, has been the education of tourists, whose primary role and responsibilities are arguably the most important. It is they alone who have deep expertise in the ways of the West, but because, like almost all Westerners, they have been imbued with the idea that there is only one path to prosperity, the Western way, they arrive blind to the possibility that it is perhaps Ladakh to whom we would do well to turn, and unaware that the poverty about which they have heard so much was an idea born of modern economic theory which has failed to develop any means of measuring the health of a society which has not traditionally depended on cash. Of the 60-70 foreigners visiting the Ecology Centre daily, a high proportion are sufficiently enlightened to join the struggle for counter-development.

Much of the recent debate around tourism as an industry has revolved around the idea of facilitating a guest-host relationship - one which is less imposing and more balanced. Before, however, this can be achieved, we have to acknowledge a few facts. Firstly, as Sonam Wangchuk has pointed out in reference to Ladakh, "20,000 demanding tourists are unleashed every year upon a small town that is meant to support only a few thousand self-sufficient farmers and some tradespeople."[16] It is hard, if not impossible, to remain 'guest-like' when you out-number your host by a factor of roughly ten to one. And secondly, what this means is that the self-sufficient local economy is forced to undergo a massive and dramatic shift to one which is hooked to and dependent on the outside, and which is actually taken over by and becomes essentially a tourism-based economy. Solutions to these problems must therefore include a general rethinking of economic development, or economic specialisation. Discussions should focus on economic diversification as a means of reducing vulnerability. This would also include the partial closing of one's national or regional doors on foreigners as has been done in Bhutan; not a very fashionable decision to take, but one which necessarily places the interests of community and society before short-term and cost-laden profits. Until there is a readiness to see tourism in its current state for what it is - as an influence of widespread destruction - and until there is a willingness to cease adapting to or accommodating societal disease, any talk about sustainable tourism as a whole will remain largely inconsequential.

Westerners, however, can put their genuine expertise about the West to good use. Our experience in and knowledge about the West must be shared if southerners are to be given any chance at all of honestly choosing their own destiny. The new and fashionable slogan being put out time and time again in the annual reports and advertisements of virtually every large trans-national corporation, "let the locals decide" must be seen for what it really is - an opportunistic manipulation of the circumstances. With companies handing out thalidomide and other drugs which have proven disastrous, pesticides like DDT, and industrial materials like asbestos, all of which have been outlawed in the West, is it not our responsibility to warn people of what is to come, based on our own experiences? We certainly believe that people must ultimately choose, but we also know, from our work in Ladakh, that they have been given only one choice. Tourists can help alert people to the fact that there is more than one way to create prosperity.

Footnotes

1 Tourism Concern Brochure, 1996
2 The Rethinking Tourism Project/The Tides Center, Project Summary, September 25 1996
3 ibid.
4 ibid.
5 Anita Pleumaron: The Political Economy of Tourism. In: The Ecologist, vol. 24, No 4/1994, p 143
6 ibid.
7 ibid.
8 Henry Osmaston, Rod Fisher, Janet Frazer, Tony Wilkinson: Animal Husbandry in Zangskar. John Crook & Henry Osmaston: Himalayan Buddhist Villages
9 Osmaston, H. : Proceedings from The Future of Agriculture in Ladakh. Ladakh Ecological Development Group. Leh, Ladakh 1989
10 Worldwatch "Climate of Hope: New Strategies for Stabilizing the World's Atmosphere" 1996
11 Study published by the UK Dept. of Health
12 ibid.
13 WorldWatch, Vol. 8, No. 6/1996, p 12
14 see footnote 5
15 Sonam Wangchuk: Impact of Tourism In Ladakh, July 1996
16 ibid.

M.S.Kohli

An Action Plan for Mountain Tourism in India

The Gangotri Conservation Project

Editors' note:

Captain M.S. Kohli's lifelong involvement with the Himalayas – including major mountaineering expeditions and an Air India worldwide Himalayan promotion campaign – culminated in 1989 in the foundation, together with Sir Edmund Hillary, of the Himalayan Environment Trust, of which he is Chairman.

1. Issues and Challenges of Sustainability of Mountain Areas

As much as ten percent of the world's population and a much larger percentage of the world's poor live in mountain regions. An additional 30 percent of the global population, besides those living in mountains, are totally dependent on and will be affected by mountain resources and their management. Viewed against this background and with the threat of environmental degradation looming large over the Himalayas, environmental problems, to quote Sir Edmund Hillary, are essentially social problems and they begin with man as the cause and end with man as victim. The main problems of the mountain regions essentially arise out of the following :

- Increasing human and cattle population;
- Accelerated destruction of biological wealth and endangered herbal and medicinal plants;
- Dwindling productivity of agriculture and forestry operations;
- Excessive soil erosion resulting in flash floods and recurring land slides;
- Shortages of fuel and fodder;
- Drying up of life-giving perennial water sources like springs and streams;
- Socio-economic problems arising out of the influx of tourists and plains people for the so-called development projects;
- Creation of slums in once scenic hill stations and resorts due to haphazard and ad hoc growth.

All these factors have combined to add hardship and drudgery in the day to day life of the hill people, particularly women and children, who have to trek for hours together to fetch water or back-breaking loads of fuel and small timber to somehow continue their existence at a subsistence level.

The development efforts - roads, hydel-power schemes, industries, mining, tourism as well as accelerated exploitation of forest resources to generate revenue and for meeting industrial raw material needs have, however, brought little benefit to the local people. Indeed, one could say that such development programmes have opened up these areas to the greedy outsiders - forest contractors, and others - with the result that the poor hill people who once were the lords and masters of their domain have been reduced to the status of hewers of wood and drawers of water, on daily wages, for the outsiders who flock to the newly opened-up hilly regions in the name of development. The drudgery, therefore, continues.

In order to save this valuable gift of nature for our enjoyment on a sustainable basis, and also to pass it on intact to the coming generations, it is imperative that we dedicate ourselves collectively to the preservation of the Himalaya. This message can best be carried by the trekkers and mountaineers who are in such intimate contact with nature.

2. Action Plan for Sustainability of Mountain Tourism in India

Since the degree of environmental degradation of various regions of the Indian Himalayas varies from region to region and activity to activity, my proposed 'Action Plan' will be discussed under the various disciplines:

Mountaineering

At present India gets about 50 foreign expeditions and about 150 Indian expeditions, comprising about 1,500 climbers and 8,000 porters. All these expeditions are controlled by the Indian Mountaineering Foundation. Each expedition has to sign an undertaking that they will look after the environment of the area they visit and will not leave any rubbish behind. By and large our mountaineers are quite responsible and disciplined people and are aware of the problems of pollution. However, there have been cases in which the visiting expeditions have not followed the guidelines. The Himalayan Code of Conduct, finalised by the Himalayan Environment Trust, has been accepted by the world body of mountaineering federations and several other organisations around the world. If the Code of Conduct is properly followed, we should be able to safeguard the upper reaches of the Himalayas to a great extent. In this context, the role of liaison officers is vital. We know for certain that many liaison officers, both in India and Nepal, do not do their jobs properly. The Indian Mountaineering Foundation, the apex body for mountaineering in India, is concerned with this problem and is taking several steps to ensure adequate action by the liaison officers in enforcing this Code of Conduct. The Indian Mountaineering Foundation is also planning to levy a deposit fee from expeditions which will be forfeited in case of any environmental lapses. Here one major problem is effective monitoring.

In respect of accumulated rubbish in the Gangotri basin, the Gangotri Conservation Project, a model project started by the Himalayan Environment Trust in India, has already cleaned several Base Camps. An incinerator has already been installed by the Gangotri Conservation Project in Gangotri which disposes of nearly half a ton of rubbish daily. The visiting expeditions have been asked to bring back their rubbish to the incinerator at Gangotri. The Gangotri Conservation Project thus monitors the environmental performance of expeditions to the Gangotri Basin, and sends all reports to the Indian Mountaineering Foundation. In respect of non-bio degradable items, the Indian Mountaineering Foundation has already issued strict instructions that teams should carry them back.

Gangotri is the most polluted part of the Indian Himalaya. It also attracts the largest number of expeditions in India. The only other high-altitude area in the Indian Himalaya suffering from degradation is the Siachen glacier in Ladakh. This, being the scene of conflict between India and Pakistan, has a large concentration of Indian troops. With constant need for compassionate evacuations, it is not easy to clear the rubbish from the area. However, the army headquarters are very much concerned about the environmental protection of the border areas and clearance of rubbish from Siachen.

Besides clearing the rubbish, the Indian Mountaineering Foundation is also discouraging large expeditions to the Himalaya. Alpine style climbing is getting more and more popular and there is an increasingly reduced dependence on Sherpas and porters.

Trekking

The Indian Himalaya have vast trekking possibilities in Kashmir, Himachal Pradesh, Uttar Pradesh, Sikkim and Arunachal. Although the number of foreign trekkers is less than 50,000, the number of Indian trekkers has reached the formidable figure of over 150,000. The Adventure Tour Operators are quite conscious of the environmental problems and issue copies of the Himalayan Code of Conduct to all trekkers. In the case of organised groups one can expect reasonable efforts towards the conservation of the trekking routes. However, in respect of the majority of the trekkers, i.e. domestic groups, monitoring is not easy. Only through general publicity and by appealing to various educational institutions and youth organisations to follow the Himalayan Code of Conduct, can we perhaps achieve some success.

With such a large influx of trekkers to the fragile region of the Himalaya, the Indian Mountaineering Foundation and the Department of Tourism will do well to start the „Trekking Permit“ as in Nepal. The Trekking Permit, as suggested to Nepal by Sir Edmund Hillary, should have the Himalayan Code of Conduct printed on the back page. This action besides reminding the visitors to follow the Code of Conduct, will generate additional funds for conservation.

Pilgrimage Tourism

One of the most important segments of Himalayan Tourism which is peculiar to India, is 'Pilgrimage Tourism'. We have a number of Himalayan shrines all over India. These include Amarnath Cave, Vaishnodevi, Gangotri, Jamnotri, Badrinath and Hemkund. More than a million pilgrims visit these shrines annually and that too in less than 6 months. Let us consider the case of Gangotri as an example. Two years ago the Himalayan Environment Trust decided to set up a model project in the Gangotri basin which had become the most populated area in the Indian Himalaya. The number of climbers and accompanying porters to the region is about 3,000; the number of trekkers about 30,000; the number of pilgrims is over 300,000. This number is undoubtedly much more than the carrying capacity of the area. As a result more than half of the forest cover has got depleted. Even the birch trees in the higher reaches, beyond Gangotri temple, are nearing extinction. The Gangotri Conservation Project started a chain of nurseries and plantations. For the birch (Bhojpatra) plantations the UNDP came to our rescue and gave us the financial support. A number of eating-places have come up all over the area and we decided to replace them with pre-fab huts and supply them with LPG (liquified petroleum gas) connections to avoid excessive use of wood. For this the PATA (Pacific Asia Travel Association) decided to support us. We have also set up a number of toilets at various halting places on the pilgrimage route. Over 100,000 leaflets containing the Himalayan Code of Conduct have been distributed in the entire area. Several rubbish-bins have been positioned all over the route. Today, after 2 years of continuous efforts and in spite of political agitations in the area, which held up our progress several times, the Gangotri Conservation Project has made a positive contribution to arrest any further pollution in the area.

Similar action is needed in respect of other Himalayan shrines. In the summer of 1996 several hundred pilgrims died on the route to Amarnath cave in Kashmir. Because of the religious fervour it is not easy to ration the number of visitors. However, proper regulatory controls can help.

The Gangotri Conservation Project is a unique integrated project administered by the Himalayan Environment Trust, the Central Government of India and the State Govt. of UP, each contributing US$ 50,000. Besides the representatives of the three organisations, six eminent experts were included in the steering committee which administers the project.

While the Gangotri Conservation Project is making steady progress, we have received offers from various experts to take up the conservation work in some other Himalayan regions. The strategy is to secure matching grants from business houses and governments of Himalayan countries. The Himalayan Environment Trust will continue to act as a catalyst and action-oriented body, and these various conservation projects function under autonomous local councils.

Himalaya Hill Stations

Most of the existing Himalayan hill stations have become concrete slums. There is an acute shortage of water in most of the hill stations, bringing suffering to the local people which has been fast dwindling. This is one of the most complicated problems and only limited action is possible. It must however be realised that any lasting action can only partially improve the situation. It is absolutely impossible to restore these hill stations to their old glory. One redeeming development is the large-scale awareness amongst the local people of these hill stations about their rights, and the need to regulate visitors and further development based on water and energy resources available.

Cultural Invasion

We cannot deny that mountain tourism has adversely affected the culture of several regions in the Himalayas. Let us take the example of Ladakh in the Indian Himalaya. Forty years ago, in 1956, I had joined an expedition to Saser Kangri in the Karakorams. At that time although some troops were stationed in Leh, no outside visitors had penetrated beyond Leh. We were the first outside visitors to enter this beautiful area in the Himalaya. The local people received us with folded hands everywhere. At several places local women, scantily clothed, moved freely without any interference. We were invited to almost every house for buttermilk and greeted warmly. Today all that is a thing of the past.

In 1971 when Ladakh was thrown open to foreign tourists without making any adequate preparations and ensuring safeguards, we soon realised that many of the rich and historic artefacts from the monasteries were bought by the foreign tourists for a song and taken out of the country. Such fragile areas should be thrown open only to a very limited number of high-spending tourists with proper regulatory controls, as is being done by Bhutan.

Himalaya glaciers

One significant development that came to our notice recently was the unprecedented recession of the Gangotri glacier. The International Commission of Snow and Ice (ICSI) predicts that if the current global temperature increases by 0.5 degrees C, the Gangotri glacier will recede further and there will be less water. The major river systems in the Himalayas are presently going through this phase, including the Ganges and the Brahmaputra.

Mr. Syed Iqbal Hasnani of the School of Environmental Sciences, JNU, and Chairman of ICSI's working group on Himalayan glaciers warns that by the year 2030 the water level in the Bhagirathi will be affected and agricultural output will suffer if the Gangotri glacier continues to shrink and recede.

After 18 years of continuous efforts the Geological Survey of India (GSI) has made an inventory of the glaciers in the Indian Himalayas under the supervision of Mr. C.P. Vohra who climbed Mount Everest in 1965 and is a former Director General of GSI. The Gangotri Conservation Project has been asked to help in the continuous monitoring of further developments in this regard through our field staff.

Principles and Ethics of Mountain Tourism

Broadly speaking, the following principles should govern the sustainability of mountain tourism:

i. Demands on energy for the foreign tourists should not be at the cost of the local population. Alternative sources of energy such as LPG, supply of kerosene and solar energy should be tapped to meet the requirements of tourists.

ii. Demands on water also should not be at the expense of the needs of the local people. If the water supply is limited, then the number of tourists should also be restricted, based on the availability of water supply position. Similarly, in respect of food items, while it will be desirable to ensure that sufficient food items are available for tourists this must not be at the cost of the local population, as otherwise children will be the first to suffer from malnutrition. Participation of the local population by giving them certain incentives from tourism must be ensured, so that they can themselves monitor the conduct of visitors.

iii. Tourism infrastructure should include provision for alternative sources of energy and incinerators to dispose of bio-degradable rubbish.

iv. No great progress is possible in respect of sustainability of mountain tourism without the whole-hearted co-operation of the local people. As in the case of the Gangotri Conservation Project, the local people should be invited to participate right from the planning stage so that they become decision-makers. It is necessary to ensure some incentives to the local people from tourism. Let us take the example of trekking in the Mount Everest area. The local people are happy with individuals and unorganised trekkers who spend less than US$ 10 per day as the entire money goes to the locals. In the case of organised tourists through tour operators, although each trekker may be spending over US$ 50 per day and although Nepal benefits more, the local people resent this, because the entire amount goes to Kathmandu. A certain percentage of the amount incurred by trekkers should be ploughed back to the local people either through co-operative associations, or in some other manner. The Government should also encourage some cottage industry in the areas so that locals can earn additional money by selling local souvenirs and products.

Judicial Support

An interesting development in India in recent years has been the invaluable support given to the conservation efforts by the Judiciary. Several public-interest petitions have been supported by a large number of „Green Judges" bringing relief. The Gangotri Conservation Project which is strongly advocating with the State Government of UP to ban movement of vehicles beyond Bhairoghati, and short of the Gangotri temple, is intending to go ahead with a public-interest petition if its recommendations are not accepted.

Growing Population in India

One of the most relevant factors is the alarming population of India, nearing 900 million today. In the next 18 years it will be 1,300 million. It is important to make a clear assessment of the water and energy requirements in the hill areas. Unless we do this, whatever is left of the vegetation, flora and fauna would disappear.

According to ICIMOD and other experts, mountain tourism requires planning, management and monitoring. Uncontrolled development is absolutely undesirable. Considering the limited carrying capacity of the hill areas, it would perhaps be in our interest to focus on high-spending tourists who visit these areas through tour operators. This will help the interests of the local people.

Most of the above activities which can be related to the carrying capacity of the area, soil, water and energy resources, cannot however be put in black and white. Each mountain area has its own problems. The most important action should be to work out a monitoring mechanism to see that the area does not get degraded due to uncontrolled tourism.

3. Recommendations of HIMTAB

One of the important developments in the field of Himalayan tourism in India was the establishment of the Himalayan Tourism Advisory Board (HIMTAB), a government organisation headed by the Minister of Tourism. The Ministers of Tourism of the Himalayan states and other members of the Board hold annual sessions to which adventure tour operators and others concerned are invited.

In November 1996 HIMTAB made the following recommendations :

1. Himalayan Tourism should be developed on an eco-friendly, nature-sensitive and community-oriented basis to sustain it in the fragile Himalayan region.
2. Architectural norms should conform to the local character and environment ambience of the area, using local construction material.
3. Vehicular movement in the Himalayan regions should be restricted and there should be proper garbage management.
4. A mechanism to prohibit/limit use of the non-bio degradable materials in the Himalayan regions should be worked out.
5. A course on Himalayan tourism should be added as a part of the curriculum in all diploma/PGD (post-graduate diploma)/degree courses offered by different universities and institutions in India.
6. The Government of India will support various sustainable developmental projects in different states.
7. All the Himalayan States and the Government of India will place emphasis on awareness creation among tourists, the tour operators, and host community on eco-friendly tourism practices and develop general awareness among people.
8. The Government of India should institute an Annual National Award for NGOs or State Governments for their commitment and contribution in the field of eco-tourism/sustainable development. It was also recommended that in the classification of hotels in the Himalayan regions the criteria of eco-friendly practices should be included.

4. National Parks and Sanctuaries

A few years ago our trustee, Sir Chris Bonington, advised that we should declare some fragile parts of the Himalaya as national parks. Due to lack of regulatory control, for example, vehicles are presently going right up to the Gangotri and Badrinath temples. Once these areas are declared national parks, the usual regulatory controls would apply to all visitors. It is desirable to declare Gangotri and some other Himalayan regions in India as National Parks and levy entry fees.

Conclusions

If I may over-simplify the problem of sustainability of mountain tourism, let us designate the tourists as "Guests" and local people as "Hosts". No tourism can be sustained if we do not take into consideration the interests of both the parties – "Guests" and "Hosts". If this attitude forms the basis of mountain tourism, planning will be on the right lines.

To end, let me narrate a Chinese story which said "if a man wanted to be happy for a day he ought to get married. If he wanted to be happy for a year he ought to have a plan for having a son, and if he wanted to be happy for life he ought to work on his environment."

The Gangotri Conservation Project: Project Outline

The Gangotri Basin, at the headwaters of the Jamuna and Ganga in Uttarakand, is a major Hindu pilgrimage destination which receives over 300,000 pilgrims a year; it is also becoming increasingly popular with trekkers and mountaineers.

The Gangotri Conservation Project (GCP) was launched by the Himalayan Environment Trust (HET) in June 1994.

It is supported by the Government of India, the regional government of Uttar Pradesh, and the American Himalayan Foundation. It has a steering committee that lays down the broad policy and tasks, which are implemented by the director under the guidance of the management committee.

Main Objectives:

- To green and clean the Gangotri Basin
- To develop simple low-cost sanitation schemes and schemes for solid waste disposal
- To develop alternative energy programmes for the conservation of the environment
- To achieve maximum involvement of the local populace

Activities (1994-1996):

1. Alternative energy to reduce firewood consumption

- Issue of over 300 LPG connections to households
  problem: reluctance of local people to stop using firewood, due to expense
  Proposed solution: stricter control through rangers and guards
- Proposals for a hydel plant at 150-250 kw capaciy have been aproved
- Briquette

problem: not followed up due to non-availability of pine needles

- Tree plantation, establishment of nurseries

2. Garbage clearance

- Clean-up operations run by NGO-organised local volunteers and Indian mountaineering clubs
- Installation of refuse bins throughout the are and an incinerator at Gangotri

problem: supervision and running expense

3. Toilet facilities

Setting up of prefabricated toilets

problem: improper use, pilfering of fittings, maintenance, destruction by floods

4. Awareness programme

Lectures for trainees; destribution of brochures, Code of Conduct for visitors

5. Alternative dhabas (foodstalls) to prevent temporary structures

Quick-erect tubular frame constructions equipped with gas burners and garbage bins to be issued (partly financed by US sponsor)

6. Involvement of local inhabitants

Preliminary discussion on the formation of a local committee

problem: local politics prevent consensus – a major threat to the GCP.

Karin Inmann

Small steps into the future

CCODER's Community Development and Tourism Projects

Editors' note

In this article the author describes the community development and tourism project CCODER (Centre for Community Development and Research), into which she has gained insight through years of co-operation. A paper on CCODER was presented to the International Conference on Sustainability in Mountain Tourism by CCODER's chairman Govinda Dhital.

The Philosophical Background

"Nobody is born in heaven
Why not try to climb up step by step."

- Govinda Dhital

CCODER is a Nepalese non-governmental organisation (NGO) which since 1991 has been active in the field of community development. While CCODER has clear ideas and visions of what rural village life in Nepal should look like in the future, it differs from other NGOs in that it does not define a path to be followed, and does not lay down a fixed time framework for its projected development. CCODER's approach is to let the villagers plan their own future, implement self-determined measures and achieve goals that they themselves have set, without having to adhere to an NGO-prescribed master plan.

The "small is beautiful" philosophy behind the whole CCODER concept evokes the ideas of Leopold Kohr or E.F. Schumacher, national economists who championed the theory that man is not able to maintain a clear overview and comprehension of a system if it is too big. If human activity is to be healthy and stable, the framework must not exceed a certain size. Although no-one in Nepal has heard of these theoreticians, CCODER's step by step village development programme echoes their approach in what appears to be a possible path to solving some major problems.

The concept rests on three pillars, all three of them sustainable in themselves and in conjunction with each other: village development; village saving and banking; and income-generating enterprises, including community tourism.

CCODER carries out projects in the Ghorka, Lamjung and Nuwakot districts. As in many other regions, one cannot escape the fact that life in rural villages of Nepal has always been difficult – a result of rapid population growth, illiteracy, insanitary living conditions, inadequate nutrition, subsistence farming and poor infrastructure. The ever-increasing pressure on dwindling resources has resulted in widespread environmental degradation. The fundamental problem, therefore, is the low, insufficient income of the poor. Hence income generating must top the agenda to help the socio-economic conditions of this sector of the population. In view of the magnitude of the problem, CCODER seeks to tackle the issue through an innovative approach to grass roots development which consists in helping the people to help themselves.

CCODER's approach is unusual in Nepal in three ways:

1. Separation of the sexes in decision-making

From its earliest village meetings, CCODER has always insisted that both men and women should participate, regardless of caste. Members of low castes are also included in all processes of policy and decision making. This approach is by no means an idealist's dream: the idea of a better, fairer society will never become reality unless it is put into practice through concrete, unassailable rules of play. The reasoning behind the principle of separation of the sexes in decision-making is that centuries of the Hindu tradition of a patriarchal social order cannot possibly be overturned within a few years by simple village development workers. Therefore men and women form their own community development committees (CDCs) in which they discuss problems separately and try to work out possible solutions. If the men's and women's groups disagree, the CCODER village development worker plays the role of arbitrator.

2. CCODER implements a step by step programme

The village communities decide the steps to be taken in the development work and determine the pace of the work undertaken. The time factor is considered to be of minor importance.

3. Maximum independence from outside

Many development projects are dependent on outside (usually foreign) funding, and the people concerned are often indifferent to the fact that their destiny may be being determined by outsiders. In many cases project goals form part of the development policies formulated by the donor countries, instead of matching the real needs of the village communities in

Nepal's rural areas. All too often, this ends with the projects collapsing as soon as the foreign donor disappears from the scene.

CCODER therefore believes that outside financial support must be kept to a minimum, as measures will only be sustainable if they have been implemented by and for the people themselves.

The project work begins with a preliminary phase, the „participatory action research". CCODER is proud that this is not a process of academic analysis, but grass-roots oriented research. Village people are the actors during the entire research process, concentrating on the most pressing issues. Problems are identified by the local people, assisted but not dominated by the researcher. The methods include group meetings, seminars, workshops, surveys and group consultations.

The project programme consists of three main stages:

1. village development activities
2. village saving and banking schemes
3. income-generating activities through enterprises – among them, community tourism

These project stages are only dependent on each other in as much as they require a co-ordinated sequence. A village community can decide whether it wants to limit its village development to improvements in living conditions (stage 1) or whether it wants to improve the infrastructure (paths, bridges, water pipes, community schools, health posts, etc.) through a savings scheme (stage 2). CCODER takes the view that a village community cannot embark on stage 3 (income-generating activities through enterprises) without having implemented stages 1 and 2.

1. Village development

There are a large number of village development projects in Nepal, all of which are trying to improve the usually desolate living conditions that leave little hope for the future. CCODER shares this aim, and its chosen path is formulated with clear pragmatism: "People, don't wait for someone to come along and help you. Do something yourselves! You must either spend some time or some money, or both."

The key word is SAVINGS:

- time: 10 minutes contribution a day towards making the village a better place to live in.
- money: for infrastructure development and economic development.

CCODER is currently running its programme in three districts, in about thirty villages in all (a total population of some 3,900). Village development begins with the establishment of an institutional framework, with the full involvement of the village people. Several community development committees (CDCs) are set up in each village community, with separate committees for men and women to avoid the women being dominated by the men, as is usually the case. There is one committee for education and social welfare, one for agriculture, one for savings and credits, etc. These CDCs send delegates to a federation of CDCs at regional level (RCDCs). Nobody is obliged to participate, but all the activities depend for their success on a large number of members.

The "10 minutes a day" programme, which requires every CDC member to contribute ten minutes of work a day, is dedicated to constructing paths, securing terraces, building toilets (under the motto "a toilet for every house"), repairing school buildings etc.

In addition, the battle against the high rate of illiteracy is being fought with the most obvious low-cost means imaginable: villagers who have learnt to read and write are trained in workshops to pass on their knowledge (non-formal education).

If money is required for village development activities, project phase two steps in.

2. Savings and banking

The success of this village savings system testifies to the validity of the CCODER model. However small the amount that is saved each month, the important thing is for it to be paid in regularly. What people have to learn in this phase is careful money-management. In addition to the savings and credit committee's careful accounting, each individual saver is required to keep exact records of how much he/she has saved. Altogether some NRs 50,000 (approx. $870) are saved through this scheme in the thirty villages every month, and the money is used for building water pipes, equipping health posts, supplying a village shop, etc.

In the initial stage of the savings system, a village was only allowed to use its own savings, but later village communities were able to lend money to each other – which, although more difficult to administrate, opened the door to a whole range of new possibilities without significantly increasing the risk involved.

In the third stage the Nepal State Agricultural Bank will make small-scale loan facilities available to village communities.

This village savings and credit system has made it possible for prises to be financed, i.e. project stage three.

3. Income-generating activities - community enterprises, community tourism

Investments have so far been made in a number of small dairies, a community fruit processing company, diverse nurseries for medical plants, community shops, community schools, etc. What all these investment schemes have in common is that they operate with minimum risk for the investor, and that the village communities receive a fixed share of the profits.

The Community Tourism Project is a new project, and the only one of its kind in Nepal. CCODER starts from a realistic assessment of Nepal's chances of getting a slice of the world tourism cake: while all the experts are forecasting huge growth rates for the world's largest industry, Nepal – particularly the mountain regions – will only ever attract a tiny bit of it. The figures speak for themselves: the country has between 300,000 and 400,000 annual arrivals, of whom 70,000 to 80,000 go trekking or mountaineering outside the Kathmandu valley.

The unpredictability of tourist trends is another aspect of the tourism industry which features large in Govinda Dhital's tourism concept. All over the world the different destinations are competing with each other to lure tourists; new trends catch on, others phase themselves out, and no-one can foresee what tourists will want tomorrow – beaches, mountains, spiritual revival? This all means that investment in tourism infrastructure is high-risk investment. And in third world countries there is not much investment capital around.

And CCODER has examples of what not to do right on its doorstep, so the CDC advisers in the Ghorka region do not have to look far afield to illustrate their warnings. In 1996 there were days and days of sit-down strikes on the Lukla airstrip: the villagers wanted to prevent helicopters from flying tourists out of Syangboche. Why? Because the investments they had made in tourist lodges had left them with huge bank loans to pay off, and they were fighting for every single tourist they could get. This phenomenon of crippling debt, in some cases even leading to the community becoming insolvent, has already been experienced in the Alps (see Luger/Rest in this book). But CCODER also knows that tourism creates jobs and additional income faster than any other industry.

The concept of Community Tourism was developed to minimise the necessary capital investment, and it is a concept which can be adapted and extended according to any specific situation.

There are two pillars to the tourism model: beautiful scenery with clean villages (the achievement of village development activities); and the region's history. The Ghorka region, with Manaslu, Ganesh Himal and Himal Chuli towering above it, has played an important role in Nepal's history. The Gurkha King Prithvi Narayan Shah had already conquered a large number of princely states in western Nepal when he set his sights on Kathmandu in 1758. After ten years of fighting, he took Kathmandu in 1769, ending the reign of the Malla Dynasty and unifying the diverse kingdoms. He is thus revered as the father of modern Nepal.

The Ghorka region is only a six-hour drive away from Kathmandu, and has something for everybody with its hikes in the footsteps of Nepali history, easy trekking and difficult high altitude treks.

The Concept

The village development work that has been in progress since 1991 is the basis of this tourism concept, and it is carried out not for the sake of tourism but for the sake of better village life. Investment in clean water, toilets, clean villages with waste disposal sites and compost systems, attractive village paths and green belts around the village already benefit the local people, and pave the way for the advent of tourism here.

There are two stages to the tourism concept:

1. individual (family) level
2. community (group) level

Individual activities

A Community Tourism Association is founded at the village level. Individual families can apply for permission to let rooms, which involves the following steps:

First the family's standard of hygiene is checked (cleanliness in the housekeeping, toilet, clean water, care of the area around the house). The family is advised on converting one or more rooms into accommodation for tourists, and if necessary they receive financial aid in the form of a soft loan. Individual members of the family, usually women, participate in workshops for hygienic cooking, simple account-keeping, and calculating costs. This presupposes that they have already taken part in literacy classes and learnt to read and write. The family is thus in a position to provide bed and breakfast without great financial outlay.

Community (group) activities

These include, first and foremost, founding a Community Tourism Association (CTA), which is encharged with consultancy, quality control, training schemes, etc., but which also co-ordinates programmes at village level such as constructing paths, maintaining a green belt around the village, culture awareness, and granting loans through village banking.

The CTA also runs a community restaurant which provides lunch and evening meals for the tourists, thus creating jobs for the local people and giving other members of the community the opportunity to sell agricultural produce to the restaurant – vegetables (vegetable growing has been being promoted everywhere for years alongside compost management), eggs, milk, poultry, and small farm animals (goats). In addition, CCODER sees the community restaurant as a contribution to fuel saving, and at a later stage it would like to extend the facilities to solar water heaters and even solar cookers.

The community restaurant building also has rooms for various workshops and an office which is responsible for networking with other villages, networking with the providers of tourist accommodation, and, as required, arranging guides and porters, providing tourist information, etc.

CCODER hopes to achieve the maximum trickle-down effect with this model, and to enable the largest possible number of families in a village community to have a share in the potential financial benefit that tourism brings.

Two model villages on the 9-day trek round the old town of Ghorka have been trying out this concept for one and a half years. A number of camp sites are also being installed on a community basis along the route to Himal Chuli base camp.

With ideas such as these, CCODER can claim to be making a contribution towards:

- reducing the gap between rich and poor
- reducing the migration problem
- strengthening the sense of community
- improving the literacy rate, thus improving people's chances in future jobs
- improving the empowerment and self-confidence of women

- improving the confidence of the whole population in their ability to fight challenges and find solutions for problems – working together and regulating themselves.

Final remarks

At present there is very little tourism in the Ghorka region. Unlike other regions which are literally suffering from a tourist invasion, the local population is well prepared for what may well be an increasing number of tourists. But the great achievement of the CCODER model is that with or without the advent of tourism, it is really doing something to improve life in the villages.

Karin Inmann/Kurt Luger

Ecotourism and Village Development

The Oeko Himal Strategy for Sustainable Tourism

> *"In order for trekking tourism to achieve the maximum positive effect on the local population, the local people must be fully involved in the whole process. This was acknowledged long ago as the basis for successful rural development projects."*
> -Toni Hagen

1.The Bottom-up Approach in Development Co-operation

"Small mountain people in co-operation with small mountain people" – this would be an apt comment on the development co-operation between the Republic of Austria and the Hindu Kingdom of Nepal. Austria's Ministry for Foreign Affairs, the government department responsible for the country's international development co-operation, has made the Himalaya one of the key regions for Austrian involvement, and has designated Nepal one of the favoured states for co-operation (Lennkh 1997). The projects in Nepal focus on education and training, technical infrastructure (energy), agriculture, tourism, and the maintenance of the cultural heritage. Most of the projects – the Thame small hydro power project, the village development project and the mountaineering school in Thame Valley, the agricultural project in the Makalu-Barun National Park, and the ecotourism project in the Rolwaling Himal – are financed from Austrian government funds and by Oeko Himal, the Society for Ecological Co-operation Alps-Himalaya, an NGO based in Salzburg and Kathmandu.

Oeko Himal is committed to a partnership approach with the maximum possible involvement of the local population and local experts in all the projects in which it is involved, including the privately-sponsored education, research and restoration projects in Tibet. The changes in Nepal's political situation during the last few years have provided a sound basis for development co-operation to proceed along these lines.

Democracy at village level

Nepal's society is intensely hierarchical, with power largely based on caste and ethnicity. It has a history of centuries of isolation from outside influence, during which the feudal relationship between lords and serfs was all that most people knew, and a person's place in society was – and this is still often the case – determined by their caste. The forms of government used to be modelled on Hindu concepts of divine rule, and the King has traditionally been considered to be an incarnation of the God Vishnu. The almost total lack of political organisation at grassroots level can partly be explained by these social relationships, together with geographical isolation and the belief in reincarnation and the possibility it offers of being reborn into a better life.

After several attempts to gain more democratic rights in the seventies and eighties, a people's movement to install a democratic system was successful in 1991: the first elections were won by the Congress party, and the King was relegated to the position of a constitutional monarch. The newly-installed parliamentary system is still weak (none of the governments elected so far have managed to survive a full term in office), and people's expectations and disappointments during the past five years have been considerable, but the opportunities to participate in politics have never been greater. People are making full use of the increasing opportunities to influence local government on district level, and a decentralisation act has given the management of resources such as water, electricity, schooling, and health care to the local governments run by locally-elected officials. All sections of civil society, including non-governmental organisations, have recognized that the scene is set for greater participation (Sattaur 1996). It is against this background that Oeko Himal aims to build up confidence in people's ability to shape their own future, both on the communal and the individual level.

The Agriculture and Village Development Project in Makalu Barun National Park and Conservation Area, East Nepal

The initial task entrusted to Oeko Himal by the project partners (the Mountain Institute (USA) and the management of Makalu Barun Conservation Area Project) was to increase the incomes of subsistence farmers and improve agricultural methods in the region of the Makalu Barun National Park and Conservation Area. Oeko Himal carried out a comprehensive feasibility study in 1993, and drew up plans for a project to run for a period of five to ten years.

"Environmental degradation is closely interlinked with poverty and underdevelopment" concluded Madan K. Dahal and Dev Raj Dahal (1993). The Makalu Barun National Park, Nepal's most recent national park, set up in 1992, was established to prevent further environmental destruction by protecting the last dense primary forest in the valleys of the Arun River, and to reduce the farmers' practice of slash and burn to gain agricultural land. This national park – a pristine landscape with tremendous diversity of flora and fauna – is the habitat of some rare species of butterflies and birds, and of bears such as the red panda. For this reason the masterplan for the Makalu Barun Conservation Project lays down particular restrictions on forest use.

As elsewhere in Nepal, the Arun region (Shankhuwa Shaba District) is completely dependent on the forest, which provides all the building materials, all the fuel, grazing land for cattle, a variety of indigenous herbs (above all chiraito) used in Indian, Chinese and Tibetan medicine as well as other plants and berries, and hunting ground for wild animals. Over-use and disregard for plant life cycles had become a threat to this diversity of species, and restrictions are now being enforced to alleviate this ecological danger.

The whole area is extremely remote. Through heavy and long-lasting monsoon rainfalls, dangerous trails, landslides, and impassable fragile bamboo bridges, the people are trapped inside their valleys for many months of the year with no link to the outside world. The people of the lower and middle sections of the Arun valley belong to the Tibetan-Burmese Rai ethnic group, one of the earliest to settle in the country. They suffer food shortages for four to six months a year (depending how high up they live), and have little understanding for the restrictions imposed on them by the park management: they are hard hit by the total prohibition on hunting, for example, as wild animals cause considerable damage to their fields and decimate their cattle stocks – yet the park management has never considered paying them any kind of compensation.

This was the situation facing Oeko Himal when it started its work in the valley areas of the Sedua and Sisuwa rivers (western tributaries of the Arun) in its capacity as grassroots consultant and provider of funding (Inmann/Luger/Rachbauer 1995). Although Oeko Himal accepts the aims of the national park administration, our point of view is that strict conservation of these mountain regions is not a viable solution. On the contrary, the protection of fauna and flora is only feasible if the areas can be developed along lines that will achieve the fundamental objective of improving the local people's standard of living. In the humid subtropical climate of the particularly steep slopes of the eastern Himalayan mountains, the vegetation cover is vital to protect the soil from being washed away in the long and heavy monsoon rains. It is indisputable that it is essential to conserve the plant cover, but at the same time the key to future development must be the full utilisation of this vegetation as a resource for the local communities.

There has hardly been any development co-operation at all so far in the whole of the Thamku sector, which is why the choice for the first project centres fell on places like Yachamka and Benchong, situated at comparatively central locations within the project area, from where successful methods could easily be spread. The work is concentrated on the upper midhills, where conflict between farmers' needs and conservation policy is most likely (Oeko Himal 1995).

Tourism is not a significant factor here: after three years of intensive work it is clear that the Thamku sector is not able to provide the necessary food for a tourism infrastructure on the main trek to Makalu base camp; and the tourist numbers are so low that tourism cannot be seen as a potential source of employment.

Oeko Himal´s human resources are limited. There are five staff in the field, one administrator based in Khandbari, and the team leader who provides the link between Salzburg, Kathmandu and the project area.

The initial village meetings in the spring/summer of 1994 produced a lot of surprises for all concerned. The farmers discussed their situations, presented the problems that affect them all, considered possible courses of action, drew up lists of measures in order of urgency of the problems, and agreed a time framework for the execution of these action plans. They were very surprised that the „tulo manche" (we foreigners) had plenty of time to listen attentively, but no ready-made solutions to offer. At no point did we interfere in their decision-making process, even though this meant that the project was very slow to move forward. The Rai farmers were accustomed to this form of community participation, being used to running their affairs according to their traditional Kipat system of communal land ownership. The Oeko Himal team were very surprised that only modest funding was required for a wide range of measures. And the people were – and still are – amazingly willing and eager to participate.

Project Activities

The project area was expanded after a large number of requests for support had come in from other villages. In 1997 it covered 18 villages, and Community Development Committees (CDCs) were founded in each one.

The project activities consist of:

- Community development and infrastructure support
- Sustainable agriculture activities
- Income-generating activities

- Local capacity-building: workshops and training, regular village meetings with discussions to present problems and find solutions, participation in activity and budget planning, etc.

Infrastructure support

In the last three years, the primary wishes in all the villages of the region have been for infrastructure improvement. Paths have been made, two chain suspension bridges built according to Swiss construction methods, a large number of water supply systems and eight traditional water mills (ghattas) constructed, several school buildings restored, and compost toilets set up in 90% of the households in all the villages. This has only been possible through the participatory approach: Oeko Himal (i.e. the Austrian Development Co-operation) provides the materials or, as the case may be, the funding; the villagers contribute their work. In each case agreements have been drawn up stipulating how much voluntary work has to be done and how many days work will be paid. What proved particularly successful was the "ten minutes contribution daily" concept: every inhabitant of the village has to do ten minutes work every day for the community. The result: throughout the region the villages can boast fully-paved paths which do not sink into the mud even at the height of the monsoon rains; clean-up campaigns have been carried out, especially around the wells and water taps; assembly places with bamboo roofs have been constructed. "Improving villagers' self-confidence in their own capabilities" is no longer an empty slogan!

Sustainable agriculture

The national average landholding is 0,92 ha, but 60% of landholdings are below average size. In Oeko Himal's project area, the Thamku sector of the Makalu-Barun Conservation Project (MBCP), the average landholding is 0,3 to 0,5 ha, not enough to feed the families. If land use is to be sustainable, slash and burn forest clearing must be phased out and non-timber forest products cultivated instead. Chiraito (a medical herb well known in arjuvedic medicine) and cardomom are two examples of plants which can successfully be produced here, without intensive labour, to bring in additional income. The fields are too small and too steeply terraced for it to be possible to use machines to reduce the burden of work – there is usually not even enough space for an ox-drawn plough. A project has been started to improve the harvest yields through permaculture and compost management, and experimental plots of land have been planted with various different vegetables. In all the villages "lead farmers" – usually women – are trying out new plants and methods and training others who are interested in following their lead.

The position of women in Nepal, in the country as a whole and in this project region in particular, is an important factor in the implementation of sustainable agricultural development. The fact that Nepali society values women less than men seems to hold true for all castes and ethnic groups. From the high mountains to the lowland Terai, women have lower status and heavier workloads. Girls are disadvantaged from birth with regard to nutrition, medical care, education, etc., and the unequal access to resources throughout their lives makes Nepal one of very few countries in which women have a lower life expectancy than men. Although this is also true of the Rai communities, some women farmers here have succeeded in achieving a high degree of independence and can support their families. Women farmers are the most active "lead farmers" in the Thamku sector. They must take credit for the success of the kitchen gardens, angora rabbit breeding, citrus nursery, etc., while men are more often responsible for the bee-keeping. Since hardly any families can live solely off their subsistence farming, husbands and sons often do seasonal harvest work in the tea plantations of Ilam (10 days' walk away), Assam or Darjeeling, or in the orange plantations of Sikkim. Many of them never return to their families.

Women's groups have now been set up in every project village, so that women can voice their needs and initiate activities. Family planning is usually top of the agenda: all the women recognise the fact that the fields are too small and their families too large, and that their children's future looks bleak if the fields are going to be subdivided any further. But how can the number of family members be reduced when activities such as farming, livestock raising, weaving, collecting fuel wood and other forest products, cooking, and trading are all full-time jobs? The infant mortality rate is high, and most of the women have lost one or more children. Yet the survival of their children represents their only insurance in sickness and old age. On the one hand large families mean more mouths to feed; on the other hand, their economic situation is usually better than that of smaller families.

Non-formal education programmes are a big success, and women make up the majority of the participants. Secondary school children in Thamku teach the literacy courses in the villages, and Oeko Himal gives financial and know-how support to the youth groups under the motto "train the trainers". At the request of the women's group, a doctor runs a first aid and hygiene course.

Income-generating activities

Even with increased harvests, the farming families in the project region have to find additional sources of income in order to buy or barter the extra food they need to see them through the year. Projects that have been initiated in this direction are: angora rabbit breeding and bee-keeping, weaving centres for allo (nettle fibre) (although there are transporting and marketing problems with this product which still have to be tackled), and numerous experiments with non-timber forest projects. The resource assessment team – six local people trained in collecting and drying plants – have sent 2,000 plants to Kathmandu in the last two years, where they have been identified and graded according to their market value. Following this, six selected medical herbs and spices have been planted in trial plots in the area cleared by slash and burn.

Local capacity building

Numerous workshops and training courses have been held over the last three years: permaculture, compost management, toilet construction, horticultural nurseries, kitchen gardening, beekeeping, seed production, etc. Excursions to farming villages outside the project region have been particularly successful: firstly, the farming families have never had time to exchange ideas and experiences; secondly, they see that others often have the same problems, perhaps even greater ones; and thirdly, the farmers are sometimes able to take on the role of consultants, which considerably raises their standing and self-esteem. Oeko Himal finances these excursions, in order to compensate the farmers for the lost work time and the extra food they need while they are away from home.

"There is no lack of challenges," says the new Oeko Himal team leader Sanjay Kapoor, "management, especially the financial management, has to be improved. People will have to work more and more independently and should continue with more and more self-initiatives. Networking has to be optimised. The co-operation with CCODER (Center for Community Development and Research), who helped to introduce a village saving system, will be continued. The co-operation with INSAN (Institute for Sustainable Agriculture Nepal) has also been very fruitful. These experienced agriculturists will put still more emphasis on the development of soil fertility management practices, winter crops, fodder, and kitchen gardening to improve nutrition among local families. Co-operation with MBCP should be strengthened on the field and research level. And we want to make people aware of their artistic qualities and give opportunities for training – both for the sake of the conservation of cultural heritage, and also for fun and relaxation."

2. Ecotourism as a Development and Conservation Instrument

Present trends in tourism, as discussed by Tirtha Shrestha, are oriented towards increasing tourist volume. As a result, certain areas are crowded while other potential destinations, in part due to their remoteness, have remained neglected by national development processes. Trekking tourism could, therefore, be seen as a potential factor in the creation of improved facilities and infrastructure. In addition the local economy could also be strengthened. Benefits from tourism can become sustainable if environmental management capabilities are in place (Shrestha 1995).

Mountain tourism in Nepal has developed into quite a considerable industry during the last 20 years. Some 80,000 trekkers and mountaineers come to the high mountain region annually. Alongside the positive economic effects such as the rise in the standard of living brought by additional income, intercultural contact and the creation of jobs, tourism has taken its cultural, social, and ecological toll (Nepal 1996, Adams 1992). It is indisputable that some of the objectives of sustainable mountain tourism are not achieved – such as alleviating poverty, avoiding poverty migration, and contributing to growth, equality and nature conservation (Banskota/Sharma 1995).

Oeko Himal, the Society for Ecological Alps-Himalaya Co-operation, is confronted with the effects of tourism in almost all its development projects, and in view of this the idea was conceived of setting up a pilot scheme, a small-scale ecotourism project, which would be involved right from the start in steering the process of opening up a region to tourism. Against the background experience of the development of tourism in the Alps, where the industry has opened up new sources of revenue for many of the inhabitants of mountain regions and thereby prevented outmigration (Baetzing/Bolliger/Perlik 1996), and after considering examples from other high mountain regions (Luger/Inmann 1995, Gurung 1992, Ellenberg/Scholz/Beier 1997), Oeko Himal started a village and tourism development project in the Rolwaling Himal area in north-east Nepal. Unlike many other tourist destinations in Nepal, this region has not so far been designated a protected area, and the almost exclusively agricultural use of the land largely disregards the fact that the ecological resources are limited.

While the initiative for a development process combining tourism and nature conservation thus comes from outside, the project aims to develop ecological awareness among the people of the region. The local population will be integrated right from the start in the development process and will thus co-steer the whole project, and training and infrastructure measures will prepare people for the future influx of tourism. It is hoped that participatory planning of the development process will help minimise negative effects.

Tourism is seen in development co-operation as an industry with a future which could in the long term bring benefit to the local inhabitants, provided it is sustainable, i.e. a holistic, ecologically-oriented approach to economic development. While the concept of sustainable tourism can be applied to towns as well as to the natural environment – to a certain extent sustainability is a basic declaration of intent which leads to particular measures being carried out within a given framework – in remote areas it would be appropriate to speak of ecotourism committed to the concept of sustainability. Ecotourism is generally understood to be a combination of various forms of nature tourism which minimises undesired environmental impacts and socio-cultural changes. Ecotourism contributes in many areas to the funding of protected zones and creates earnings potential for the local inhabitants (Ecotourism Working Group 1995 3). More broadly, the term is used to mean tourists visiting a relatively untouched natural area in order to enjoy and study the scenery, flora and fauna, or to observe and experience the local culture. The core of the sustainable tourism concept, however, is that the local population should be involved and should derive material benefit. This also requires directives and legislation to keep the negative effects of tourism on the local culture and the environment to a minimum (Ellenberg/Scholz/Beier 1997). The fusion of the concepts of ecotourism and sustainable tourism is expressed by the Ecotourism Society, one of the most important non-commercial NGOs in this sector, which defines ecotourism succinctly as responsible travel to natural areas that conserves the environment and sustains the well-being of local people (Strasdas 1997).

In its report on protected areas for the German Ministry for Economic Co-operation and Development, the Ecotourism Working Group underscored the importance of this concept of tourism in development co-operation. In the context of development assistance, the promotion of tourism (i.e. ecotourism) can be justified, providing it takes economic and ecological aspects as well as the interests of the local communities into account. The following conditions must be met:

- Ecotourism contributes to an improvement in the standard of living of the inhabitants.
- Innovation potential is generated which can be harnessed to solve regional or sectoral problems.
- Distribution mechanisms exist or can be developed which assure that the population within and bordering the protected area receives the largest possible share in the income from tourism.
- The development of tourism is undertaken by responsible enterprises.
- Sufficient control possibilities for monitoring the environmental and social impacts of tourism can be established and put into practice.

The authors propose implementing this concept through "concerted protected area management (CPAM)", which regulates the co-operation between official authorities, local communities, private tourism enterprises and non-governmental organisations. Their fundamental assumption is that ecotourism can be established as an independent strategy through multidisciplinary co-ordination and the integration of individual strategies. This involves identifying and fostering ecologically and socially sound, soft forms of tourism in natural or semi-natural protected areas, or in areas deserving protection – as is the case in Rolwaling Himal.

3. The Rolwaling Ecotourism Project (RETP)

The following presentation reflects the development approach as well as the guidelines for sustainable tourism followed by the draft operation plan, which was worked out by the project leaders Kurt Luger and Max Petrik. In 1996 Oeko Himal conducted a feasibility study on an ecologically, culturally and socially acceptable model for tourism in the Rolwaling region of the Himalaya with crossings into Khumbu (Thame Valley) in the east and the Lapchi Kang region in the west. This research defined the following premises as a basis for an ecotourism project in this area (Oeko Himal 1996):

- The development of tourism in this area must be carried out giving special consideration to the ecological aspect.
- The promotion of tourism must be subjected to a carefully planned procedure which will rule out any negative effects in the socio-cultural field.
- The creation of jobs in tourism must be seen as a contribution to the expanding subsistence economy and not as an alternative to the al-

ready existing economic forms. All measures must be planned so as to be of use to the local population, irrespective of tourism.

- Special attention must be given to the creation of jobs in the region in order to reduce the pressure of migration on the larger towns and Kathmandu. At the same time, this may help to support families or keep them together, as the men will have the chance to find work locally. They will no longer be forced, to such an extent, to earn a living as migrant workers or to seek employment in the trekking industry in Kathmandu.
- The sustainability of the measures must be taken into account in all investments.
- Extensive training programmes (including hygiene, quality of food, ecological management, economic running of lodges etc.) for those employed in local tourism will be particularly necessary. Training programmes for guides and porters will also have to be arranged.
- The development of tourism must be organized in such a way that the local population receive the biggest part of the earnings.

Integrated tourism also includes such objectives as reducing the level of illiteracy, lowering the poverty rate and improving the health care system, and investing part of the income obtained from tourism in such areas.

Apart from individual involvement in tourism, community-building action should be promoted in order to allow as many village inhabitants as possible to share in the development.

3.1. Area description

At present two generally known routes in the region are used for tourism.

One route leads up from Charikot along the Bhote Kosi Valley, and then ascends steeply up into Rolwaling Valley. Roughly 400 tourists passed the checkpoint/police station in Simigaon between March 1995 and March 1996. This main route runs eastwards through the valley to Beding and over the Trashi Labtsa Pass into the Thame Valley, and thus into Khumbu.

A second route crosses Bahrabise and the Tinsang La Pass into the valley of Amatal Khola and rejoins the first route either in Gongar or at Jagat.

Both starting points can therefore be reached by bus. Bahrabise is situated on the Chinese road (Arniko Highway), Charikot is on the road to Jiri (an extension of this road up to Singati is planned).

The central element of the trek is Rolwaling Valley, which is 180 km as the crow flies north-east of Kathmandu. It runs east-west, parallel to the border with the Autonomous Region of Tibet. The valley is about 30 km long and lies in the shadow of the holy mountain Gaurishankar or Jomo Tseringma (7,146 m.). The Gaurishankar massif and a chain of mountains 6,000 m (18,000 ft.) high. border the valley to the north. On the south side a range of peaks from 4,000 to 6,000 m (12,000 to 18,000 ft.) shelter Rolwaling from the monsoon. To the East the valley ends basin-shaped just past Lake Tsho Rolpa and the Trakarding Glacier at an altitude of roughly 5,000 m (15,000 ft.) above sea level, at the foot of Bigphera Go Shar (6,730m). From here, two more glaciers branch off with a steep track crossing them and the Trashi Labtsa Pass to Thame Valley and from there into the Sagarmatha National Park.

In the lower area the valley is covered in a dense jungle of rhododendrons, conifers, bamboo and thick undergrowth. The Rolwaling stream drains the valley, which is considered sacred and in which no animal may be hunted. In the upper region of the valley, conifers and deciduous trees with long hanging lichen predominate. The forest ends just before Beding at an altitude of about 3,500 m above sea level, where it changes into bush vegetation with dwarf shrubs. Higher up the land consists mainly of fields for growing potatoes or pasture for yaks. Apart from transfer payments from external tourism (employment by agencies as porters or guides) as well as from local trekking and expedition tourism, which is also organized from Kathmandu (e.g. from the sale of food or providing accommodation), farming and livestock are the main sources of income for the local ethnic Sherpa population (Baumgartner 1980).

The mainstream of trekking tourism has hitherto taken a wide detour around the area described, despite the fact that is lies close to areas much frequented by tourists. Charikot is on the road to Jiri, for example, where the Khumbu trek starts. Only one pass separates Rolwaling from Sagarmatha National Park, the second most popular trekking area in Nepal. One reason why Rolwaling has not been used for tourism is the fact that it is only separated from Tibet/China by a chain of 6,000m - 7,000m mountains (with passes that are difficult to cross): in view of the complicated political situation, the Nepalese Government therefore declared it a restricted area. Another reason is probably the difficulty involved in crossing the Trashi Labtsa pass (altitude, rock fall, crevasses), which can lead to accidents. For years it was only possible to enter the area with a special permit which was only granted to expeditions.

Furthermore, as agencies could more or less determine the prices themselves in places that were not officially declared trekking areas, they showed little interest in seeing the area opened up for individual tourism. They offered full service tours, which meant that everything was organized in and brought from Kathmandu, including the crew. The local inhabitants hardly benefitted at all from this form of tourism, except for selling some extra food to the groups or occasionally providing a place to sleep. This is also why no tourist infrastructure developed: so few tourists came to the area that it was not worth investing in infrastructure, and there was no prospect of earning any additional income. Even Thame Valley on the Khumbu side, which, although it does not lie along the highest mountains in the world, still offers exceptionally beautiful scenery (nearby mountains and glaciers and lovely pastures) and is also culturally interesting, did not profit greatly from the tourism boom in the rest of Khumbu, which is concentrated along the main route.

Rolwaling's seclusion all these years could turn out to be its advantage. Compared to Khumbu and other regions where the damaging effects on culture, society and the ecology are becoming more and more evident, culture and nature in the RETP area are still more or less untouched. The local people make a living from farming and breeding livestock but not from tourism, unless the men are employed as guides or porters by trekking agencies in Kathmandu.

Yet the local people in Rolwaling and those living further down the Bhote Kosi River could organise trekking tourism themselves. There is a potential of about 40 more or less trained guides with experience in expeditions in Rolwaling Valley alone, and several dozen other young men who could be available at any time as high altitude porters.

Similarly, the lower section of the trek from Bahrabise or Charikot to Simigaon does not have any tourism worth mentioning. One comes across farmland and beautiful scenery in the area of the hills (up to 3,000m), and a large part of the trek runs along the river. Conversations with lodge-owners in Bhote Kosi Valley indicate that there is hardly any individual tourism beside the fully-organized group trekking tours, and so for want of tourists the existing extremely modest infrastructure is hardly used. Tourism, so far, cannot be considered a wealth-increasing business: "Agriculture, so far, brings more benefit than tourism" is how a hotel owner in Singati summarized the present situation.

However, all the people interviewed for the feasibility study declared an interest in more tourism, which would mean an improvement in sources of income and more contact with the outside world ("indeed, it is a very remote area", said Thundu Sherpa, teacher and lodge-owner in Simigaon). The people hope to receive financial help for carrying out various community duties (schools, bridges, regulating streams, supplying electricity, health care). It appears that no money is available for building up or expanding the tourism infrastructure in the area below Simigaon. Due to transfer incomes the financial situation in Rolwaling Valley is said to be much better.

Without external financial and logistical assistance, the development of the tourism infrastructure seems almost impossible. The local people in Bhote Kosi and Rolwaling Valleys are more or less waiting for outside support. The idea of „integrated tourism planning" may be foreign to them, but they are fully capable of coherent and integrative thinking.

There are some advantages of the area, which allows the assumption that RETP can contribute to sustainable tourism development:

The treks are near to roads and bus connections. Most of them are easy routes, very few dangerous ones (exception: Trashi Labtsa). It is a relatively short trek (approx. 10-14 days) with many good and new bridges. The landscape is of unique beauty (wonderful views, dense jungle with a variety of growth, terraced fields), the culture mainly unspoilt, no environmental or waste problems induced by tourism. On the trek close contact with local inhabitants is guaranteed (paths go through villages, accommodation in shared rooms). Tourists can experience the "real" culture-rich Nepal, away from crowds and mass tourism. In general, it is a new, extremely attractive route, connecting two scarcely developed valleys (via a pass).

The disadvantages lie in the unclear situation with regard to opening up the area, and the fact that there is almost no tourist infrastructure, which means difficulties for individual tourists (food and board). The main attraction Trashi Labtsa (for experienced trekkers only) may be unsafe (according to season there may be dangerous rock fall and crevices, dependent on weather) and the Tsho Rolpa lake is below the pass, endangered by a glacier lake outburst.

3.2. Model concept for the development of ecotourism in the region

Oeko Himal's approach to sustainable tourism is committed to "integrated planned tourism development". Integrated means that planning is not focused on one sole object or goal, but contrasts with the old approach to tourism planning in which tourism was regarded as an autonomous, self-contained microcosm of hosts and guest. Tourism, therefore, is not seen as an industry in isolation.

"Moreover, integrated planning has to be embedded in a regional development programme. It links tourism to other sectors of social and economic policy making:
- protection of the environment and of the cultural heritage, alternative land use in agriculture, energy production, housing development, road construction and traffic planning
- education and mental welfare of the local population, i.e. improving the quality of life of the local people" (Mazanec/Alkier 1985 277).

All these goals widen the scope of tourism planning and the responsibility for all decision-makers, for politicians and lodge owners as well as for tourism project managers.

A concept that especially aims at an ecologically and socially responsible form of tourism must:

- Give maximum consideration to the needs of the local people
- Call for an intact environment
- Call for economic productivity
- Give consideration to the wishes of the tourists
- Aim at optimum communication

3.2.1. Objective: to give maximum consideration to the needs of the local people

In order to do justice to this aim, tourism will have to be seen as a complement to the present subsistence economy. This means that the building up and expansion of tourism in the region will broaden the previous income basis, which is almost entirely farming and breeding livestock.

The organization of tourism should, as far as possible, be the responsibility of Tourism Development Village Committees, either alone or on a co-operative basis. This democratic arrangement guarantees the participation of all and their right to have a say in any decisions. Oeko Himal works primarily in co-operation with these committees. In particular, the women of the villages should be motivated to participate.

The following projects are to be organized on this basis:

- a local "sustainable tourism development project"
- improvement of drinking water supply and sanitary facilities

- construction of community tourism service centres (for training courses, tourism management courses, local culture promotion, etc.)
- management of money which the Austrian Development Co-operation has made available for investment loans (roll stock-credits) for the local population
- maintenance of trekking routes, bridges, etc.

3.2.2. Objective: intact environment

At present the area is not a protected zone or national park with conditions comparable to those of the Annapurna or Langtang regions, although such protective measures seem imperative for harmonious tourism development. More tourism would necessitate using more wood and other resources. According to the Ministry for Tourism and Civil Aviation, there are no plans at present to place the area concerned under protection, so it seems that ecological tourism management is most likely to be possible if lodges are required to follow certain conditions. Enforcing these conditions requires a model for participation, i.e. granting suitable privileges to lodge owners or tenants for respecting ecological measures. In this connection kerosene depots will have to be set up.

A participation model for a network of eco lodges could be implemented as follows:

Oeko Himal would work out a memorandum of understanding with the village committees of individual lodge owners, which would provide for certain measures for the protection of the environment. The granting of loans or supportive measures (know-how transfer) will depend on whether or not the conditions are adhered to. These conditions correspond more or less to those that are applied in the Annapurna Conservation Area Project, but will have to be suitably adapted for the project region. The lodges are required to join together in co-operation. A logo has to be designed to display on buildings as a "seal of quality". This seal guarantees high recognition value (a "branding" similar to the green lodges on the Khumbu Trek) and full observance of the ecological conditions. Oeko Himal will take charge of training those involved in the project (instruction with regard to ecological lodge management), provide loans, give help and support in building work, promote or conduct joint marketing, check the standard of quality in the lodges (whether kerosene is used for cooking, no trees are cut down for firewood for cooking, compost toilets are built, etc.). All lodges will be required to display information on ecologically correct trekking behaviour. In areas where there are no lodges, Oeko Himal will build model lodges which will be run on a joint or tenant basis. The tenants or lodge owners will co-operate with Oeko Himal on the basis of a franchise system, and will work on their own account while keeping to the conditions in the contract. Oeko Himal's share of any possible profits will be allocated to community jobs or put towards other projects.

These model lodges are based on the original building methods and use passive solar energy, through which a much higher level of living comfort can be achieved. This technology can be copied in the construction of private houses. The central concept is an "energy saving house" compatible with the conventional architecture of the region. Simple, mainly local building materials will be used. The lodges will follow the concept of ecologically sound houses promoted by the Ladakh Development Project (see Goldsmith's article in this book; Norberg-Hodge 1992).

3.2.3. Objective: economic profitability

The higher quality and better facilities of the lodges justify the higher prices, which will hardly be a problem for tourists. The price rate for services in tourism in the Annapurna or Everest region is at least two or three times higher than in the project area at present. Farming families who do not actually offer meals or accommodation or run a teashop could also profit from tourism by supplying cereals, vegetables or meat, thus expanding the basis of their income. Although no comprehensive study on food supply has been conducted, the fact that it is an agricultural region suggests that it could easily feed a few thousand tourists in addition to the local population. Larger villages nearby where many additional products can be bought guarantee a further source of supplies. At the same time tourism would provide more jobs and reduce underemployment, and thus become a source of income for porters.

Apart from providing accommodation in the lodges, the village committees could also be responsible for maintaining and running the campsites near the villages, for which a fee could be levied. This is not common practice at present, except when tents are put up in inner courtyards of private homes. At the moment campsites represent great competition for the lodges, as tourist groups pay for „full service" and do not want to pay extra to stay in lodges. Another reason is that the quality and standard of hygiene in the lodges is lower than that of camping packages in which a toilet tent is usually provided.

3.2.4. Objective: taking the tourists' wishes into account

The wishes of trekking tourists can be summed up in the following central points:

- value for money
- clear advantages over other destinations (such as better accommodation, more attractive mountain views, closer to local culture, fewer tourists, etc.)
- hospitality
- impressive and ecologically intact environment
- a certain standard of hygiene and modestly comfortable accommodation
- despite what appear to be adventurous conditions, safety requirements on mountains must be met

While the first four points are without doubt largely fulfilled in the region, the last two points cannot be guaranteed at present. The standard of hygiene and the level of comfort regarding accommodation (if available at all) are totally underdeveloped even in comparison with other regions in Nepal. This is because on the whole there is no infrastructure for tourism, and the standards correspond to those of the local inhabitants. As far as safety is concerned, there are obvious problems, especially in the higher regions, due to the poor level of training for porters and guides. It would not be advisable, at present, to hire porters anywhere in Bhote Kosi Valley to cross the Trashi Labtsa Pass. For this reason most tourists turn to the trekking agencies in Kathmandu, which provide a greater sense of security. The guide (Sirdar) is usually very experienced, having acquired his know-how from working as a guide on previous tours. Very few, however, have a sound training as a mountain guide (using ropes, orientation, first aid etc.).

For this reason the improvement of accommodation facilities and a more highly qualified training of guides and porters must be defined as an important development objective, which, at the same time, will bring advantages compared to other regions. In collaboration with the RETP, a mountaineering school in Thame Valley run by Oeko Himal, the Mountain Association of Nepal, the Trekking Agents Association of Nepal, and the Hotel Management and Tourism Training Centre, courses for local guides and porters will start in 1998. The curriculum includes technical training (rock and ice climbing, handling of equipment), rescue and first aid-skills as well as education in hygiene and environmental awareness. Austrian mountain guides together with local experts will be the instructors and contribute to the long-term improvement in training. Oeko Himal considers investing in training to be an essential element in the improvement of safety standards and in the move towards professionalization in tourism.

3.2.5. Objective: optimum communication and marketing

The starting point is to establish optimum communication between tourists and the local population. This demands of tourists that they respect the hosts' culture, and assumes that tourists are suitably informed. The necessary groundwork will also have to be done by the local inhabitants, such as defining definite aims as to what forms of tourism should be on offer. Moreover, agreement will have to be reached in the villages. Thus a corresponding process of awareness will have to be promoted or initiated in order to develop a master plan for the region. Distinctions should be made between Bhote Kosi Valley, Rolwaling Valley, Amatal Khola (with the biggest Buddhist nunnery in Nepal) and Thame Valley (where Oeko Himal is running another village development project including a small hydro power plant), as each region is able to offer something slightly different. How can long-term success, in the sense of sustainable tourism, be safeguarded?

As tourists do not come to a region specifically because of a village or lodge (at most because of a mountain, as the example of Everest shows), the introduction of a "brand name" has been suggested, based on a service package. The name "Rolwaling" would seem an obvious choice as it has already been introduced and is marked on maps as a tourist destination. The whole product must be unmistakable. Where else in Nepal is there so much change in scenery, ethnic groups and culture in just a few days, as well as views to discover, and all this more or less untouched by western civilization? By using the logo, a clear and unmistakable sign for ecotourism can be established and at the same time an image created or developed.

With reference to the analysis of strengths and weaknesses, opportunities and threats (SWOT analysis), and bearing other marketing strategies in mind, the basis for positioning the product "Rolwaling Tourism" must be established.

On the strategy level this means "follow the leader project" (in this case the Annapurna Conservation Area Project) by introducing a new product and carrying out an integrated concept: "ecological lodges". With an eye to the competition with other regions, Rolwaling offers opportunities for making certain distinctions. Rolwaling/Oeko Himal is a new product with a particular image of adventure, which stands out against other products (Everest trek, Langtang trek etc.) on account of its comparative advantages. The scope of action for the strategy is medium to long term, extensive, and limited to one region.

A focus on quality is necessary in order to make the most of the basic features of the product "Rolwaling". As to communication policy, an independent positioning and an image have to be developed, and a brand name established. Once ecological quality has been achieved, the aim must be to build up a true preference. Instead of offering the cheapest treks (price-quantity-strategy), the focus should be on the highest quality in the sense of ecologically sustainable tourism (preference strategy).

Key aspects in establishing this environment-oriented concept can be defined as follows, and solutions must be found regarding brand names and a seal of quality:

- ecological damage in target area
- eco-friendly facilities for lodges (energy and waste programme, sewage, toilets etc.)
- environmental awareness and behaviour of guests (information)
- attitude of locals to tourism and the environment (training)
- attitude of partners in tourism (trekking agencies) to environmental questions (training)
- visible damage to nature and landscape (renovation, developing alternative energy, kerosene, maintaining paths etc.)
- clean water supply
- burden of traffic (public transport, avoidance of flights)
- financial support for environmentally friendly facilities
- image of country and region
- strategies of immediate fellow competitors (co-operation and competition)

Environment-oriented marketing aims are to develop a new market segment by acquiring an environmentally aware and culturally sensitive holiday target group for the area; and to publicise a consistent ecological policy as a development project in order to achieve an image lead.

To stress the ecological aspect of the product, the marketing strategy must focus on the core of the product (geography and climate of target area, landscape, culture/folklore, traffic situation, water supply and quality, sewage and waste disposal, energy plan) as well as the tourist infrastructure (facilities and additional services) and travel care and assistance, accommodation, catering, information and services etc. Only in this way can a high-quality tourism product „Rolwaling/Oeko Himal" become a symbol for a standardised performance of constantly high ecological quality and thus a unique selling proposition (USP).

The project's communication policy must present the tourist package to the public and propagate it with the aim of influencing knowledge, behaviour and attitude. Thus communication policy should not be regarded separately, but as a necessary complement (Roth/Schrand 1995). Co-worker communication, advertising, direct advertising, sales promotion, public relations and sponsoring all serve as instruments within communication policy. As far as the development goals are concerned, co-worker communication will be made a point of emphasis. This involves forming village committees, training and informing villagers, porters, and owners of lodges and teashops, motivating by creating incentives and rewards (income gains), showing benefits and explaining disadvantageous subsequent costs, realistic assessment of expectations etc.

3.3. Prospects for the future

The number of trekking tourists in Nepal has not changed drastically since the beginning of the nineties and is now stagnant at 80,000. These are concentrated on the three main trekking routes: Annapurna, Everest and Langtang, whereby the Annapurna area attracts around 60% of the total number of tourists and the three together over 80%. The opening of new routes in the last few years (Dolpo, Mustang, Kangchenjunga, Manaslu) has not slowed this development down because very high fees are charged for these tours. Efforts are now being made in connection with „Visit Nepal Year 1998" to make tourism in Nepal more attractive through improving the quality of the tourism product, and through the addition of new destinations to the well-worn tourist trails. Recently the Federation of Nepalese Chamber of Commerce and Industries boasted a list of more than 70 new tourist spots across 30 districts. While the local people seem to be enthusiastic about selling their areas, the private tourism sector has problems with new products. Most of the places lure adventurers with their natural and historical importance, but they lack basic tourism infrastructure. They are inaccessible, do not have enough water and energy, and have poor communication, transportation and accommodation facilities (Khadka 1997).

A certain amount of tourism infrastructure is essential to meet the requirements of trekkers, the majority of whom come from the western industrial countries and from Australia and Japan. Building up sustainable tourism in these regions requires a carefully planned, comprehensive development process which integrates the hosts in the planning and implementation of tourism strategies. If this is not the case, there is a great danger that the mistakes made in the past will be repeated and that the disadvantages of uncontrolled development will outweigh the potential positive effects. Numerous examples of development in the wrong direction can be seen in the Alps; and in Khumbu, too, the modernisation brought by tourism has been largely uncontrolled (Adams 1992). The lodge owners of Namche and the surrounding area are now burdened with heavy debts, the lodges with tourist facilities are only fully occupied for a few weeks a year, and the process of transformation into a society increasingly dominated by economic interests (a process begun with the advent of tourism) is leading to social and cultural tensions (Vorlaufer 1996, Hauck 1996).

These mistakes should be avoided in the Rolwaling Tourism Development Project. Over the next three years, an increase is planned in the number of tourists from the present figure of some 400 a year to between 1,000 and 1,500. Through careful monitoring of the ecological, social and economic effects of the project and the tourism it generates, developments in the wrong direction should be recognised at an early stage and corrective measures introduced (Hopfenbeck/Zimmer 1993). An evaluation of the individual stages of the project is being carried out, both as a case study report for scientific research and in order to gain more comprehensive information on the region. This includes drawing up a register of natural disasters and threats to the entire region as well as taking stock and analysing the region with regard to the ecological basis of land use, settlement and demography. These statistics form the basis for the calculation of the carrying capacity of the region, which quantifies the maximum amount of tourism that an area and its population can absorb without detrimental social or ecological effects.

The foremost priority of the project is the implementation of measures for village development, such as building up a network of committed local inhabitants, literacy and education programmes for young and old, the improvement of sanitary facilities, and the introduction of alternative forms of energy (biogas and solar power). In this way the foundation is laid for ecological tourism, in co-operation with the local population and Nepalese NGOs, who can bring their knowledge and experience into the development process. But even if gently phased in this way, tourism inevitably brings cultural change. An advance in wealth status – a general aim of development co-operation – is bound to lead to a change in lifestyle and social patterns. The measures planned and in part already introduced in the RETP should assist the local people to forge ahead with the development of their region in a spirit of self-reliance and with respect for the environment, without allowing the rhythm of the Himalayan villages to be unduly disrupted.

References

Adams, Vincanne: Tourism and Sherpas, Nepal. In: Annals of Tourism Research, Vol. 19, 1992, pp 534-554

Baetzing, Werner/Martin Bolliger/Manfred Perlik: Staedtische und laendliche Regionen in den Alpen. In: Berichte zur deutschen Landeskunde, Bd. 70, 2/1996, pp 479-502

Banskota, Kamal/Bikash Sharma: Tourism for Mountain community Development. ICIMOD Discussion Paper Series No. MEI 95/11. Kathmandu 1995

Baumgartner, Ruedi: Trekking und Entwicklung im Himalaya. Zurich 1980

Dahal, M./D.R. Dahal: Environment and Sustainable Development. Issues in Nepalese Perspective. Kathmandu 1993

Ecotourism Working Group: Ecotourism as a Conservation Instrument? Making conservation Projects More Attractive. Weltforum Verlag, Muenchen-Koeln-London 1995 (Research Reports of the Federal Ministry for Economic co-operation and Development Germany, Volume 117)

Ellenberg, Ludwig/Mar: n Scholz/Birgit Beier: Oekotourismus. Reisen zwischen Oekonomie und Oekologie. Spektrum Akademischer Verlag, Heidelberg-Berlin-Oxford 1997

Gurung, Chandra Prasad: Annapurna Conservation Area Project, Nepal. In: World Wildlife Fund For Nature (Ed.): Beyond the Green Horizon. A discussion paper on Principles for sustainable tourism. London 1992, pp 37-39

Hauck, Dieter: Trekkingtourismus in Nepal. Geobuch, Muenchen 1996

HMG: Nepal Environmental Policy and Action Plan. Kathmandu: Environmental Protection Council 1993

Hopfenbeck, Waldemar/Peter Zimmer: Umweltorientiertes Tourismus-Management. Landsberg 1993

Inmann, Karin/Kurt Luger/Dieter Rachbauer: Partnerschaftliche Entwicklungszusammenarbeit auf dem Dach der Welt. In: Luger/Inmann 1995, pp 287-308

Khadka, Navin Singh: A Hard Sell. Don't expect Tourists to head for new destinations in Nepal any time soon. In: Spotlight, April 18 1997

Lennkh, Georg: Die oeffentliche Entwicklungszusammenarbeit in Oesterreich. In: Liebmann, Andreas/Werner Amon (Eds.): Dimensionen 2000. Umwelt Friede Entwicklung. Vienna 1997, pp 361-392

Luger, Kurt/Karin Inmann (Eds.): Verreiste Berge – Kultur und Tourismus im Hochgebirge. Studienverlag, Innsbruck 1995

Mazanec, Josef/W. Alkier: Tourism Planning in Highly Developed Mountain Areas. Recommended Methodology. In: Singh, Tej Vir/Jagdish Kaur (Eds.): Integrated Mountain Development. New Delhi 1985, pp 275-292

Nepal, Sanjay K: Tourism, Environment and Sustainable Development – Reflections on the Nepal Himalayas. In: Weiermair, Klaus (Ed.): Alpine Tourism – Sustainability: Reconsidered and Redesigned. ITS-Series Studies in Tourism and Service Economics. Innsbruck 1996, pp 156-173

Norberg-Hodge, Helena: Ancient Futures. Learning from Ladakh. Rider Books, London 1992

Oeko Himal: Annual Report 1994. Internal report of the project „Increasing Rural Incomes of Subsistence Farmers in the Makalu-Barun Conservation Project Area". Salzburg 1995

Oeko Himal: An Integrated Concept for Tourism in the Rolwaling Region. Feasibility Study, Salzburg 1996

Roth, Peter/Axel Schrand (Eds.): Touristik-Marketing. Munich 1995

Sattaur, Omar: Nepal. New Horizons? Oxfam Country Profile, Oxfam 1996

Shrestha, Thirtha B.: Mountain Tourism and Environment in Nepal. ICIMOD Discussion Paper Series No. MEI 95/4, Kathmandu 1995

Strasdas, Wolfgang: The Ecotourism Society. In: Ellenberg/Scholz/Beier 1997, pp 259-266

Vorlaufer, Karl: Tourisms in Entwicklungslaendern. Darmstadt 1996

Guenter Mussnig

Austria's Hohe Tauern National Park

Sustainable Tourism in a large European Protected Area

In 1971 a contract was signed in Heiligenblut, a mountain village at the foot of Austria's highest mountain, Grossglockner, to set up the Hohe Tauern National Park in the federal states of Carinthia, Salzburg and Tyrol. It was another 10 years before the first part of this protected area came into being in Carinthia in 1981, followed by the sections in Salzburg (1983) and Tyrol (1992). These long delays were not due to the somewhat complicated division of competencies between the states and the central government, but to conflicts with the electricity sector and reservations on the part of the landowners in the planned protected area. On the one hand, there were plans for huge hydroelectric power plants in the Hohe Tauern region, from which some of the local population hoped to derive more economic benefit than from a protected area – for example through the potential large-scale technological development of tourist facilities such as glacier ski resorts. On the other hand, the farmer-landowners rejected the national park for fear of expropriation and restrictions on agricultural land utilisation.

By persisting with efforts to inform the local population and gain their acceptance for the idea of a national park, the advocates of the idea succeeded in overcoming most of these objections and winning round the local communities.

Today the Hohe Tauern National Park, which covers an area of 1,800 sq. km, is the largest protected area in central Europe. Although it is a recent establishment, it has seen the implementation of several internationally acclaimed projects and now has a good chance of being awarded the designation „Category II National Park" by the International Union for Nature Conservation (IUCN).

In view of the wide range of experience gained in the last few years through working towards the development of sustainable tourism in the national park, coupled with the numerous similarities – both cultural and natural – between the Alps and the Himalaya, it is worthwhile considering the possible replicability in the Himalaya of some of Hohe Tauern's successful projects.

1. The Work of the Hohe Tauern National Park

Our experience can be considered under three headings:

- Zoning of the protected areas
- Integration of the local people in protected areas
- Visitor management and tourism

1.1. Zoning of the protected areas

The Hohe Tauern National Park comprises three zones:

a) the core, or nature zone: this consists of the untouched high-mountain natural areas, with no economic activity and the strictest protection status;

b) the outer, or conservation zone: the traditional areas of mountain agriculture with alpine pastures;

c) the national park region, or conservation development area, which is outside the actual protected area and includes the inhabited valleys. National Park funding is available for projects here although it is not part of the protected area.

Replicability in the Himalaya

The concept of zoning is already being implemented in the more recently established protected areas of Nepal such as the Makalu-Barun National Park with its "National Park" and "Conservation Area". The idea could be developed further along the lines of the Austrian model. This would bring several advantages:

a) The core, or nature zone comprising the untouched natural scenery of the high mountain areas, can be more effectively protected. Within the framework of management planning the visitor activities can be better monitored and planned (for example, a complete prohibition on access to ecologically sensitive areas).

b) The outer, or conservation zone, comprising the agricultural mountain areas, is utilised by the local people, primarily as high pastureland. Establishing a conservation zone here would increase the importance of regarding these cultivated areas as an integral part of the whole ecological system, instead – as has been the case – of presenting them as an obstacle to the implementation of a protected area policy. This would undoubtedly also raise the acceptance level among the inhabitants of the region. Traditional and ecologically sound forms of agriculture and other projects can be promoted and supported here.

c) In the national park region, the main aim is to extend and improve the infrastructure and to promote tourism and other economic activities (as is already being done in some of Nepal's conservation areas).

In our opinion, this zoning concept could initially be implemented in the Himalaya when a new protected area is set up; if it proved successful, it could be adopted in the existing protected areas.

1.2. Integration of the local population in protected areas

In contrast to the North American or African national parks, the Hohe Tauern National Park was set up mainly on private land. Over 70% of the protected area is owned by individual farmers or communities. This made it essential for the national park project to integrate the local people affected. Without their co-operation the idea could never have been realised.

This model of a "democratic" national park has proved very successful and has received international acclaim. Over 70% of the local people identify with the national park, and 95% are in favour of its continuation.

The most important institution in the development of the protected area and the integration of the local population is the Committee, which decides on the focus of protected area policy, management policy, the budget, and the implementation of projects. It also fulfils a supervisory board function for the national park administration.

The principle of this Austrian national park model is that these committee decisions should be taken primarily by representatives of the local community. The Carinthian Committee includes six mayors, twelve representatives elected by the local community and one representative from the agricultural sector, with only eight representatives altogether from the state of Carinthia, the Austrian Government, and the Austrian Alpine Association. Thus in every vote the nineteen local representatives have a majority over the eight public sector representatives. Nevertheless, most decisions are reached through consensus, which reflects positively on the protected area.

Application to the Himalaya

In our opinion the National Park Committee model could work very well in the Himalaya. Our experience has been that a smaller number of members makes a committee of this type more efficient, but the local representatives must always retain the majority.

The competencies of the committee depend, of course, on the situation and conditions in the protected area in question. Unless the participation of the local people is laid down in the institutional framework (in Carinthia the committee is fixed in the national park statutes), a protected area will always remain a top-down project with low acceptance among the local people.

1.3. Visitor management and tourism

Since the Hohe Tauern National Park was established in Carinthia at the beginning of the 80s, a large number of tourism projects have been implemented. We have selected some that are potentially applicable to the Himalaya:

1.3.1. Visitor management

In contrast to Nepal, we do not have the option of charging a permit fee for entry into the Hohe Tauern National Park. It is therefore necessary to regulate the stream of visitors through measures such as special information trails, selective information material or guided hikes.

From the planning point of view it has proved advantageous to concentrate the visitors in certain areas and to keep other ecologically sensitive areas closed to tourism. In this way it is possible to maintain better control over the impact of tourism and to build optimal facilities for the areas visited by large numbers of people.

Replicability in the Himalaya

The tourism infrastructure could be modernised in the areas which already receive large numbers of tourists (e.g. Annapurna, Langtang, Everest regions). Areas suitable for future tourism development (above all the lower Himalayan regions) could be developed as pilot projects. And areas where the dangers of tourism development are greater than the potential benefit (e.g. Mustang, Dolpo, the far west) should only admit tourists on a very restricted basis.

1.3.2. Infrastructure

The development of an infrastructure appropriate to a national park is laid down in Carinthia's national park statutes. Setting up visitor centres and modernising the alpine huts for climbers and hikers have been key programmes in the last few years. These are two examples of features which might be worth considering in Nepal.

- **Visitor centres**

Our visitor centres have proved very successful in the past few years. They now fulfil a number of important functions:

- they are information centres for the visitors
- they provide visitor education on ecologically appropriate behaviour in the park
- specifically targeted information helps to steer visitor behaviour
- income is generated through the sale of national park products, including local agricultural produce

The visitor centres owe their success to two factors:

- they are centrally located at the sites with the highest concentration of visitors
- they are equipped with modern facilities and feature interactive design.

Replicability in the Himalaya

Visitor centres could play an important role in the future in Nepalese tourism. It would be necessary to set up a small number of modern, spacious centres. The tourist centres Kathmandu and Pokhara would be appropriate locations. The visitor would be able to get information before setting off on his/her trek, which is particularly important. In addition, income generation through the sale of local products could benefit projects in the protected area.

- **Alpine huts**

In the protected area of the Hohe Tauern National Park there is a network of alpine huts for climbers and hikers. Thanks to these huts, which are modern although not luxurious, there is very little camping in the park. In this way it has been possible to reduce the environmental problems considerably, since all the huts are equipped with environment-friendly energy supplies (small hydropower stations, solar energy, biomass power) and small biological sewage plants.

Replicability in the Himalaya

In the Himalayan regions with a large number of visitors it would be appropriate to set up central huts (lodges) for the following reasons:

- reduction of environmental damage through the use of alternative sources of energy and central waste disposal
- better distribution of the tourism revenue to the entire village community, by supplying the lodges with local produce and operating them on a community basis. The lodge could be run jointly by local residents, or, as in the Hohe Tauern National Park, leased by the village to tourism experts – which would also bring revenue to the village community.

1.3.3. Training

The park rangers are an important aspect of the visitor service in the Hohe Tauern National Park. They are responsible not only for guiding tours in the park, but also for most of the visitor information service. The Hohe Tauern National Park is therefore keen to keep up the further training of these rangers, and to this end has founded a "National Park Academy".

The courses cover both environmental and cultural studies, and didactic skills and language training. The National Park Academy is attended by the park staff, and also by others working in the field of tourism and people from the region.

Replicability in the Himalaya

An institution of this kind would certainly be worth considering for the Himalaya. Not only the national park staff but also the trekking agencies' sirdars would be a target group for this further training. Trekking tourists look to their sirdars for information, so the sirdars fulfil an important function. If, in addition to their knowledge of the local region – which is usually excellent – they could increase their knowledge of fields such as cultural heritage, social and cultural geography, ecology, and environmental protection, significant benefit could be derived:

- better information for tourists
- prevention of negative impact on culture and the environment
- increased status for the sirdars through an improved job profile
- better control of trekking tourism: e.g. permits for sensitive areas only being granted to agencies whose sirdars had been trained in the academy.

2. A Democratic Protected Area

The protected area of the Hohe Tauern National Park is not publicly owned as in the USA: most of the area is the property of individual mountain farmers or mountain farmer associations. This structure made it essential to plan and develop the National Park from the bottom up, i.e. in co-operation with the local people and especially with the property owners in the protected area. In view of the economic interests in the protected area, it would not have been possible to set up the National Park without the co-operation of the local population.

The statistics for the Carinthian section of the National Park (which do not differ significantly from those of the Tyrolean and Salzburg sections) show the diverse structure of property owners:

The Carinthian section has 273 different property owners. The area is owned by:

- 1% Austrian Forestry Company (owned by the Republic of Austria)
- 13% Austrian Alpine Association (which co-operates very well with the park service, especially in questions of nature protection)
- 18% individual mountain farmers (a total of 209 farmers)
- 66% mountain farmer associations (a total of 47 associations with maximum 95 members each)
- 2% other owners, non-farmers (non-agricultural sector)

A structure like this requires close co-operation between the local people and the park management, not only during the initial phase of setting up the park, but also during its development. For this reason the new National Park law requires a National Park Committee. The National Park Committee functions as a kind of National Park parliament, taking all the important decisions on the development of the park.

Representation in the National Park Committee:

The mayor of every National Park community: 6 members
Two representatives of the property owners (elected) for every National Park community: 12 members
One expert (delegated by the state of Carinthia) for every National Park community 6 members
One representative of the Austrian Alpine Club 1 member
One representative of the Republic of Austria 1 member
One representative of the Chamber of Agriculture 1 member
The total number of members of the National Park Committee is 27.

This means that the local people have the majority with 18 out of 27 members, and thus no decisions can be taken against the interests of the local people.

The Committee has very broad responsibilities. As laid down in the National Park law, they include consultation with the park management and decisions on financial support for projects. The Committee also has to discuss the reports of activities, the financial report, and the estimated budget for the following year, and report back to the park management.

The Committee's 5-year term of office coincides with the local elections in Carinthia. There are also National Park Committees in the Tyrolean and Salzburg sections of the National Park. There are some differences in the distribution of the representatives, but everywhere the local people have the majority.

During the last 14 years, the National Park Committee has been very important for the development of the National Park Hohe Tauern. It has always been possible to find a compromise between the park management and the interests of the local population. The park has become more widely accepted, since the local people have the feeling that their position is represented. The park has enjoyed more and more popularity, both national and international, which has made it a leading model of a protected area based on the principle of bottom-up development.

3. Financial Structure

The Hohe Tauern National Park is mainly financed by the states of Carinthia, Salzburg and Tyrol and by the Republic of Austria. Each of the three states is responsible for financing their section of the park, and the following report explains the financial plan of the Carinthian section.

The State of Carinthia set up a National Park Fund in the year 1993 to improve the financial support for the park. The State of Carinthia pays its contribution to the funds annually. Further income is generated through the economic activities of the park-management, such as selling National Park products in the visitor centres, entry fees for guided tours, seminars and other education programs.

The fund is available for:

1. The management and administration of the National Park, i.e. the visitor centres, information trails, the National Park infrastructure, the mountain trails, the park-rangers and the seasonal staff. The management staff are not paid out of the fund, but by the state of Carinthia direct.
2. The support of projects run by others than the park management, such as the local farmers or tourist enterprises. Most of the projects are agricultural, tourism, scientific or nature protection projects and are decided on by the Committee.
3. The nature protection agreements with the property owners. Contracts between the property owners and the park management regulate the non-use of certain areas or the lease of former hunting reserves (to transform them into no-hunting reserves).

The funds total 12 million Austrian schillings AT$ (approx. one million US dollars) annually. The National Park Hohe Tauern is also supported by the Republic of Austria, in accordance with an agreement between the Austrian Government and the three states (Carinthia, Salzburg and Tyrol).

The annual contribution of the Republic to the National Park is 30 Million ATS (approx. US$2.7m) for the whole park; for the Carinthian part it is 8.12m ATS (approx. US$700,000).

The central government's financial contribution is mainly used for major projects, such as building visitor-centres or to buying ecologically important properties in the protected area.

Thanks to the co-financing of the state of Carinthia and the Republic of Austria, in the last four years (1993-1996) 88.2m ATS (approx. US$ 8m) were invested in the Carinthian part of the park. 58.8m ATS (US$5.2m) were raised by the National Park Fund and 29.4m ATS (US$2.8m) by the Republic (Ministry for Environmental Affairs).

Expenditure 1993 - 1996

Nature Protection	US$ 560,000
Cultural Landscape, Agriculture	US$ 1.3m
National Park Tourism	US$ 2.0m
Public Relations, Education	US$ 2.3m
Science, Planning	US$ 700,000
Contracts with property owners	US$ 750,000
Others	US$ 220,000

The Hohe Tauern National Park is not only supported by public funds, but also by private initiatives.

The Association of Friends of the Hohe Tauern National Park was founded some years ago, and supports projects in the park. The association has more than 3,000 members, mainly private individuals but also big companies which often contribute sums of over a million ATS (US$ 80,000). The projects of the club are very often nature-protection, wildlife-protection or cultural projects.

Another organisation supporting the park is the Austrian Alpine Association, which is the largest property owner in the park and has always been an active supporter of the park's aims. The Alpine Association has founded a sponsorship program through which members of the Alpine Association (which counts over 350.000 members) can buy a symbolic square meter of the protected area. The money collected through this very successful program is used for nature protection and educational projects.

To sum up, the co-financing of the Tauern National Park from public and private sources provides an adequate financial basis. In the last few years it has been possible to implement some very important projects, such as internationally acclaimed projects for environmental education, infrastructure (visitor centres, information trails etc.), and initiatives to maintain the traditional cultural landscape in the mountain valleys. In addition, some important projects have been set up to promote the international recognition of the National Park (nature protection agreements, no-hunting areas).

However, the tourism marketing of the National Park needs to be improved. It has not been possible to build up an efficient tourist organisation and structure and to transform the forms of tourism in the park communities into a real "national park tourism". Tourism in and around the park has been declining during the last few years, above all due to the nation-wide tourism crisis in Austria, and so the economic input to the park communities has also decreased.

List of Contributors

Renton de Alwis, Tourism Consultant, UNDP, Nepal/Singapore

Sunderlal Bahuguna, Environmentalist, Save Himalaya Movement, India

Narendra Bajracharya, General Secretary, Hotel Association of Nepal, Nepal

Siddhartha B. Bajracharya, Project Director, King Mahendra Trust for Nature Conservation, Nepal

Kamal Banskota, Dr., Director, Centre for Research and Environment Studies (CREST), Nepal

Wendy Brewer Lama, Ecotourism Consultant, The Mountain Institute, Nepal/USA

Les Clark, Tourism Consultant, New Zealand

Kanak Mani Dixit, Chief Editor, Himal South Asia Magazine, Nepal

Patricia East, Dr., Professor in the Faculty of Tourism, Fachhochschule Munich, Germany

Zac Goldsmith, International Society for Ecology & Culture (ISEC), England/Ladakh

Harka Bahadur Gurung, Dr., Director, Asian and Pacific Development Centre, Malaysia/Nepal

Karin Innman, Dr., Managing Director of Oeko Himal, Salzburg/Austria

A.R. Basit Khan, Co-ordinator Northern Areas, World Wildlife Fund, Pakistan

Capt. M.S. Kohli, Chairman Himalayan Environment Trust, India

Kurt Luger, Dr., Professor for Intercultural Communication, University of Salzburg, Austria

Guenter Mussnig, M.A., Deputy Director, National Park Hohe Tauern, Austria

Malcom J. Odell, Dr., Environmental Advisor and Trainer, Kali Gandaki Environmental Management Unit, Nepal/USA

Nina Rao, Tourism Researcher, India

Franz Rest, Dr., Prof. for Communication Studies, Austria

Axel Schrand, Dr., Tourism Researcher, Germany
Yogendra Shakya, President, Hotel Association of Nepal, Nepal

Bikash Sharma, Tourism Researcher, Nepal

Pitamber Sharma, Dr., Tourism Researcher/Regional Planner, ICIMOD (International Centre for Integrated Mountain Development), Nepal

Ludmilla Tueting, Journalist, Germany/Nepal

Friedrich Zimermann, Dr., Professor for Geographic and Regional Studies, Austria

The Editors

Patricia East, Dr., Professor in the Faculty of Tourism, Fachhochschule Munich, Germany; Board Member of Oeko Himal

Karin Inmann, Dr., Managing Director of Oeko Himal, Salzburg/Austria

Kurt Luger, Dr., Professor for Intercultural Communication, University of Salzburg, Austria; Chairman of Oeko Himal

HOTEL VAJRA